To Roger

SOUL-ESTEEM
The Power of Spiritual Confidence

Phylis Clay Sparks

Soul-Esteem™ Publishing
Maryland Heights, Missouri

For information write:
Soul-Esteem™ Publishing
105A Progress Parkway
Maryland Heights, MO 63043

Or call: 314-576-5508
Fax: 636-536-4730
e-mail: soulesteem@aol.com
www.soul-esteem.com

ISBN: 0-9665284-0-9
Library of Congress Cataloging-in-Publication Data
is available from the publisher.

Edited by
Nancy Bardenheier

Cover photo by Suzy Gorman, St. Louis, MO
Cover design by Phylis Clay Sparks and Michael Adkisson

Acknowledgments

Thank you from the bottom of my heart to those who have participated in the creation of this book.

My husband and spiritual partner, Roger Sparks, has never let up on his encouragement, enthusiasm and love.

My editor, Nancy Bardenheier, has shared my commitment to communicating the principles in this book as clearly as possible. I deeply appreciate her ideas and demand for excellence, her dedicated attention to detail, the time she has invested in this project and her friendship.

Thank you to Gary Heebner for his guidance in getting this off the ground, and to Dorothy Northrip and Chris Bryant for their constructive suggestions and proof reading work. Thank you, Chris, for always being there to help in any way you can as an associate and treasured friend.

My love and gratitude to Michael Adkisson for his computer expertise in designing the cover, and for the beautiful job he has done as our webmaster and audiovisual director every Sunday morning.

Thank you to Nancy and Scott Spencer and Jere and MariLouise Wilmering for believing in me.

I lovingly acknowledge my family for their unwavering love and support throughout my life and especially now. My mother, Thelma Kehres, and my aunt, Marcella Vogel, have shared a celebration of life with me and have always inspired me to reach for my dreams. My dad, Philip Kehres—and my memories of his unconditional love and support—have been a guiding light and constant companion on my spiritual journey.

My spiritual family has provided me with a forum to teach what I have learned and has been a major force in allowing me to pursue and fulfill this goal. Thank you to everyone at The Soul-Esteem Center.

Whatever degree of soul-esteem you achieve from reading this book, everyone who helped make it possible will rejoice with you because we're all in this together.

CONTENTS

About the Author

Phylis Clay Sparks is a professional speaker, teacher, artist, workshop facilitator, spiritual counselor and author. As an ordained minister, Rev. Phylis is the spiritual director and founder of The Soul-Esteem Center in St. Louis, Missouri. She is a graduate of Washington University in St. Louis, and the Ernest Holmes College School of Ministry in Orlando, Florida. She was a Dale Carnegie Course instructor for seven years and has written many articles on self-development for various publications. She has written and conducted the *Power-Presence Courses and Workshops* focusing on personal skill development, self-empowerment and spiritual confidence. She is actively teaching, lecturing, counseling and conducting a weekly Sunday Service called *The Gathering* at The Soul-Esteem Center in St. Louis. Phylis lives in Chesterfield, Missouri with her husband Roger, and is available for speaking and workshop engagements. You may contact her by writing to her at:

Soul-Esteem™ Publishing
105A Progress Parkway
Maryland Heights, Missouri 63043
(314) 576-5508
e-mail: soulesteem@aol.com
Web site: www.soul-esteem.com

Introduction

It must have been almost thirty years ago when a very insightful person said to me, "Phylis, you're a square peg in a round hole. Now, you can try to be like everybody else and make yourself miserable, or you can march to your own Drummer and lead an extraordinary and joy-filled life."

I've thought about that advice over the years, and I have noticed that when I followed it I always felt "on purpose." I was okay. I was happy. But when I conformed too much to the world around me, or when I tried too hard to please other people, I began to lose myself in a sea of sameness that took my identity with it. When I listened to the beat of my Inner Drummer, my life flowed like a clear mountain stream, and everything seemed to fall into place. I seemed to tap into the harmony of Higher Energies that supported me in everything I did. When I didn't listen to my Inner Drummer, I became scattered and vulnerable to outside energies that didn't resonate with my uniqueness.

In thinking about that long-ago advice, I realized that it wasn't just what I did or didn't do that made me feel right with the world, it was how I looked at that which I did, and how I felt about that which I did, that made the difference. I've come to realize that the journey of self-discovery and fulfillment is not so much about exploring new places, doing new things, and being successful in the eyes of the world, but in seeing with *new eyes* and hearing with *new ears*: eyes and ears that are tuned to the Inner Drummer.

This book is about learning to march to your own Drummer. It's about cultivating "soul-esteem." It's about letting your own *rhythm of life* surface—really allowing a kind of *spiritual freedom* to happen with every thought you think, every feeling you feel. I'm talking about finding your authentic self among the hodgepodge of tribal confusion that may have caused you to believe yourself to be something you're not. I'm talking about rediscovering and honoring your own soul.

Marching to your own Drummer with soul-esteem means rediscovering the lightness of the Spirit within you. It means believing in yourself down to your toes and learning to be your own leader. You may have heard a lot about "self-mastery," which sounds like a tall order. But self-mastery is simply learning to lead your life from the Self of Spirit. It's not a self-improvement technique, nor is it something that is measured by end results. It's not some gimmicky strategy for success, nor is it shutting out the world in which you live. It is the discovery and revealing of your Divine Center and the translation of that into your human expression. It is soaring with spiritual confidence and learning to enjoy your life beyond what you have come to think of as normal.

Soul-esteem is a "consciousness tone" beyond a better self-image, beyond self-love and self-confidence, and even beyond the all-important self-esteem. There is a spiritual depth to you that must be discovered and brought to a conscious awareness. It is a spiritual depth in the realm of soul. Marching to your own Drummer is a journey into soul-esteem—into spiritual confidence.

I'm convinced that people who decide to march to their own Drummer and lead with soul-esteem, remember why they're on the planet a lot faster than those who stay emotionally tied to the tribal mind. By tribal mind I mean the group mind: the societal or ethnic group, the family or religious group or any other group consciousness that influences your choices and decisions.

I'm not indicating that groups are wrong or bad. They are not. In fact, we all need other people. All too often, however, the mentality of the group can keep you in chains when it comes to following your heart's desire. When you conform to something that is contrary to your authentic self, you can create "baggage" in the form of resentment, judgment, positioning, guilt and anger: baggage that makes it more and more difficult to soar with spiritual confidence.

You may be sitting there saying to yourself, "Well, the message of this book isn't about me. I already march to my own Drummer. I have lots of soul-esteem. I'm independent and self-reliant, I think for myself, and I don't try to please everybody else. I'm my own person."

But I ask you why, then, do you compare yourself to other people? Why do you expect them to treat you a certain way? Do you worry about what other people think of you? Do you rely on someone else to make most of your choices for you? And why are you so unsure of yourself at times?

Perhaps all of these questions do not apply to you personally, but I suspect that at least some of them do.

This book is not about telling you which Drummer to march to. It is about helping you to do the spiritual work that will enable you to find the rhythm of your own Divine Center. And as you find it—as you hear that familiar beat—you will be surprised by joy.

Now is the time for you to begin marching to your own Drummer. Everything that has happened in your life up until now is important and has brought you to this moment in time. Now is the time to stir your spiritual sensitivities and arouse the dormant potentials and unlimited resources that lie buried in your soul. Now is the time to build spiritual confidence and soar with soul-esteem.

Now is the time to begin using the human mechanism as a true instrument of your spiritual essence—a true instrument of the soul.

I invite you to climb the ladder of soul-esteem above and beyond the obstructions of the third-dimensional world. What are your buried dreams? What "beat" do you hear whispering at the center of your being? Where would you like to go and what would you like to see? What would you like to feel and discover? What would make you feel fulfilled? Useful? Creative? Alive? What's going on inside your soul—deep inside where the Drummer sits?

Phylis Clay Sparks

Part One
Getting to the Soul of the Matter

*If a man does not keep pace with his companions,
perhaps it is because he hears a different drummer.
Let him step to the music which he hears, however
measured and far away.*

— Henry David Thoreau

Chapter One
Marching Into Enlightenment

Have you ever longed for something—waited for it—
worked for it—and when you got it, noticed that you felt much the
same as you did before you achieved your goal? Maybe you felt
as unfulfilled as you did before you accomplished that which you
thought was going to bring you blissful contentment. But even if
the accomplishment felt wonderful, it wasn't enough. Before the
curtain came down on your latest performance, you were off and
running toward the next drama on the stage of life.

This isn't something about which to be disappointed. You
will continue to create meaning for your life by establishing goals—
goals that revolve around education and career, family, financial
success and creative fulfillment. But it doesn't seem to matter
how many goals you accomplish, the result is never enough. Why?
Because you may have missed the one great goal that underlies all

the human goals. It's a goal that you don't have to create because the Creator created it and planted it in your soul. It's a built-in, inherent longing that is embedded at the core of you. It calls out from the center of your being, but stays buried in the subconscious until you recognize it and bring it to the surface. Once you acknowledge it, all other goals pale by comparison. This all-pervasive goal is the desire for enlightenment.

The word "enlightenment" is typically used in a general way to describe many different experiences. It might be used to describe a level of knowledge or wisdom, mental poise and balance, or a spiritual plateau. However it's defined, it is usually thought of as something you seek, something you must find. But enlightenment is not something to search for—it is something planted in your soul that you have been longing to express. Enlightenment is a level of spiritual maturity that you are compelled to grow into. It is a profound shift into soul-esteem. It is a spiritual confidence that understands that what you seek you already are. Enlightenment is not just a peak experience like the emotional high you feel when looking at a sunset or watching the birth of a baby or letting music touch your soul. It is a clear, alert awareness of the *new now moment* that represents a long-lasting level of spiritual confidence. It is a refinement of consciousness.

You were not born enlightened. You were not born with spiritual maturity and confidence. You were not born with mental clarity, emotional maturity, or a grasp of your personal responsibility as a co-creator with God. But you were born with the seed of enlightenment inside you, beating its relentless rhythm in the soul of your being and demanding your attention. Now is the time. Now is the time to march to your own Drummer and march into enlightenment.

Growing towards enlightenment closes the gap between you and your God. It is the remembering of your oneness with all that is. It is the process that enables you to notice the longing cry from the core of your being, and it will find its way to the surface only when the mental and emotional baggage which you have gathered is dissolved and transmuted into the Light Itself. Growing into enlightenment is the very rediscovery of God's perfect harmony that dwells at the center of your being.

To live an enlightened life is to live with soul-esteem. It is to march to your own Inner Drummer with such profound spiritual confidence that you can maintain a mental and emotional calm in the midst of uncertainty and cynicism. It is to discover great peace in the midst of chaos and injustice. It is to live your life according to the truths which you have come to understand—to express your inner harmony in every area of your life.

Enlightenment

A cosmic glimmer comes suddenly.
It thrills your mind and startles your senses.
It comes when you least expect it
and in a split second you understand.
You penetrate the veil
and pierce the illusions of humanhood.
From your mouth comes the breathy sound, "Ah-ha!"
and your heart beats to the rhythm of the Drummer.
The shroud of mystery falls away
as you glimpse the higher realms of knowing.
Your spirit soars and your pulse quickens
and you delve deeply into the space between your thoughts.
You lose the little self in the Infinite Sea of Oneness
that frees the beat of the Drummer.
The ecstasy is deafening.
And behold, you are changed in the twinkling of an eye.
You will never be the same again.

Listen to the Drummer

Greetings, My beloved. Be still for just a few moments and turn your attention inward, away from the outside world. Breathe deeply, relax your body, and let your ego-mind slow down. Come with Me into a time of quiet reflection as we become reacquainted with each other. I am the Drummer that sits at the center of your being. I am the Divine Spark of Spirit that calls to you from deep inside. I am your Holy Self that beats a steady rhythm as the heartbeat of your soul. Retreat with Me into a safe and quiet realm of oneness where you can fall into step with My divine rhythm.

Lay down your doubts, My dear one. Surrender your resistance and march with Me into the depths of your own divinity. Lay down your defenses, My child, and acknowledge the unity and wholeness from which you came. Step out of blame and guilt and walk with Me into a realm that is beyond fear, where your difficulties are dissolved by the flame of My Divine Presence.

I am your Divine Self. I am Love. I am Truth. I am the One Mind that will think as you—if you but let Me. I am the wisdom behind your choices. I am the compassion behind your judgments. I am the Holy of Holies that fills your cup to the brim in this precious present moment. I am the Drummer.

As My holy pulse beats stronger and stronger within you, let enlightenment dawn upon your consciousness like the light of day rises above the horizon. Let it spread itself across your mind and heart smoothly and evenly, just as the sun spreads itself smoothly and evenly across the sky and gradually lights the world. Child of Light, magnificent is the Truth of your beauty. Remember your holiness.

Understand this, My beloved: You are My special creation, fashioned out of Myself and set free to take My Infinite Potential into the playground of experience. Experience Me, My dear one. Experience Me as the hidden splendor that is rising up from the center of your being to fulfill itself in everything you think, everything you feel, everything you say, everything you do. Experience Me as the longing within you to be the best you that you can be. Let your eternal longing evolve into a full realization of your oneness with Me. Let your awareness deepen into a trust that never wavers. The Holy Grail lives within you. It is the priceless treasure of your real Self.

Let there be no fear in marching to your own Drummer, My child, for you will be marching to the beat of My rhythm of Life. You will be marching through life with soul-esteem. Go forth, My beloved, with My peace as your peace; with My faith as your faith; with My joy as your joy. Go forth knowing that My Presence is always with you and within you.

I love you. All is well.

—The Drummer

We feel the self to be deeply private, tucked away,
an intangible something that peeks out at the wider
world beyond and that might enjoy all manner of
capacities and freedoms but for the body's limitations.

—Danah Zohar, *The Quantum Self*

Chapter Two
Where the Drummer Sits

More and more people are noticing an urgency to march to their own Drummer; to find a deeper meaning in life; to go beyond the routine world into a sense of fulfillment beyond the job, beyond tribal expectations, beyond "should" and "have to," beyond what has been known and experienced thus far.

The beat of the Drummer seems to be louder and louder, stirring within many people a restlessness with things as they are, even a total dissatisfaction with one or more areas of life. Does this sound familiar to you?

Perhaps you are like the increasing number of people who are refusing to settle for the status quo that no longer fits for them, whether it has to do with relationships, career, family ties, organizations, present environment or old friendships. There may be a feeling of being different, of not being understood, or of lacking identity. Sometimes there's a sense of loneliness or separation, along with anxiety and fatigue. There may be a longing to discover who you really are, what your purpose is in coming to planet Earth in the first place, and a deep desire to bring meaning to your life.

There are many reports of people noticing that it takes less and less time for something that they envision in their minds to manifest in the physical world. Have you noticed this to be true for you? People are discovering that they are channels for healing energy and that they are truly ready to move out of victimhood and into the authentic power of a spiritual being having a joyous and happy human experience. Can you relate? More people are experiencing what used to be called *paranormal phenomena*, but which is fast becoming just *business as usual.* Have you noticed? Can you deny the increasing intensity of the rhythm being pounded out by the Drummer that sits in your soul?

When I say that the Drummer sits in your soul, I'm not suggesting that It's hiding behind your liver, or that It's tucked away among your kidneys and gallbladder. Let me ask you a question. Are you your body? I'll bet you're thinking, "No, I'm not my body." Let me ask you another question. Do you *have* a body? More than likely your answer is, "Yes, I *have* a body." Here's the next logical question: Who is the *you* that has a body? Who are *you*, really?

You are consciousness. You are energy. You are a soul. Your soul is your divine essence, and it is made of God-Stuff. What is God-Stuff? It is the invisible, untouchable, loving and very real Energy in back of all that is. It is that which expresses as and supports all form. This Energy is the all-pervasive Presence of God. Beyond the veil of human illusion and delusion, this Energy exists as the very vibrant and alive spiritual essence that is your soul. We might think of it as a piece of God, a spark of God, or an individualized expression of God. It is the core of who you are.

Your essence, or soul, has been infused with and molded out of Infinite Potential and is having a physical experience on this earth plane. It can experience itself as any part of the Infinite Potential that it chooses. Despite this physical experience, you are more than your body. In fact, you are not your body at all, any more than you are your car just because you're driving it. If you can but recognize the difference between your divine essence and the temporary personality and body that represent you during this lifetime, you will remember who is in charge—who is in the driver's seat during this ride through the human landscape.

But just in case you have forgotten, the Drummer is sounding Its beat with a steady pronounced rhythm pulsating throughout your being. It can no longer be denied.

Your veil of human perception conceals, separates and screens like a curtain, anything beyond your three-dimensional reality. To go beyond the veil means to penetrate the barriers between your physical world and the world of Spirit. Beyond the veil is a world of many dimensions, many realities, and many levels of consciousness. Jesus said, "In my Father's house are many mansions." It was Plato who said that the visible world is not a reliable measure of reality—that anything physical is not a principle or law. In fact, everything begins in the invisible, beyond the veil, beyond logic, beyond appearances.

As you begin to get glimpses beyond the veil, you will come to understand that you live a dual existence. You are dealing with two selves. There is the self that is the personality, and there is the Self that is invisible, infinite, eternal—your true Self—your soul Self. The personality self is your mask. The word *personality* comes from the Greek word *persona*, which means mask. It is important for you to learn that the ego-self, or the personality, is your lower self, your outer self, your human self. That human self is active on the stage of the human drama. The invisible Self beyond the veil is the higher or divine Self.

The individual soul is a microcosm of the macrocosm that is the Soul of God. As a microcosm, it has the potential of growing and expanding its energy and consciousness to become more and more like the macrocosm, or God. We might refer to this as the evolution of the soul. The ultimate goal is to expand this individualized energy and consciousness into the fullness of expression that exemplifies the wholeness of God.

The spirit is not the same as the soul. The individual spirit is the microcosm of the macrocosm that is the Spirit of God. The Spirit of God is the Universal Life Force. It animates and gives life and vitality to Its creation. The individual spirit is the Spark of God, the Drummer, that lives within and gives vitality to the individual soul.

It has been said that everything is Energy, or God Energy. This God Energy is Spirit. It is the *I Am*. The soul might be considered condensed God Energy, or the individual's field of consciousness and divine potentiality.

Every human faculty has a counterpart that exists in the realm of soul. I'm talking about the *knower* beyond the believer; the *listener* beyond the ears; the *voice* beyond the vocal cords; the *feeler* beyond the touch; the *thinker* beyond the brain. During the last century, the science of quantum mechanics and the new physics have proven what metaphysics, which means *beyond the physical*, has said for ages: that everything is part of a unified reality, with many realms, many facets, but all connected and interwoven into one universal fabric. There is One Mind, One Infinite Intelligence, from which everything emanates, and within which everything lives and moves and has its being. It is also That which lives within you and within all that is. And That which lives within you pulsates to an all-pervasive "tone," or frequency, that unites everything. It has been described as the Great Hum, or the One Song.

When you tune in to your soul and begin to develop your spiritual faculties and taste your spiritual freedom, you will look upon your world through the eyes of the soul—from beyond the veil. You will see beyond the surface of the physical world and you will hear the whisper of the Great Hum as it emanates from every plant, every animal, every human being, and from your own soul. And even though you will begin to live from the invisible, you will learn to honor your physical body more than ever before because you will see it as your most sacred resource available through which to *experience* your soul. "Know ye not that ye are the temple of God, and that the Spirit of God dwelleth in you?" (I Cor. 3:16)

Lay aside your doubts and your fears. Surrender unto your own soul and life will become a wonderful journey—a soul journey—filled with joy and a sense of incredible awe. And that part of you that has lived for so long on the self-projected stage of the human drama will begin to see, hear, touch and experience from an entirely different perspective. You will come to know yourself as you really are. You will come to know the Drummer that sits inside you.

The Living Drummer

Spirit of the Living Drummer that beats within me,
I turn to you in holy reverence.
Today I give up my illusions of human control
and I surrender my compulsions.
I begin to move to the beat of the Drum
that pounds in my heart and my mind,
the Drum that I've come to recognize as your Divine Will,
throbbing within my very being.
Whatever I do, whatever decisions I make,
whatever responsibilities lie before me,
I know that it is You through me doing the works.
It is not that which I think
with my own intellect that matters,
but the mystical awareness of the power
that lies beyond anything I can think or do on my own.
The Drummer beats as my own power of will
that I've come to understand as
an extension of your Holy Self.
I open myself to Your magnificent expression through me,
and I resonate with the vibrations
that thrill my being.

Listen to the Drummer

Take a few moments to rest, My dear one. Take a deep breath and let yourself feel expanded. Do nothing—just sit quietly and experience the expansion. Let all the mind-chatter stop, and listen. Allow yourself to float in the infinite ocean of My Presence. I am the inside of you, the outside of you, and all around you. Notice Me. I am the Drummer. Notice Me in the beat of your heart, in the breath you breathe, in the longings of your own soul.

Be present with Me, My dear one. Feel My Love wash over you. Feel My Divine Energy all around you, through you, in you, and as you. Drop the anxieties and burdens to which you have become so attached, and open yourself to the idea that I know exactly what to do and how to do it—and so do you, My beloved.

Allow My power to flow through you, and let the sound of My holy rhythm stir within you a new awakening. You need not settle for that which lulls you to sleep and steals from you the remembrance of your true nature.

I am the Infinite Potential that pulsates through you with a steady, pronounced rhythm that cannot be denied. I am that from which you are crafted, My child. You are a spiritual being and heir to My Kingdom. Allow My power to flow through you, transforming any painful memory into the joy that My gift of love offers you right now. Let My power transmute any hurt or injury into wholeness, and what may look like a fearful problem, into peace.

I've told you so many times before, I will never leave you or forsake you; even when you try to separate yourself from Me—or put blinders on—or create blockages and barriers to protect yourself from intimacy with Me—intimacy with your holy Self. I will never leave you or forsake you. You will find that at any moment, night or day, whether you make your bed in hell or in heaven or whether you walk through the valley of the shadow of death, you may turn and find that I am walking beside you.

I am the everlasting arms underneath you. I am the soft whispers in your ear that guide you out of harm's way. I am the ocean of love in which you live and move and have your being. Come, notice Me, My beloved. Notice how good you feel as you come into My Presence. Come into My Presence in your everyday world— in the midst of whatever is happening in your human experience. Come to Me often, My child. Walk with Me. Talk with Me. Unburden yourself. And remember —I know what things you have need of before you ask.

I love you. All is well.

—The Drummer

There is one spectacle grander than the sea, that
is the sky; there is one spectacle grander than the
sky, that is the interior of the soul.
                                        —Victor Hugo

Chapter Three
Becoming Reacquainted With Your Soul

The first step in lifting the veil between your human
personality and your soul is to acknowledge that your soul exists.
To then engage the soul you must value it, respect it and nurture it.
When you nourish your soul, you begin to exercise it and develop
your spiritual faculties. You begin to integrate spirit, soul and body
into a dynamic power-presence. You become a divine human.

Conventional wisdom conceives of the soul as *in* the
human being. This is backwards. The human being is in the soul.
In other words, the soul expresses itself in material form, but exists
beyond the physical form as a field of consciousness within the
Universal Consciousness. It has often been referred to as the higher
self, or the superconscious.

The soul is the bridge between Spirit and body—it unites. It connects, and it yearns for connection. When the soul is neglected it functions like an old washed out bridge that no longer serves to get you from one side to the other. Neglecting your soul magnifies or amplifies the illusion of separateness—of being cut off from your Source—from the fountainhead of your divinity.

Could it be that those who commit horrible crimes are those whose bridge back to Spirit is washed out? Could it be that they have lost contact with their souls? Is this what being desensitized means? Is this what being morally insensitive means?

It's so easy to fall into the human trap set by the responsibilities of everyday life. Whether it be meeting the quota, paying the bills, getting the kids off to school, closing the deal, shopping for groceries or getting the car washed, your human responsibilities may take priority over the needs of your soul. This is a world where productivity is a standard by which the worth of one person is compared to another. Productivity, rewarded by money, is the standard for worldly success. Being productive usually means being driven in some labor intensive or task- oriented way with little concern for spiritual balance. When this happens, you may just shut the door on your soul and fall spiritually asleep. When you go to sleep spiritually, the beat of the Inner Drummer becomes dimmer and dimmer and all but disappears under the heaviness of human burdens, stress and competition. And before you know it you're trapped in the human world, on the body side of the bridge, having lost contact with Spirit.

Loss of contact with your soul always causes a void to manifest within you. It's an emptiness that many people fill with addictive patterns. When you've lost contact with your soul, it's easy to follow the path of least resistance and bring work home from the office every night, or stare zombie-like at the television, or fall into patterns of grumpiness and grumbling because you never have time for yourself. When you lose contact with your soul, you seldom hear the Inner Drummer and instead, gravitate toward becoming a fearful and judgmental victim, instead of a magnificent soul enjoying a human adventure.

One evening as my husband and I were shopping at the mall, I kept an eye out for a pair of comfortable shoes. We came upon a store with a large display of sturdy sandals with the thick, tire-tread soles. I went into the store and selected a pair with substantial arch supports and extra shock absorbers, and asked to see them in my size. I sat down and the salesman placed them on my aching feet. When I stood up and walked, I felt as though my whole body had been transformed. I paid for the sandals, asked to have my old shoes boxed up, and walked out of the store a new woman. As I glided through the mall with a smile on my face, my husband said to me, "See honey? It pays to take care of our soles."

Cute. Real cute. But the minute he said it, I began thinking about the similarities between how we treat our soles and how we treat our souls.

Have you noticed how you take your feet for granted? You may even abuse them by putting them in shoes that don't fit, shoes that make no sense except to make a fashion statement. You may expect them to take you where you want to go and support you for hours on end without rest. You might ignore them, never realizing how much easier it would be to walk through life with happy, cared for soles. If you were to acknowledge your feet and love them more, they would do their job of supporting you in a healthier, more comfortable way. The same is true for your soul. In fact, I'll bet your soul is many times more ignored than your soles. If you are like many people, you may have gone through your entire life, up until now, not even aware that you have a soul. If so, you may have shaped your life from a limited, fearful human perspective.

In Mark 8: 36–37, we read: "For what shall it profit a man, if he shall gain the whole world, and lose his own soul? Or what shall a man give in exchange for his soul?"

Whether or not you've fallen spiritually asleep, and whether or not you've become oblivious to the needs of your soul, it's time to make soul-work part of your life—part of your moment to moment awareness.

Soul-work means paying attention to life. It means noticing the beauty and the joy as well as the grief and the pain. It means listening to your Inner Drummer. Every experience where you allow your soul to participate expands your experience of life. Although there aren't any set rules or prescribed maps for nourishing the soul, the secret lies in embracing life, opening yourself to life, and being fully alive. It is a journey of constant activity that requires your willingness to accept life's challenges with an enthusiastic spirit. It is a journey away from fear. It is an inward journey. It is a shift from being ego-dominated to being Spirit directed. It is a soul journey to the beat of the Inner Drummer.

The one sure way to nourish your soul is to experience awe. The American Heritage Dictionary defines *awe* as "A mixed emotion of reverence, respect and wonder inspired by authority, genius, great beauty, sublimity, or might." When you can say you have felt awe, you can say that you have touched the presence of God, or put on the mantle of Spirit.

One of my favorite places to go when I want to be awe-inspired is Sedona, Arizona. I find Sedona so amazingly different from almost any other place. It's almost magical.

We recently flew into Phoenix, rented a car, and drove to Sedona, a drive that can be a rather colorless landscape for almost two hours. But at some point the road turns and you are presented with one of the most spectacular sights one can imagine. The red rocks of Sedona loom up before you, and the only way I can describe the feeling that surges through my being is awe, incredible awe.

Every time I drive into Sedona, I become like a little child as I wait for that first glimpse of the red rocks. And it always happens. The minute I see them I get that mixed emotion of reverence, respect and wonder that can only be summed up as awe. It awakens the little child in me every time. The Master said, "Except ye be converted and become as little children, ye shall not enter into the Kingdom of Heaven." The Kingdom of Heaven is a state of consciousness. It's not a place with physical boundaries, but instead represents that which transcends physical definition.

That little child that you may so often neglect is that part of you that can touch the magic of life and the majesty and wonder of nature. That little child is part of your soul; it's always there, never aging, never changing, always watching, knowing nothing of judgment or hatred. You may have heard a lot about the *wounded* inner child, but what is *that* but a human illusion that has lost the lightness, innocence and wonder of the original child created by God that lives within your soul?

The Master's advice to become as a little child wasn't meant to suggest that you be childish, immature or simplistic. The idea is to become childlike in the sense of being nonjudgmental, loving, accepting, and open— filled with awe at the magical qualities of life. The ancient sage Heraclitus once said, "Man is most nearly himself when he achieves the seriousness of a child at play." The little child part of you knows how to look with love at everyone and everything. The ageless child within you doesn't notice unimportant comparisons. It just observes, allows, and is always ready to recognize something glorious and bask in the awe of it all. What better way is there to nourish your soul?

Letting yourself feel a reverence for all life, a respect for everything around you, appreciating every moment, and feeling a sense of awe, may require that you distance yourself from the routines of your everyday world. You may find, as I have, that you can put space between yourself and your daily life and create "soul moments" by returning to nature. My favorite and most awesome soul moments include the sounds of surf crashing against the rocks, the sound of seagulls, the feeling of freedom as the wind moves through my hair, the wonderful feeling of grass under my feet, or sand between my toes. Nature fills my soul with awe when I see the color of a sunset, or feel the warmth of the sun upon my face, or experience the thrill at seeing a rainbow. I feel awe at the power I sense from simply leaning against a tree. I feel awestruck at the sound of sails as they fill with the wind, the bow as she slices through water, or the majesty and incredible energy emanating from the red rocks of Sedona.

Another way to distance yourself from your third-dimensional world is to meditate, pray, reflect, and spend time in the silence. If you haven't already done so, create a "nest," or a personal sanctuary to which you can go that will be conducive to getting in touch with your soul and the living Presence of God.

A few years ago my husband, Roger, and I purchased a new home and decided that it would become a soul-sanctuary. On the third floor there is a loft area overlooking an atrium with a skylight and a big third-story window offering a lovely view. We decided this would be our nest. We furnished the loft with two wing chairs with a lamp and table between them, and next to them our sound system with tapes and CD's at arm's reach. The area is lined by shelves loaded with books and sprinkled with meaningful things. On the table you will always find a candle and incense ready to enhance the mood. Our "meditation nook" is our favorite place in the house. Each of us has claimed our own chair, and both of us return often, sometimes individually, sometimes together. We have both experienced incredible insights and sharing, sitting in this special place.

The value of creating a nesting area where you do your spiritual practices has to do with energy. When you return to the same place over and over again, you build an atmosphere that draws you back into it as soon as you sit down. As you build positive energy that nurtures your soul, you will find it easy to get in touch with your soul when you visit that spot. I encourage you to create a private soul-sanctuary. Fill it with those things that inspire and calm you, comfort you and enrich you. Make it a safe haven that can facilitate peace and quiet and accelerate spiritual awareness—an inviting place to welcome your soul.

What about times when you feel nothing? What about times when you go back to nature and try to stir yourself into feelings of awe and reverence, but to no avail? What about times when your soul-sanctuary doesn't do the trick—when you seem to have tuned yourself out and have become numb to the glory that surrounds you? If and when this happens, it just may be a signal from the universe that you have been neglecting your soul. Remember that your body and the world you live in are always giving you feedback. They are always telling you how you're doing in consciousness. If you have closed yourself off from feeling awe, you have closed yourself off from your soul. It's time to get back to spiritual practices.

Get back to prayer. Get back to meditation. Listen to inspiring music. Be with people who are uplifting. Do some soul-searching and look for the feelings that you may be trying to deny. Talk to someone and bring those buried feelings up to a conscious level. Let yourself feel the emotions, and then transmute those emotions into something higher and lighter. When you operate out of the higher, lighter emotions, you will find it easier to stay in touch with your soul. You will hear the beat of the Drummer and be empowered to make new and wiser choices. Once you do that, you will have opened the channels so that the higher emotions of awe, love, reverence and faith can be felt with depth and clarity.

The secret is, instead of trading your awestruck inner child for adulthood, make your journey a progressive one. Learn to take with you that childlike part of your soul that always maintains a sense of delight, joy, spontaneity and innocence. Allow these attributes to expand into a spiritual maturity and confidence that go so deep that they might be called soul-esteem—a confidence that isn't afraid to experience life to the fullest.

When you find yourself responding to what you think, see, hear and feel with a rush of incredible bliss and wonder at life that brings goose-bumps to your flesh, you will know you have touched your soul. Allowing yourself to be deeply touched in this way is a kind of living, moving meditation—a vital, rich spiritual practice. Find something beautiful to reflect upon. Find a baby to hold, a rose to smell, a tree to hug, or music that fills your soul. Marvel at a beautiful sunset, gaze at a candle flame—whatever moves you into reverence. For me, it's gratitude.

Gratitude is the key to the higher emotions of reverence, love, compassion and faith. Take a moment to sit down, get comfortable, take some deep breaths, direct yourself to let go of what has been happening around you, and move into the new now present moment. Don't allow yourself to think about the future, just the present moment—where God lives. Then start writing down those things for which you are grateful. Let yourself begin to lift out of the dullness and notice the beat of the Drummer. As you do so you will not think about what your personality is doing, nor will you fret about your problems. You will experience a higher level of love, and you will not judge anyone or anything because you cannot march to the Drummer and at the same time think about hate or injustice, remorse or guilt. You will simply be immersed in soul, luxuriating in your true Self.

You will know that you are in touch with your soul and operating out of soul-esteem when you experience a sense of peace about your choices and make firm decisions based on the highest good for everyone concerned. You will know when you respond to circumstances instead of reacting to them; when you are vital, alive, creative and loving, instead of stagnant and unhappy; when you find yourself in a mode of forward movement, comfortable with change and uncertainty, and when you can give up your insecurities and trust in the process of unfoldment and transformation. You will know you are operating out of soul-esteem when you learn to identify your intuitive promptings and act upon them with spiritual confidence; when you understand that you cannot "own" anything, but have access to unlimited good to use freely; when you can look upon and observe your human experience with peace instead of feeling victimized by it, and when you can take responsibility for your life instead of blaming someone or something outside yourself. You will know, when you can transform outer control into inner mastery.

The soul is your transcendent consciousness, your spiritual body, your invisible essence—that immortal part of you that longs to project love, wisdom, caring, compassion and peace. It's time that you become reacquainted with your soul as the connector between your human self and the Universe. Consciousness evolution is speeding up, and if you don't want to be left at the gate, pay attention to how deprived your soul may be.

Find your soul by noticing the parts of yourself that have atrophied from lack of use. Think about what gave you pleasure as a child, and consider doing those things in order to resurrect the child within that holds the key to the Kingdom of Heaven. When you remember or rediscover something that nourishes your soul and brings you joy, honor yourself enough to make time for it in your life. In the midst of a soul-nourishing activity, you will become liberated. Your creativity will emerge and you will fall into a kind of spiritual syncopation. You will march to the beat of the Drummer with soul-esteem.

Listen to the Drummer

Greetings to you, My dear one. Take a moment to relax and open your awareness to the thickness of Spirit. Breathe deeply and let everything else go, as you surrender into this present moment and into My outstretched arms. Be silent and listen for the Drummer. Listen for the rhythm of the Silence.

It is My deepest desire in this beautiful moment of communion that you experience a greater sense of Me and a greater awareness of the goodness and wholeness that is your very soul. Let Me help you, My dear one, as I remind you to notice Me in the songs of the birds, the warmth of the sun upon your face, the aroma of flowers. I am present wherever you turn to notice Me. Listen for My voice as it whispers in the wind, and let yourself open to My love as it speaks from the eyes of another.

I am present in everyone, My dear one. In every person you meet—there am I. I am present in you, and that part of you that is Me is your very soul. Notice Me. You need not try so hard to come into My Presence for I am the soul of you. Just open yourself that I may fill you with My Living Spirit. Let Me live through you— speak through you—think through you—love through you. Let Me light your path— direct your way —and take you to the mountain top of spiritual awareness. Remember this, My child: "I have not given you the spirit of fear, but of power, and of love, and of a sound mind."

I am the Spirit of God within you and I give you peace. I am the Spirit of Truth within you and I set you free. I am Divine Love within you and I cast out fear.

Clear the way, My dear one. Let My Life flow through your soul and into your human vessel with ease that your light might shine and be a beacon to those who have lost their way. Notice how easily the difficulties of the world slip away as you follow the steady beat of My drum. Let My rhythm guide you into peace— right now—in this precious moment of holy communion.

Use your mind to think on these things: "Whatsoever things are true, whatsoever things are honest, whatsoever things are just, whatsoever things are pure, whatsoever things are lovely, whatsoever things are of good report; if there be any virtue and if there be any praise, think on these things." And as you direct your mind and your heart to dwell on these things, we will come into conscious union. And you, My dear one, will feel the thickness of Spirit. Your pathway will be filled with sunlight, and the air will be sweet with the fragrance of Pure Spirit. You will be so in tune with Me that you will become oblivious to everything but your oneness with Me.

I am always here, My beloved. I am here, closer than breathing and nearer than hands and feet, waiting to share with you your next moment of joy. Remember to take time out in your busy day to renew yourself with My Love and to lift yourself into My peace. Go forward this day taking with you the sweetness of My Presence and the sound of My rhythm.

I love you. All is well.

—The Drummer

In quietness and confidence shall be your strength.
—Old Testament

Chapter Four
Beyond Self-Esteem

However valuable various self-esteem teachings may be, they generally focus upon the ability of the human being to acquire more of that which is desired at the physical or material level. There's nothing wrong with that, but you might notice that your objective often becomes *getting*, and a getting consciousness fosters an attitude of competition and striving. This leads to an experience of outer struggle because when you are in the getting mode, you usually become fearful about keeping what you already have. The next thing you know, you feel as though it's you against the world, instead of you living in cooperation with the world.

Your degree of self-esteem is obviously important, but self-esteem is confidence at the level of personality. There is a confidence level within you that is even deeper than self-esteem. That deeper level is soul-esteem, the state or tone of consciousness that is expressed when your soul is allowed to grow and evolve, and to shine forth in all its splendor.

When you learn to believe and trust in your invisible inner support system, that part of you that is plugged into the unlimited Source, you act out of soul-esteem, not just self-esteem. When you recognize your soul and begin to operate from soul-esteem, you can function in the world without feeling that you are controlled by the world. Instead, you follow the beat of your inner Drummer. When you do that, you accomplish things in the human world that you never thought possible. You find yourself making decisions with ease, and you are able to maintain a sense of peace in the midst of everyday life.

As your individual soul is allowed to more fully express, it will embrace more and more of the Infinite Good. It will then produce happier and more harmonious conditions and experiences in the physical world. Your physical world is really a kind of "consciousness barometer" or human indicator of your state of soul-consciousness or soul-esteem. The important thing to understand is that *your soul is not something separate from the Source, but is an individualized expression of God.* It is God Energy taking a condensed form—as your soul, then as your body. When your soul is expressing its authentic Self, the result will be you as a fully integrated being in expression as a "power-presence."

Several years ago I attended a lecture in Denver, Colorado. The surroundings were contemporary, the mood was upbeat, the people were positive. The building structure was round, and the auditorium seats wrapped around the speaker's platform in a semicircle. I immediately responded to the uplifting music. The lights dimmed and the speaker stepped up to the lectern. His silver-white hair was impeccably groomed and he was wearing a crisp white suit. As the spotlights focused only upon him, his appearance was dramatic against the surrounding sea of darkness. Something about him was instantly likeable. Something about him tore down any walls of resistance between him and his audience. His voice was strong, his message inspiring, and his humor delightful. The person next to me leaned toward me and said in a strong whisper, "Now THAT'S a power-presence!"

I'll always remember the impact of that speaker and the

words that were whispered in my ear. Yes, the lighting was effective. Yes, the "image" was impressive. Yes, the speaker was compelling and the staging obvious. But it was more than that. There was something that radiated from that person that could only be described as a power-presence. What was it? It couldn't be misconstrued as egomania or the kind of power that one person might impose over another. It had nothing to do with control or manipulation. I *wanted* to listen to that man! I *liked* looking at him. It had nothing to do with physical strength or masculinity, or cleverness that maneuvers people or situations. This person exuded the competence and worth of self-esteem. He was not only competent—he *knew* he was competent. He believed in himself, and he possessed a high degree of self-respect. He was aware of his own worth. But there was something more.

That which emanated from the speaker that day was energy directed toward a purpose, an energy that carried with it the qualities of an unencumbered soul. He projected love and trust and strength to each member of his audience. There were no barriers. Some part of him, beyond his personality, was speaking to us beyond our personalities. He was speaking from his soul. He was speaking with soul-esteem. This transformed his ordinary personality into a power-presence.

The best world leaders have learned to turn the ordinary personality into a power-presence, which is so much more than self-confidence. They let the power-presence be who they are. They let it shine forth as it proclaims itself through their voice, their language, their manner, their personality, and their purpose.

I was so taken by the idea of the power-presence that I named the work I was doing at the time, *The Power-Presence Courses and Workshops*. During one of the classes, I encountered a woman who was in the military and worked in an office environment populated predominantly by men. She approached me and said, "Teach me about power words. I want to know how to get these unreasonable, obstinate, male chauvinists to pay attention to my suggestions and ideas." My response was, "I can't help you. I don't know any power words."

Sadly, many people think of power as their ability to tell other people what to do, or as a method of getting their own way by brandishing control over another person. They think of power as something they *get* from somewhere. It is so much more than that. It is much more subtle than that.

The power-presence is the personality of the soul that shines forth as a result of solid soul-esteem. It is something you already have—not something for you to get outside yourself. The trouble is, you may be unaware that you have the gift of personal power already built-in, beyond your limited concept of self. The good news is that you can discover or become reacquainted with it and learn to express it in a way that is authentic, effective, and unique.

The first step toward cultivating soul-esteem and expressing yourself as a power-presence is to *believe* that you already *are* a power-presence. After all, how can you express something you don't believe you are in the first place?

Does it seem difficult to believe that you already *are* a power-presence? If it does, then you have more than likely come from a background rooted in fear and ignorance and you are sabotaging yourself by operating from that limited perspective. You may be accustomed to using manipulative techniques, and you may allow your emotion-backed reactions to control you. You may be like so many who are afraid of being victimized, and as a result you may tend to react out of raw, lower level emotions. Fear-based emotional reactions keep you from believing that the power-presence can even exist for you. To build soul-esteem, you must practice exercising your soul. You must cut through the crusty layers of fear and surface struggle and dig down into the depths of unlimited possibility. You must tap into the radiance of your own soul—where the Drummer sits.

As you become more conscious about the truth of your being and lay aside fear, you will begin to notice the beat of your Inner Drummer. You will begin to emit soul-esteem. Soul-esteem then gives birth to the power-presence, and the personality of the soul begins to shine forth through you as you cultivate and use it.

The diagram at the end of this chapter, *Anatomy of a*

Power-Presence, illustrates this ideal. You express yourself in the human world as a power-presence when your human self recognizes and allows your soul to shine through the human expression. The amplitude of the power-presence depends upon the soul-esteem that is liberated at the soul level. This can only be accomplished by exercising your belief and trust in your soul's oneness with the Universal Power, and by getting in step with the Grand March.

Soul-esteem is developed as you learn to trust the qualities of the soul such as its intuitive abilities, its power to bring into your physical world the desires of your heart, its responsiveness to your needs, its unlimited resources, and its unconditional love and support of your human experience. When you have soul-esteem, you use the world to discover—not to survive. When you live a truly spiritual life with soul-esteem as your base of operation, then the human world will never be a problem. You will know that you are a spiritual being having a human experience. You will be *in* the world but not *of* the world. You will cease being dependent upon the world, and you will stop giving the world power to control your experience of it.

Self-esteem without the recognition of the soul and its potential power leads to an ego-based human experience. As a result of this shallow perspective, there is bound to be imbalance, struggle, emptiness, and ultimately, a sense of futility and fear. A personality without soul-esteem can exist on its own power only for a short time. It will eventually feel the effects of its spiritual disconnection.

Cultivating self-esteem is the building of confidence and trust in the outer personality, resulting in a kind of *horizontal development.* Soul-esteem is the result of building trust and belief in the soul, or a kind of *vertical development.* The two together create an upward and outward expansion of self-awareness that encompasses your spiritual nature *and* your human nature. This results in a magnificent human experience and an expanded consciousness that goes with you when you graduate from Earth school.

Anatomy of a Power-Presence

The Whole Self has two aspects:

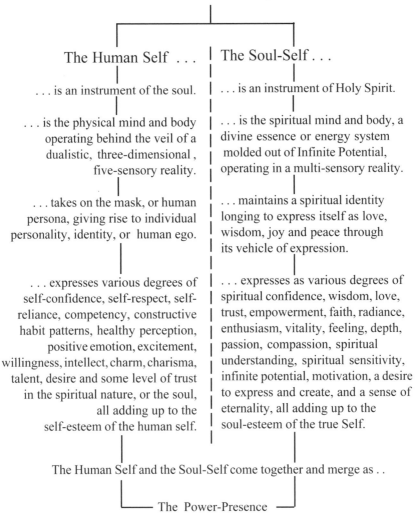

The Human Self . . .

. . . is an instrument of the soul.

. . . is the physical mind and body operating behind the veil of a dualistic, three-dimensional, five-sensory reality.

. . . takes on the mask, or human persona, giving rise to individual personality, identity, or human ego.

. . . expresses various degrees of self-confidence, self-respect, self-reliance, competency, constructive habit patterns, healthy perception, positive emotion, excitement, willingness, intellect, charm, charisma, talent, desire and some level of trust in the spiritual nature, or the soul, all adding up to the self-esteem of the human self.

The Soul-Self . . .

. . . is an instrument of Holy Spirit.

. . . is the spiritual mind and body, a divine essence or energy system molded out of Infinite Potential, operating in a multi-sensory reality.

. . . maintains a spiritual identity longing to express itself as love, wisdom, joy and peace through its vehicle of expression.

. . . expresses as various degrees of spiritual confidence, wisdom, love, trust, empowerment, faith, radiance, enthusiasm, vitality, feeling, depth, passion, compassion, spiritual understanding, spiritual sensitivity, infinite potential, motivation, a desire to express and create, and a sense of eternality, all adding up to the soul-esteem of the true Self.

The Human Self and the Soul-Self come together and merge as . .

──── The Power-Presence ────

The Power-Presence is the fully integrated Divine Human and emerges as a spiritual being having a human experience. It displays Itself as poise and balance, delivering a graceful response to the world of form.
It stands out as a gentle power and attractive individuality.
It shines through the eyes, proclaims Itself through the voice, extends Itself through the mannerisms, and exalts Itself through action.

Listen to the Drummer

Greetings, My cherished child. Be still and rest. You've been searching for a long time in terms of your Earth years. And, My dear one, you aren't even sure what it is for which you search. Could it be for the beat of your Inner Drummer? Could it be for a closer relationship with Me?

As you have walked the path of your own awakening, you have never been alone. Oh, I'm not speaking about the company of those with whom you interact on the third dimensional plane. I'm speaking about the angels of My Presence who surround you and awaken within you that mystical place wherein the Drummer sits. Such stirrings bring the message of new life, eternal life, wholeness, and oneness.

Lift up your heart, My child, and raise your eyes; throw back your head and sing praises for the dawning of the Now Age. Walk with Me in partnership. Let your old beliefs and your thoughts and feelings of confusion or distress vanish with the past, and let the freshness of this new now moment blossom in your heart and mind.

As you come into these new times, you will be transformed by the renewing of your mind, and you will be lifted up as the wholeness of spirit, soul and body that constitutes your holy expression. You are My beloved. You are that which I have created out of Myself. You are part of Me. You are heir to the Kingdom. Let yourself become the clear, unobstructed channel for My Love that you were created to be, and your life will be a demonstration of the power-presence that I had in mind from the beginning.

Let the tone of your consciousness vibrate with faith as old hurts and anger are transmuted into peace. Trust in your inner support system that is always directing you toward a purpose. Forgive yourself and all others. As you stand cleansed and free in the New Now you will be transformed for "Behold, I show you a mystery; You shall not sleep; but you shall be changed in a moment, in the twinkling of an eye, at the last trumpet. For the trumpet shall sound, and the dead shall be raised incorruptible, and you shall be changed."

The time of transformation is at hand, My beloved. You have always known you are more than your body, and now you will see that you are. You have always intuited that you are immortal; now you shall know that you are, and you shall voyage into the unknown with trust and confidence. You have always felt unfinished; now you are evolving before your very eyes. And in the twinkling of an eye, you shall be changed.

You are a miracle, My child. You are a power-presence born out of My wholeness. Go forth knowing that I have filled your cup to the brim with new understandings—with patience and endurance that you may fulfill your dreams.

I love you. All is well.

—The Drummer

Part Two
The Wake-Up Call

If you look at life one way, there is always cause for alarm.
—Elizabeth Bowen

Chapter Five
It's a Whacky World

Whacky isn't a misspelling. I don't mean *wacky* as in crazy, strange, irrational or eccentric. I mean *whacky* as in sharp, resounding blows.

I remember working at my desk one day, grumbling about expenses, feeling self-pity over my hectic schedule, and exhibiting a generally surly attitude. The telephone rang. It was an in-law calling to tell me about my twenty-two year old niece, who fell to the floor with a fatal heart attack the night before. She was tending her five-month old baby when it happened. The news literally jolted me out of my self-indulging doldrums. What a whack. I felt the blow in my head, my heart, and my knees. Suddenly my *attitude* vanished.

I've noticed that every time I get too consumed by my own human affairs, an Earth school "pop quiz" slaps me in the face. It's as if *something* is always watching and monitoring me. When I fall too deeply into the trance of self-pity, it shouts, "Oh, you think you got it bad? Try this on for size!" ... *WHACK!* The cosmic two-by-four strikes again.

Think about the enormous amount of energy wasted on self-pity, anger, frustration, gossip, anxiety, worry. You squander your mental, emotional and physical resources, and then wonder why you feel tired and bedraggled. Several people I know have gone through nasty divorces and it's interesting to be a spectator, observing these real-life dramas. Along with the pain, they experience various physical symptoms including fatigue, lined and drawn faces, stomach disorders, depression and general moodiness. Their creativity and productiveness suffers, and everything they do feels to them like a struggle. They don't laugh or have much fun. Spending just a few moments in their company makes me want to curl up in a corner and go to sleep. They radiate a mental and emotional smog that reaches out and grabs anyone within range and zaps that person's energy. I know. I've been grabbed more than once. It can be exhausting.

I have watched people become so consumed and obsessed with loss and pain that they shut down. They disconnect from their soul. They literally turn off their power. Their power is used up feeding the emotions of hurt, grief, anger, self-pity and fear. Some of these people are great performers. They practice stuffing their emotions and walk around dead inside, pretending to be fine on the outside. In time, after practicing and rehearsing over and over, they become class-act performers. What happens then? They need bigger and bigger whacks in order to feel anything at all at the soul level. Most of the time it takes a king-sized head-banger to wake them up. Sometimes it takes bottoming out and losing everything to get their attention. These people have chosen the toughest courses in Earth school.

I'm reminded of the game where a group of kids asks someone new to the game to sit under a blanket. The group asks the new person to take off something that isn't really needed, and toss it out on the floor. The gullible kid under the blanket usually removes a hat, a shirt, a bracelet, or a belt. That same person is asked to remove something else—and something else—until he or she finally catches on that it is the blanket that can be thrown off as unnecessary.

That's how most of us function when we are wearing a problem. We keep throwing off our energy, our health, our emotional stability, until we realize that it's the *problem* we don't need. We do not *need* pain and loss. We do not *need* to be fretting and worrying about our disappointments, and about all the bad things that haven't happened yet. Most of the time it takes a *whack* to wake us up and send us back into present time consciousness.

I remember browsing in a book store a few years back and happening upon a wonderful book called *A Whack in the Side of the Head,* by Roger von Oech. It's a book about how to stimulate creativity. The author talks about a teacher who couldn't get her student to understand what she was talking about until she picked up a stick and gave him a whack on the side of the head. The jolt caused him to grasp the ideas she was trying to convey. It got him *thinking something different.*

In this day and age, it isn't advisable for one person to whack another in the side of the head unless someone wants to go directly to jail. But the point is, sometimes nothing short of a whack on the side of the head can dislodge our stuck, stale ideas. Not a whack from another person, but a whack that we attract to ourselves from the reciprocal universe. Like the student in von Oech's book, we all need an occasional whack on the side of the head to shake us out of our routine, addictive patterns.

This universe delivers up *whacks* in all colors, all sizes, and all shapes. They usually show up when you least expect them, anytime night or day. All *whacks* have one thing in common—they force you, at least for the moment, to think something different. Sometimes you may get whacked by a challenge, sometimes by what looks like a failure, a change, or some event. Many times you will be whacked with situations that seem humanly impossible to meet. Everyone has these experiences at one time or another.

Actually, everything that you experience which is different from the comfortable routine that you have established for yourself can be considered a *whack.*

Whacks come to us in three ways, the first being *random acts of whacks*. That means whatever comes down the pike. We can get whacked any minute, out of the blue. You see, most of us are asleep to the fact that we can take charge of our lives. Until we wake up to this truth, start acknowledging our power, and start making conscious intelligent decisions based upon soul-esteem, we will remain subject to the *law of averages*.

The first time I was made aware of the law of averages was in Thomas Troward's book, *The Edinburgh Lectures on Mental Science*. Basically, the concept refers to large numbers and a wide margin of error, or accident, or failure. It is a principle that says probability will influence everything in the long term. So when someone operates according to the law of averages, that person is subject to the collective consciousness—to the toss of the dice—to whatever comes up.

In the animal kingdom, for example, there is a margin of destruction that corresponds to reproduction perpetuating the species. This is the law of averages in action. No individual animal or insect knows which ones will die or which will live to keep the balance.

Troward suggests that as intelligence advances at the human level, the individual is less and less subject to the law of averages, and has more and more power over determining and controlling the conditions of his or her own life. But if you are asleep to the power of Universal Law and to your own power to use it, you tend to take no conscious part in your own destiny. You go through life blowing in the wind, thinking you are powerless to control your experiences. People who live their lives subject to the roll of the dice are usually unhappy much of the time. They worry about when the next whack will hit. What will it be? A fire that burns their house to the ground? A mugger in the mall parking lot? A dreaded disease? A germ? A pink slip at the office? There isn't much time for joy, or peace, or creativity, or spiritual awareness in the midst of all these concerns. As we gain more soul-esteem and hook up with Infinite Intelligence, the margin of accident narrows.

Stephen Covey, author of *Principle Centered*

Leadership, points out that everything is created twice: first in thought, second as form. If you are not in charge of your first creation, meaning your ideas and thoughts, you will live most of your life by default, or according to someone else's idea.

At the soul level we are all connected, somewhat merged with each other. This creates the soul life of all beings collectively, sometimes called the *collective unconscious*, the *seat of all memory*, a record of everything that has ever happened. This collective memory makes up the subconscious tendencies expressed through the individual. People who take charge of their own first creations can change these tendencies in themselves. Through a constant awareness and an effort to take charge of one's thoughts, feelings, beliefs and actions, each person can use the gift of choice and rise mentally and spiritually above the law of averages into self-mastery.

The second way in which whacks come to you is through self-imposed *lessons*. These are *wake-up* whacks, or lessons, that you will repeat like a student who flunks a course and must keep repeating it until he grasps the material. You finally get the idea that life would be much easier if you had learned the lesson the first time.

The third way in which whacks might come to you is by the *Law of Attraction*. You will literally draw to yourself that which you believe. These are like the whacks you get when you look in a mirror the first thing in the morning. There you are looking back at yourself. The mirror shows you exactly what you believe is true. Just like the mirror, your life—surroundings, environment, people, experiences—all serve you by showing you the content of your consciousness. The life you are living is like a barometer, indicating the atmospheric pressure of your belief system. Your life will always reflect what you believe without fail.

There's a law in the universe that says, "That to which you give your attention grows." So guess who has the most accidents, the most illness in the family, the most difficulty getting along with other people, the most problems in general. The person who conceives of them in the first place. Napoleon Hill made the statement, "That which we can conceive and believe, we can achieve." He meant it with respect to success, but it goes both ways. If you conceive of and believe in disaster, disease, worry and dread, you attract more and more disaster, disease, worry and dread. The universe always supports your beliefs. You get back what you give out. You reap what you sow. What goes around comes around, and the boomerang always comes back.

The bottom line is, until you rise above the law of averages and start taking charge of your own creation of life, you will go around whacking yourself in the head—and the heart—and the solar plexus. All lessons in life are self-lessons. All learning is remembering and revealing your true Self.

How do you handle the whacky world in which you live? You learn to use your power to control how you react to what is going on around you. When an event comes your way that you appear to have no control over, it is vital to realize that you *do* have control over your response or reaction to that event. You can use your power to detach yourself. I don't mean ignore what's going on, I mean look upon the circumstance as though viewing a motion picture. Look upon it with interest, but don't get stuck in all the sticky *stuff.* That's the difference between sympathy and empathy. Sympathy makes you part of the problem; empathy makes you a compassionate onlooker. From a detached position you can use your power to make a constructive or positive change for the better. You can change your consciousness. The trick is to be *in* this whacky world, but not *of* it.

If you have been misusing your power or giving it away, you can turn things around through an act of will. Realize that the situations in which you may be stuck really have no power unless you fuel them with your energy. Understand that no other person can stop you or hold you back unless you give that person your power by not taking charge of your own thoughts, feelings and beliefs. The good news is, you don't have to live your life by default.

Actually, you have many opportunities to wake up before you get whacked by something big. Some of the silliest things can happen to you when you are asleep, and I don't mean literally asleep, I mean spiritually unaware. When you become so distracted by the human world that you no longer hear the sound of your Inner Drummer, and fall out of step, you will be gently nudged to notice the dumb things that you may have done when you weren't awake. These little eye-openers often show up as harmless, funny, no-brainer things that are really timely whacks to wake you up. When you listen, wake up, and tune back into the Drummer, you won't need to attract a head-banger to get your attention. But if you don't wake up as a response to these nudges, you will eventually experience the *big whack*. When you can wake up in the middle of one of these big whacks, laugh at yourself, get back into step, and watch life flow.

Christine, a friend of mine, told me about a wake-up nudge she received from a police officer —or was he an angel? She related how she had just completed a business appointment and was driving her car up a ramp and onto the highway. She pounced on the gas pedal, blended with the traffic, and was cruising along thinking about her day. She looked up and saw flashing lights behind her and finally realized that it was a police officer trying to get her attention. She pulled over onto the shoulder of the road and nervously removed her driver's license from her wallet.

The policeman approached her car on the passenger side, made no reference to her driver's license and said, "Do you have any idea how fast you were going?"

"No sir, I don't," was her reply.

"Do you have any idea how long I've been following you?"

"No sir, I don't," she said in a timid high-pitched voice.

"I have been following you for more than a mile," he said.

Then he looked her in the eyes and said firmly, "Pay attention to what you are doing," and walked away. His wake-up message was so powerful that Christine promptly burst into tears. She told me she felt she had been "visited."

One day I was backing out of the garage in my new Jeep. There are parking spaces across from our garage, and I had become used to pulling straight back into the parking spaces as I turned to exit the parking lot. Until that day I had been only partially aware of the blind spot at the back of the Jeep where the spare tire rests. I was only barely conscious of the way smaller cars, when passing me on my right, are so low that they become almost invisible from my perspective in the Jeep. The point is, I was not nearly awake enough to really look and see what was around me from these unfamiliar perspectives. So I got to experience a wake-up nudge that was serious enough to get my attention.

On this particular day I remember looking over both shoulders and thinking, "Boy, you really have to be alert in order to see around the blind spots in this vehicle." However, even though I *looked*, I didn't really *see*. I accelerated. *THUD*. I had backed into Barbara's Dodge Shadow. Barbara was our tiny little dynamo who ran the cleaning service that kept our home presentable. The little Shadow didn't have a chance. I poked both of its tail lights out, smashed the bumper, and the trunk looked like a big grimace. My big Jeep Grand Cherokee was unscathed. I felt terrible. Since that incident, I have become very awake about the blind spots. It's as if my awareness about learning to look more carefully had been lurking at some level of my consciousness, but it didn't have my full wide-awake attention until I experienced a wake-up whack.

Poor Barbara had just gotten her Shadow out of the body shop the day before. It had undergone major repairs for the same thing— being attacked while driverless. After the repairs were complete from the impression I had made, the Shadow was once more attacked while sitting innocently and driverless at the curb side. Could this have been Barbara's wake-up call?

There are so many minor wake-up whacks that protect you from the bigger whacks. When they happen, they are often annoying and you may think of them as nuisances, but they are really angels in disguise. Think about it: the times you have tripped and caught yourself and blamed someone else for leaving something in your path; the time you weren't paying attention as you ran down the stairs, slipped or lost your balance, and caught yourself just in time before you fell headlong down to the bottom. What about the time you barely escaped an accident when you were daydreaming in your car? These whacks woke you up, didn't they? Perhaps it was an angel tapping you on the shoulder. Why did these things keep happening? Because you kept sliding back into a semi-consciousness, into sleep, into laziness, into drowsy living, into spiritual dullness.

Learn to bless these precious moments that jolt you awake so that you can protect yourself from a disastrous occurrence—one from which you might not wake up at all. More important, begin taking charge of your own first creation—your own thoughts—your own feelings—your own beliefs—your own consciousness. Turn toward your own soul, that part of you that is in direct communication with Spirit, and listen to it, love it, care for it, lift its burdens and let it shine.

Running Toward the Light

I'm on the path.
The eternal path to everywhere and nowhere.
The path where Holy Spirit guides me
and holds my hand.
Sometimes the path before me
takes on a shroud of mystery
and I walk into a fog of thick, gooey doubt and fear
that chokes and strangles.
My feet feel heavy
as though I'm walking through tar,
as I struggle to lift one foot and place it in front of the other.
But I look up and notice a beam of Light
that pierces the illusion of fear.
It's just a tiny beam of awareness,
but it gives me hope.
And soon, the fog begins to clear
and I notice that my feet are moving faster than before.
There is grass under my feet and I'm running.
Running toward the Light.

Listen to the Drummer

Greetings, My beloved. It is I. The One that loves you. Make yourself as comfortable as possible. Take a deep breath, let your face muscles soften and relax, and tell your neck muscles to let go. Let your shoulders drop as you let go of the tension that's been held there.

Enter into this safe and holy place that is the present moment, My child. Let yourself sense and feel the sacred space all around you. Can you feel My Presence surrounding you? Filling you? Loving you? Can you let yourself relax into the sweetness of My Presence? Let Me lift you into joy, My child. Let Me lift you into a higher place. Come with Me into a realm where all restlessness is calmed—and where you remember that I fashioned you out of Myself.

I know your confusion as you experience what seems to be lessons in your human world. It is not I, My beloved, who sends you the lessons, but you yourself. My creation contains those laws that operate on your behalf to bring you back into the awareness of My kingdom. I have blessed you with everything you need to enjoy your experience on Earth, but you must realize that you are the creator of your every experience. As you transmute your sorrow, confusion, doubt, and fear, into joy and lightness, you will begin to feel the energy of My Presence enfolding you, ready to respond to your every desire.

The key to My Kingdom, to creating a heaven on earth, is to let My Love move freely through your mind and your emotions. In this safe and sacred time of communion, can you allow your pain and anger to melt in the fire of My Spirit?

Can you allow your fear and insecurity to be transmuted into courage and faith? My Love flows freely through your consciousness and into your world of experience in proportion to your forgiveness and acceptance of yourself and all others. Be not afraid My child. Remember that all things whatsoever you pray and ask for, believe that you have received them and you shall have them.

I withhold nothing from you, My beloved. You, who have chosen to turn your eyes from the darkness to the Light, are blessed by My grace right now. You, whose heart has longed to create a heaven on Earth, to see love instead of hate, are a part of My desire to bring wholeness and healing to your world. Everything in the world blesses you. The very planet you live on is blessing you. Honor your relationship with the Earth.

And so for now, go forth My dear one, open to My blessings that will take form according to your every need. Take time out to sit in the silence with Me every day, yea, many times a day. I am always here. I am your Source. I am closer than your breath and nearer than hands and feet.

I love you. All is well.

—The Drummer

I arrived at Truth, not by systematic reasoning
and accumulation of proofs but by a flash of light
which God sent into my soul.
                                        —Al-Ghazali

Chapter Six
Truth or Consequences

Part of the waking up process has to do with becoming aware of the truth. There are two versions of truth—the personal and the impersonal. Both are true, but personal truth is *your* truth, and impersonal truth belongs to everyone.

When you first think of the word truth, you might think of that which conforms to the facts as perceived by the five senses or that which is the opposite of a lie. You might think of honesty, and you know that if you tell a lie or you're dishonest, you will face the consequences. You will reap what you have sown. But personal truth varies from individual to individual based upon beliefs, customs, and perceptions. In other words, your truth may not be the same as my truth. What is true for me may be different from what is true for you. This is personal truth as opposed to Universal Truth. There are also degrees of truth. Mark Twain said, "I am different from George Washington, I have a higher, grander standard of principle. Washington could not lie. I can lie, but I won't."

On the human level, people play many games with truth. They manipulate it so that it appears to be truth—so that it *feels* okay. To understand what I mean, all you have to do is bring to mind one of the many *fish stories* about the "one that got away." One man, after fishing all day and not getting a nibble, packed up and headed for home. On the way he stopped at a store with a sign in the window that said, "Fresh Fish." He went in and told the man behind the counter to *throw* him several of the biggest fish he had. When the man asked the fisherman why, he replied, "Because it's important that I catch them. I'm not much of a fisherman, but I'm certainly not a liar." You can convince yourself that things are true by creating your own version of the truth.

It is *true* that the central nervous system cannot distinguish between what is real and that which is imaginary. In other words, if you think something long enough, your body will respond as if it really happened—whether it happened or not. This is what happens in hypnosis. If you're a good hypnotic subject, you can be told that you're being burned by a flame and a blister can appear, even though the flame is imaginary. Hypnosis can also produce anesthesia as well as manifest any number of other suggestions that the subconscious mind accepts as true.

Have you ever gone overboard in telling the truth? Have you ever told the truth knowing that it would hurt someone or enable you to get even with them? Such an obsession has been referred to as *compulsive truth telling*. When you're dealing with personal truth, it's a good idea to examine the *intent* of the truth you're about to tell. Some truths may be better kept to yourself. Poet William Blake said, "A truth that's told with bad intent beats all the lies you can invent."

As you look at the bigger picture, you'll see that there is a higher truth that is impersonal Truth, which can also be referred to as Eternal Truth or God's Truth that applies to everyone. Personal truth, the human level of truth, changes as you change. But you can never change Universal Truth because it remains constant regardless of variable external factors. In many metaphysical writings, what is true in the relative world is indicated with a small "t," and that which is God's Truth is indicated with a capital "T." The Truth is all-pervasive and accessible to everyone who tunes into it. But each person processes the Truth through the filters of his or her own personal truth, or individual consciousness.

It's been said that the truth hurts. This may be true of personal truth—or compulsive truth telling. But the Truth has never hurt anyone. The Truth knows only how to heal. Those who resist Truth resist healing, and those in need of healing can find it by embracing Truth. The Truth brings with it a peace and a satisfaction that falsehood cannot imitate. This Truth can do no harm. Truth cannot harm, and it cannot contaminate. Divine Truth empowers. You need the Divine Truth in order to expand your consciousness and grow, in the same way that you need sunshine, vitamins, love and affection.

It has been said that Truth is a synonym for God and can carry only one message—the standard of God. Truth cannot be qualified as bad Truth, good Truth or better Truth. Truth is just Truth and never changes.

I've heard it said that the universe could thrive on the foundation of Truth alone—even if there were no God. So for those of you who might find the idea of God, or the word God objectionable, you can still make use of Universal, Eternal Truth. "Ye shall know the truth, and the truth shall make you free." This passage in the Bible doesn't just say the truth shall make you free, it says, "Ye shall KNOW the truth, and the truth shall make you free."

To know the Truth is to be tuned into the Inner Drummer. When you hear the rhythm of the universe, no one can take it away from you. To know the Truth means you have expanded your awareness beyond the five-sensory world. You begin to use your spiritual senses to see and hear as though sensing things from the God perspective. Your human world begins to harmonize and you march to the Drummer with no hesitation or fear. You rise above the confusion of the human world, and when you are called upon to face a problem, you quickly see that there is no problem, simply an opportunity to respond with trust and faith.

Al-Ghazali was a second century Islamic philosopher. He said, "I arrived at Truth, not by systematic reasoning and accumulation of proofs but by a flash of light which God sent into my soul." That's the way you will KNOW the Truth. It's the same as hearing the beat of your Inner Drummer. You sense it as it comes like a flash through the channel of your consciousness, and you *receive* that truth with a knowingness that is intuitive. But if the Truth comes through intuitive channels that have been contaminated with your fears and doubts, you might rationalize the Truth to be what you want it to be. The stream of Universal Consciousness is always expressing through you, and in doing so it takes on the tone of your own consciousness. It takes on the tone of your thoughts, feelings and beliefs.

Throughout this book I will talk with you about bringing your hidden thoughts, feelings and beliefs up to a conscious level so that you can reeducate yourself with the Truth. When you have accepted the Truth on all levels—mind, body and soul—you will have gone through the process of being born again.

You will more than likely recognize the Truth through your feeling nature, because you will generally sense or *feel* Truth more than you will think it. You will *know* it, even though you may not be able to understand it or explain it. To turn away from Truth will lead to struggle. To turn toward Truth will give you life and peace. When you truly align yourself with the Truth that you are one with God, that there is no separation, you will begin to see Truth pour Itself through your consciousness. It will display itself in your human world as love, compassion, integrity, strength, wisdom, joy and peace. You can find descriptions of Truth in books but you will never find Truth in a book, because the Whole Truth cannot be described, contained, confined, or formatted into something that serves only a few. The Truth is free to everyone and cannot be possessed. No religion, no philosophy, no teacher, no group has exclusive possession of the Truth. The Truth is inclusive of all and no one can be excluded from it. Jesus, Buddha, Moses, Mohammed, and the other great ones have all taught the same Truth. There are many paths, but there is only one Truth. The Truth cannot be altered, bought, sold, or traded. It can only be embodied and lived.

If you want to know what Truth is, put aside your textbooks for a while and walk outside under the trees. Watch a child play in the park. Lie in the grass and look at the stars. Be amazed by your very breath. Listen to your favorite music. Dance. Be. In the words of David and Jamil: "The dance is never done, and the song is never completely sung, 'til the love of the Truth has made us One."

Listen to the Drummer

My dear one, I once again welcome you into an awareness of My Presence. Let yourself slide into a beautiful, peaceful place of peace. Breath deeply and let your body and mind relax. Ride on the waves of My breath that is your breath. Let it flood your being so that you can forget your physicality for just a few moments as you lift into the higher dimension that has been called My Kingdom.

Open your heart, My beloved, and notice that My Truth is that which is the governing principle of all life. Understand, My precious one, that I am Life. Life is that which I am. And that Life which I am is within you. It lives through you and as you. Can you sense the magnitude of that understanding? Can you lift yourself to see that you are Me happening? This is the Truth that never changes, My child. This is the Truth of your being.

My Truth is not the same as the human sense of truth, which is relative to each human being's perception. Eternal Truth is that principle which operates in accord with the Will of the Divine. It is the same yesterday, today and tomorrow, and exists at the center of every living thing. The Truth is free to everyone and cannot be possessed. It is inclusive of all, for there is but one Truth.

Do not make the human mistake of believing that it is I who punishes you for your erroneous stumblings, My child. From My perspective you are whole and perfect. It is only from your vantage point in the human dimension that you appear to falter and fall.

Your faltering seems to carry with it a punishment. But that so-called punishment is simply the reciprocal action of the universe in which you live, My dear one. It has nothing to do with My judgment of you. In My eyes you are My beloved in whom I am well pleased. As you rise above the veil of human perception, you, too, will see with My eyes and the corruptible shall put on incorruption.

Do not blame yourself, My dear one, when you sink down into the density of the human drama and forget your Divinity. You need but come to Me and have a talk as we are now doing. Breathe in My life, and breathe out the heaviness. Let the illusions fall away as you turn your attention to My Love that surrounds you and infills you and embraces you and soothes you. Your spiritual confidence lies in a conscious unity with Me, My child, in your awareness that My good is always available, that I am always accessible. It is the turning toward Me that dissolves all shadows. Come as often as you will, My beloved, for these moments of Truth and remembering. I love you. All is well.

—The Drummer

*We check and repress the divinity that stirs
within us to fall down and worship the
divinity that is dead without us.*
                              —Henry David Thoreau

Chapter Seven
Spiritual Responsibility

The word responsibility can be thought of as the ability to respond, or response–ability. Spiritual responsibility has to do with responding to what is happening in your world in such a way that it is in harmony with the intention of Creation. Responsibility was given to you as an inner impulse to use your endowments. What are endowments? Natural gifts. In other words, you have certain abilities built into your nature which are intended to enable you to behave and respond in certain ways that are unique to you. Before you can truly march to your own Drummer, you must learn to respond to these gifts and put them to use in your life. If you do this, you will not be envious of someone else's talents or abilities, and you will not compare yourself to anyone else—you will simply do whatever is necessary to develop your own hidden treasures and experience the joy of freedom in the process.

Think about this. Birds relate and respond to the air and fish relate and respond to water. Birds are not responsible to swim in the ocean, and fish are not responsible to fly in the air. Cattle respond to grassy pastures. A cow does not feel it a duty to dive into the ocean and swim, nor does a cow feel the impulsion to soar through the clouds. "This is ridiculous," you might say, "Cows were not intended to fly or to swim." Exactly. There isn't a stalk of corn growing in the cornfields of the Midwest that you would expect to produce apples and you have yet to see a fish digging a hole next to a gopher. "This, too, is ridiculous," you say, "Corn was intended to be corn, and fish were intended to live in water." Exactly. Likewise, there are many things that *you* were intended to do as well as many things that you *were not* intended to do. In other words, you should feel no responsibility to go against your innate nature.

The reason for responsibility is to provide an impulsion within everything toward a coherent, orderly and unified relationship with everything else. Each creature and each person is responsible to be that which they were intended to be and nothing more. Responsibility is an inside job. Unfortunately, it has been distorted to mean only outside duty, obligation, burden, or accountability having to do with human expectations. When what you have done does not meet society's expectations or the expectations of your family or your circle of friends, you often feel guilty and inadequate. Much of the time these self-imposed responsibilities have nothing to do with your natural responsibilities—your spiritual, internal responsibilities.

It is important when someone tries to hand you something to do, or when you look around and see where something needs to be done, that you listen to your own heart and mind and soul. Ask yourself, "Is this something that resonates with my innate impulsion toward my soul's fulfillment? Will doing this thing support my life purpose? Is this in harmony with that for which I am intended?" If you respond honestly to these questions, you will know if that which is before you to do is in alignment with Creation's intent for you and you will have the courage to say "No," if it doesn't feel right. Don't become imprisoned by imposed responsibilities. Don't go against Creation by taking on the responsibility to save other people or the world. When you try to protect others from life experiences that offer them opportunities to grow in consciousness, you interfere and suppress that person's soul from revealing itself through its lessons.

I'm not espousing the idea that you give up all sense of obligation. This would be irresponsibility. To be irresponsible is to be immature and egocentric. But spiritual responsibility is recognizing Creation's impulsion within you and listening to it, knowing within yourself what task there is for you to do regardless of how hard it seems or how long it will take. When you are fulfilling your spiritual responsibility there will be a knowing within you—a feeling that you are resonating with life. Synchronicities (God's clues) show up to support you, and you notice how easily life flows. There is undeniable energy-synergy.

Until now you may have been reliant upon something outside yourself to help you respond to life's happenings. You may have largely relied upon a God that is outside yourself to fix things for you and to manifest what has been called *miracles* in your life. You may have operated out of the awareness, opinions and beliefs of the group, or collective consciousness, with which you have identified. It might be the family group, the societal group, the religious group, or some other group or groups. Up until now.

All of us are, one by one, growing *out* of group consciousness, and growing *into* individual self-responsibility. You may have noticed that you are relying less and less upon the group mind to direct you, and you are responding to the longing to be more responsible for your own choices and decisions.

You are part of the new consciousness movement that could be described as the New Energy. You are moving out of feeling helpless and reliant upon someone or something outside yourself, and moving toward becoming a conscious co-creator with God. It is time to accept the new gifts of Spirit and begin taking full responsibility for what is happening to you. It is time to put on the armor of Light and take action to create your desire, your passion. The Master said, "With God all things are possible." He didn't say it isn't possible for *you* and *only* possible for God. He said, *with* God all things are possible—that is, in *partnership* with God all things are possible.

The *now* times are about partnership with God and about taking responsibility to hold up your end of the bargain. You have for so long been taught to "let go and let God," with a sense of giving up and surrendering any responsibility. This no longer applies. Yes, you must let Spirit move through you, work through you, speak through you. Never again can you treat Spirit as something outside yourself to which you give yourself up. Why? Because God is happening as each one of us. God is happening *as* you! It is your responsibility to put God back where God belongs in your consciousness. It is your responsibility to put God back into your actions. It is your responsibility to practice the Presence of God and experience the Presence in every action, every behavior, every word you speak, every idea you entertain, every intention you embrace. It is your "now" responsibility to let all of life be an opportunity to see God and to put God into action. With every action you must accept Spirit's poise. In the words of author, teacher and healer Frederick Keeler, "Pick up that pen as though you were doing it for God. Tie that package for God. Eat for God. Live with God for the moment until these moments become your days, and your days become God's days." This is spiritual partnership.

Where do you *do* this practice of the Presence of God? You do it right where you are—in the midst of your human experience. It may be nice to go off once in a while to a mountain or a cave or some sacred place and renounce the world in order to do soul-work. Isolation and sitting in the silence can be like recharging your soul-batteries or refreshing your spirit just as you would recharge the batteries in your car or your cell phone. But once a battery is recharged and ready for use, you don't keep recharging it. Likewise, once you are recharged, it is time to put yourself into action.

You are intended to put God into action. You are intended to put your gifts into action. Your awakening is to realize that your spiritual responsibility is as a co-creator with the Infinite. You don't create Creation itself, but you do create your experiences of Creation. When you begin to fully realize that, you will begin marching to the Drummer that sits at the center of your soul. You will march on with your head held high because you are marching with soul-esteem. You will march on fearlessly, wearing your mantle of Spirit, donning your armor of Light, clothed in your robe of magnificence. The only thing that can hold you back from putting on the robe and claiming your partnership with God is the level of your own spiritual confidence.

Begin now to affirm your divinity. Begin now to integrate your human self with your Divine Self and wake up to your oneness with God. Let yourself recognize the power-presence that you are and move into true partnership. Move out of total surrender and reliance into commitment—commitment to take spiritual responsibility of your life as you partner with God.

To some of you, it may seem blasphemous or irreverent to put yourself on such a level with the Supreme Being. But for those who are from traditional backgrounds, let me remind you of the words of the Master when he said, "Is it not written in your law, I said, 'Ye are gods?'" (John 10:34)

It was Jesus who called God "Father." As he used the metaphor of the divine parent, he said, "I of my own self can do nothing, it is the Father in me that doeth the works." Jesus represents the evolution of consciousness into the awareness of the Spirit within. The Father within. The Creator within. Unity. Oneness. And now we are making a transition into a new era; a new understanding; the next step in consciousness evolution, which is spiritual responsibility—an era of Divine Partnership.

So what does co-creation really mean? Co-creation is the duty, or responsibility, that requires you to believe and accept that with God all things are possible. It means having enough soul-esteem to be able to respond to your world with actions that bring God into everything that you say and do. Here are some powerful words from Lee Carroll's book, Kryon Book VI, entitled *Partnering with God.* "No longer see your boat of life drifting in a sea of frightening uncertainty. Instead, take the tiller of the rudder in your hand with wisdom and power. Watch the giant hands of spirit—your own golden angel of Higher Self—wrap its fingers around yours, and together, steer an anointed course to home. This is the real partnership!"

What are the spiritual responsibilities of this holy partnership? The first responsibility, as *The Course in Miracles* puts it, is to make peace your single goal. It is to create peace in your life by committing yourself to the idea that you can start to have peace even in the midst of terror and chaos, even in the midst of painful memories that have engraved themselves in the tone of your consciousness and the biology of your body. It is to create peace so completely that your countenance becomes a mirror of God's wholeness. This shift in consciousness will let peace shine through your eyes, show itself in the expression on your face, display itself in the confident posture of your body, and in your attitude and demeanor.

If you commit yourself to creating peace in your life, then during those moments when your humanness moves you into anger or frustration, you will be conscious of your Partner's Presence saying to you, "Be peaceful with Me. Don't be rocked off your center by these things that are your lessons. The bigger picture is that there is only Love and it is the most powerful force in this universe." Take responsibility in your partnership by listening to that still small voice. Let the arms of Spirit protect you, lift you, and create for you the peace you desire as the partner of Love Itself.

Another spiritual responsibility is to have no other gods before you. Gods such as worry, anger, and other forms of fear. It does seem to be human nature to become angry once in a while or to worry about what's going to happen next. But neither of these emotions serves you. No form of fear serves you, except for the few moments when you must be alert to physical danger. Otherwise fear does not serve you and doubting your self-worth is a form of fear.

Fear goes against the very commitment to create peace in your life and to rely only upon the God within. To rely on external influences is infidelity of enormous spiritual magnitude. Anger, worry, doubt, all go against the principles of your new partnership. When you let anger or worry or doubt get the best of you, you begin to fall back into the old energy of looking outside yourself for help and solution. And when you look to something or someone outside yourself, to something or someone other than the higher part of yourself, you literally create infidelity with God, infidelity with your Higher Self.

Henry David Thoreau wrote these words in his journal: "We check and repress the divinity that stirs within us to fall down and worship the divinity that is dead without us." This is saying that we ignore the divinity within ourselves in favor of making false gods of worldly things. It speaks of the ego-self that claims you are less than a partner with God, less than one who has the capability of responding to change and becoming new, fresh, alive and forward-moving. It is that which most people bow down to and worship. It is the lie about life.

Your spiritual responsibility is not about seeking, but revealing your own unique expression of life. It is about seeing the Presence of God in all things and all people and in whatever you are doing. It is not about taking the burdens of others or the world on your shoulders, but about staying true to yourself. Do not engage in self-blame but in spiritual accountability. When you become accountable, you acknowledge that you had something to do with what has happened to you, that you played a part in creating, promoting or allowing it all to happen. When you take responsibility, you take control. You claim the power to make your own choices and to develop your personal endowments so that you can participate in the *Law of Circulation* and give back to life.

In order to realize your dreams you must become the person who you think deserves the greater good or greater experience. You must believe that you *can* activate the fantastic potential inside you, your soul potential. Then you must turn your attention away from lack, limitation and inadequacies, and turn toward the unlimited, wonderful possibilities. Such a transformation is not created over night. It takes persistent commitment to spiritual responsibility and fidelity to Truth. It takes soul-work to gain the kind of attitude and behavior that produces positive results, and it takes soul-work to maintain that attitude and behavior. But it is made easier when you become conscious of your soul and its power and understand that you do not have to force, compete or manipulate in order to win in life. Your soul is always there to support you, your gifts are there to bless you, and your outer world is always there to show you how you're doing.

Keep dreaming wonderful dreams and believe that they can come true. Accept that the powerhouse within you is ready and waiting to become more. It is true that you must earn your dreams, but you do not have to earn your potential, your uniqueness, your individuality, your specialness or your God-given endowments. You were born with these things. You must dig out from under false conclusions, misperceptions and negative self-image, and free yourself to be more. You must send out into your world that which is more positive, more loving, more creative and more vital. If you do these things, you will begin enjoying your life more, and you will reap the rewards of creative thinking and behavior. And when someone says to you, "Just who do you think you are?" you can respond with, "I am a child of the universe. I am Spirit personified. I am a spiritual being enjoying a human experience."

Go forward, committed to knowing that "with God all things are possible." Rededicate yourself to the practice of the Presence of God, no matter what you're doing, whose eyes you are looking into, what situation you're dealing with, and regardless of your human temptation to become angry or worried or doubtful. Rely only upon God—your Senior Partner, your ally, your beloved, your Divine Self. Come into the knowing that you are in essence a whole being that no longer looks outside itself with questions, but stands ready to celebrate the answers within. You have reached the summit of the mountain and it's time to don the mantle of Spirit, put on the armor of Light, and fulfill the function for which you came into the world.

Spiritual Responsibility

As I wade through the burdens
which rest upon my shoulders,
I feel their weight holding me in place.
It's as if in a bad dream
when my feet are running as fast as they can
but I'm going nowhere.
And then I hear a sound in the distance—
not from outside myself,
but from the depths of my being.
It's the beat of The Drummer
dissolving these self-imposed expectations
into the nothing from whence they came.
I stand free and unburdened,
with an inner impulsion toward higher ground.
This is my soul's responsibility,
and none other.
My human responsibility becomes
as light as a feather
as I let Spirit move through all that concerns me.
I accept the gifts of Spirit
and uphold my end of the bargain
in my new partnership with God.
The Presence of God fills me, guides me
and moves me to put my gifts into action
as I march to the Drummer
that sits at the center of my soul.

Listen to the Drummer

Still yourself for a few moments, My dear one. Make your body as comfortable as possible, take a deep breath, and enter into our sanctuary of oneness where tensions of the day melt away. Let your face muscles soften and relax, tell your neck muscles to let go, and allow your shoulders to drop. Notice the mind-chatter slowing down and dissipating so that you can bring your attention fully and completely into this present moment. As you enter into this present moment, you enter into a holy moment. You enter into sacred space. Let yourself sense and feel this sacred space all around you, and notice that it fills your being with light and love.

Are you ready, My beloved? Are you ready to claim your divine heritage and take joy in your spiritual responsibilities? Are you ready to do your soul-work, to deepen your inward journey, to give up your illusions of worry and doubt? To do so is to take responsibility for the gifts of Spirit which represent the full potential of your Divine Self.

Take a leap of faith, My child, and embrace the new now with spiritual confidence and divine grace. Come into My Presence with singing and honor your-self as a spiritual being. Listen to the Drummer as it beats out the desires of your own heart and mind and soul. Recognize Me as your Divine Partner. Accept and appreciate the wonders of your God-given characteristics, and know that whatever you are doing, whatever decisions you are making, whatever responsibilities lie before you, I am in the midst of it all.

I call you, My beloved, to journey the path of Light and heal the separation that you have perceived between us—a separation that you have invented, that you have imagined. Step into the Light of our oneness and into your rightful place as a partner in Love and Life. As you take on the mantle of Spirit, you will more and more hear the rhythm of My whisperings as they empower you and lift you into grace.

Listen for My voice, My dear one. Respond to My leadings. I send them on the wings of love through My holy messengers. I give voice to the wind and send My greetings through the dancing leaves on the trees. I am there in the sunrise and in the love of a friend. My words may come to you through the pages of a book or a rain drop on your cheek. I may inspire you and come to you in many ways. So listen. Listen. I am your Inner Drummer. I repeatedly and eternally strike a cadence at the center of your soul and invite you to march with Me, My child. Remember the splendor of your soul.

I love you. All is well.

—The Drummer

Part Three
The Soul-Math Formula

The final mystery is oneself ... When one has
weighed the sun in the balance, and measured the
steps of the moon and mapped out the seven heavens
star by star, there still remains oneself.

—*Oscar Wilde*

Chapter Eight
The Soul-Math Formula
A Map of the Creative Process

The Soul-Math Formula is a map of the creative process in the individual. It is the creation matrix that offers you a tool with which to understand the creative process that you've always been using, although perhaps unconsciously. It will help you explore and systematically uncover that which has motivated your creative process up until now. As if you were a spiritual archeologist, you will dig deeply into your own psyche and unearth those buried beliefs that have caused you to make your life decisions up until now. The Soul-Math Formula will also act as a creative tool to help you make corrections so that you can change and expand your consciousness and thereby become a conscious co-*creator*, or conscious co-*operator*, with God. Until now, you may have been an unconscious co-creator. Or you may have been semiconscious. Well, no more. As of right now you can let go of the old patterns and move into the driver's seat.

To do that you must recognize that you will be moving from where you *are* to where you *want* to be. You will be moving from one life strategy to another, or from one game plan to another. Until now you have been operating according to a strategy which has been defined by various people and things in your life. This includes your immediate family, friends, siblings, talents, career, joys, sorrows, and lots of material possessions or lack thereof. All of these elements have played roles in the approach to life that you are now taking.

If you are ready and willing to change your life strategy in order to experience more of life, to be more prosperous, healthy, happy, loving and lovable, an entirely new game plan is required. You can't just recreate it using the same terms and conditions as the strategy you are leaving. You've heard the saying, "Keep doing what you've been doing, and keep getting what you've been getting." Something has to change. You must leave behind the old energies and define the new now game plan in terms of the higher frequencies of Spirit. Soul-Math can help you do that.

You are a unit of energy, or a point of consciousness, that vibrates to a particular frequency within the One Energy, or Universal Mind, or God. Your consciousness determines that frequency as well as your experience of the physical world. Your level of vibrational frequency is determined by several *factors* that work together to shape your consciousness. To shift, or change your consciousness, you must change the factors. The factors are *thought, feeling, belief* and *action*, and these comprise the Soul-Math Formula. This formula can help you set a course to change, expand and raise the frequency of your consciousness, thereby enabling you to create something different in your physical world.

Soul-Math is a mental and emotional *archeological tool* as well as a *creative and corrective* tool. It enables you to analyze the strategy you are using in your current game plan, identify the ways in which you are spending your power, and guide you in handling your life force energy more effectively. It excavates the ways in which you have been creating your life *unconsciously* and brings that information up to a conscious level—

out into the open where you can observe it. After all, how can you change something unless you know what needs to be changed? Soul-Math helps you discover hidden patterns and beliefs that have been sabotaging you. It points out to you what you must do to shift strategies so that you can rise up out of the sticky, cloudy, heavy energies which have negatively impacted your creative process. Your new strategy will propel you into the lighter, freer energies where you will be creating with the higher energies of Spirit. And it will help you understand the power of your will and how to use it properly in a co-operative effort with God.

I have been teaching this process to people for the last several years, and it has proven to be a fabulous tool of insight and creative motivation for the people with whom I have shared it. It will assist you in assessing a current situation so that you can make adjustments, initiate change, and transform any circumstance. It may surprise you to find that you have been living a game plan that you didn't even know you have been living. You may have been marching to someone else's drummer more than you realized. It may surprise you to find out that your priorities are not what you think them to be.

Soul-Math will assist you in building soul-esteem and releasing it to operate in your life. This process is fun, insightful, challenging, necessary and rewarding. Once you get the hang of it, you'll see the depth of this wonderful tool, and you'll use it often.

The Soul-Math Formula

$$\text{Thought} \times \text{Feeling} \times \text{Belief} \times \text{Action} = \text{Experience/Result}$$
$$\text{Power of Will}$$

The Soul-Math Formula summarizes the creative process and contains the primary factors that create any experience or result. The equation becomes more complex as we study each factor and take a closer look at the way in which the various factors affect each other.

The Soul-Math Formula

The Soul-Math Formula

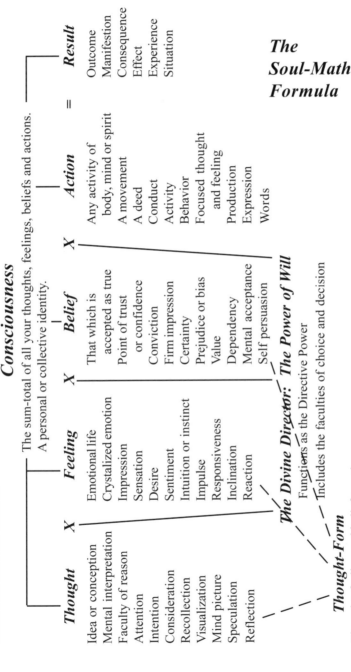

Consciousness

The sum-total of all your thoughts, feelings, beliefs and actions.
A personal or collective identity.

Thought	X	*Feeling*	X	*Belief*	X	*Action*	=	*Result*
Idea or conception		Emotional life		That which is accepted as true		Any activity of body, mind or spirit		Outcome
Mental interpretation		Crystalized emotion		Point of trust or confidence		A movement		Manifestion
Faculty of reason		Impression		Conviction		A deed		Consequence
Attention		Sensation		Firm impression		Conduct		Effect
Intention		Desire		Certainty		Activity		Experience
Consideration		Sentiment		Prejudice or bias		Behavior		Situation
Recollection		Intuition or instinct		Value		Focused thought and feeling		
Visualization		Impulse		Dependency		Production		
Mind picture		Responsiveness		Mental acceptance		Expression		
Speculation		Inclination		Self persuasion		Words		
Reflection		Reaction						

The Divine Director: The Power of Will

Functions as the Directive Power
Includes the faculties of choice and decision

Thought-Form

Thought, feeling and belief together
create a "seed thought" or "thought-form."

Let's examine the possibilities with respect to the Basic Formula. Suppose you engage a *thought* about something, and you consequently have a congruent *feeling* about that same thing. But suppose your belief system is opposed to the thought and feeling. The contrary belief will throw up a block, and no action will be taken on the thought and feeling. For instance, let's say you've fallen in love. Your thought might be, "I want to marry this person." Your feeling nature agrees, "Yes, because I feel great love for this person." But rooted in your belief system is your perception, "I'm afraid of commitment." As a result, you make no wedding plans. In other words, you take no action to bring the congruent thoughts and feelings into manifest form. The equation now looks like this:

$$\text{Thought x Feeling} \quad \text{x Belief} \quad \cancel{\text{x Action}} = \text{Nothing New}$$
$$(\text{ Congruent })\quad (\text{Incongruent})$$

The above equation has become a formula for daydreaming or fantasizing, not a formula for creating something new.

Now let's say you entertain a *thought* about something, but you don't pay any attention to your *feelings* about the subject, and decide to take *action* based only upon your thought. For instance, suppose you are thinking about a career choice. Your logical thought might be, "I'm really good at math, biology and calculus, therefore I should become a scientist." But your feelings are saying, "I hate science, I would love to be an artist." Your belief system in the meantime might have rooted within it the idea, "Artists make no money." So you decide to act on your thoughts backed by your belief and become a scientist. But you are miserable because you are not motivated by your feeling nature. The equation would now look like this:

$$\text{Thought x } \cancel{\text{Feeling}} \text{ x Belief x Action} = \text{Short-lived}$$
$$\text{or forced result}$$

Now the equation has become a formula for temporary

results, or forced outcome. It lacks the congruent *feeling,* which is the motivator, or the yeast that makes the bread rise. The only way the outcome of this equation could last very long would be through sheer willpower, a process of struggle and striving and force.

Another possibility is to ignore your *thoughts* and your *beliefs,* and just go with the *feelings* about something, and then take *action* based only upon your emotions. For instance, consider being on a first date in a romantic situation where the other person proposes having sex. Your emotions are crying out, "Yes, go for it!" But your thoughts are countering with "I won't think much of myself in the morning," backed by the belief, "Sex without love makes me no better than a prostitute." But you get carried away with the emotional surge and take action anyway. The result is that you don't think much of yourself in the morning, and you further reinforce the belief that you're no better than a prostitute. The equation would now look like this:

~~Thought~~ x Feeling x ~~Belief~~ x Action = Disappointing result

Now the equation becomes a formula for emotion-backed reactions, which override the balancing factor of mental clarity and the belief system. It becomes the formula for addictive, impulsive behavior. This is clearly not the path to peace and balance.

The point is none of these combinations will create a happy, healthy, reliable outcome, because they do not have all the factors in agreement. All factors must be active and consistent with each other, and the will must be activated to keep all of the factors in alignment. There must be congruency across the board. Only when all factors are in agreement with each other will you get a result that is consistent with the intent. For example, in order for a result to be *positive,* all factors must be positive. The *congruent, positive* equation would look like this:

Positive Thought x *Positive* Feeling x *Positive* Belief
x *Positive* Action = *Positive* Result

But the creative process works both ways. In other words, *negative congruency* will produce *negative results*. The *congruent, negative* equation would look like this:

Negative Thought x *Negative* Feeling x *Negative* Belief
x *Negative* Action = *Negative* Result

An incongruent equation, or an equation that mixes positive factors with negative factors, will produce results that are confusing, immobilizing and unreliable— outcomes that will more than likely look like mistakes.

Now that we have had an overview of the Soul-Math Formula, let's take a closer look at the component parts, beginning with the *thought factor.*

The Puzzle

Ah, how good it feels
to find another piece of the Puzzle of Life
and to turn it this way and that
until it falls snuggly into place.
How exciting it is
to take the puzzle apart
and hold each piece in my hand
like a valued treasure and look at it,
turn it some more,
and let it speak to me its truth.
How wonderful it is
to see deep inside each piece
with my microscope of pure intuition and realize
that each piece itself is made of many other pieces,
and each of those pieces still smaller pieces,
so that I continue to be drawn into God.
Into universe within universe—layer after layer—
of pieces that comprise the Great Mystery.

You truly are the world, and your thoughts do make all the difference in this world. Have reverence for your mind. Treat your invisible inner reality with sacred blissful appreciation, and know that you are capable of bringing about real magic in our world, and that every thought you have of love and harmony is one more atom aligning itself toward the phase transition that is inevitably occurring even now as you read these words.
                                              —Wayne Dyer

Chapter Nine
The Thought Factor

Thought x Feeling x Belief x Action = Experience/Result

There has been so much attention given to the power of thought. I suggest to you that thought is not a power but simply a movement of energy that is formulated into an idea, an image, a visualization, a conception. Thought is virtually powerless unless combined with the other creative factors. It is the result of processed Energy—Energy that is the raw material of the creative process. To produce an effective thought, the stream of consciousness must become an unbroken and sustained energy pattern. A hazy thought that is an undulating, shifting, unclear pattern of energy will be useless in helping condense energy into manifestation.

Let us first consider thought from the perspective of Universal Intelligence, or Infinite Possibility. Thought at this higher level takes the form of archetypal images, or divine blueprints, of all creative possibility. These divine archetypes carry an energetic *charge* that knocks at the door of each soul, and when embodied by that soul, is revealed through the individual consciousness and integrated into the human world. In order for this to happen, however, there must be an alignment or cooperation that takes place between the individual consciousness and the Universal Consciousness.

The archetypal image of humankind, for example, is whole, perfect and complete from the Higher point of view. But as the stream of Universal Consciousness moves through your individual awareness, you inevitably interpret and reshape the archetypal energies based on your own perceptions. Your biocomputer, or your brain, performs this processing of information by applying memory, reason, judgment, analysis and emotion to the stream of Universal Consciousness. And the more congruently your own consciousness is aligned with the Universal Consciousness, the more likely this entire creative process will result in a manifestation in the physical world.

In other words, that which you may generally *think* of as new ideas or thoughts, is really the recollection of stored information by your brain. The brain acts as a warehouse or data bank that records everything you have learned and experienced. This means that when you think with the brain, what you're really doing is recalling the past in the present moment.

The point is you rarely produce a truly new thought because you are mainly reorganizing stored information— reshuffling the same deck of cards. To create something truly different, you need a new deck of cards. In other words, you need a clear path of awareness, unpolluted by previously stored information which may be negatively affecting your creative process. You must be willing to purify your consciousness by using your power of will to produce higher thoughts. These higher thoughts will enable you to tap into the Universal creative dimension.

What thought should you shoot for in order to launch the creative process toward happiness and fulfillment? You should always shoot for the highest possible thought. What is the highest possible thought? The thought that is most closely aligned with the Divine Standard, or the Archetypal Divine Blueprint. When you think you have thought the highest possible thought you can think, go higher. And then go even higher. When your objective is to live in a state of greater faith for instance, the highest creative thought you might think is, "God is all there is" or "With God anything is possible" or "God is *happening* as me."

When in the creative mode, strive to think the highest spiritual thought about the vision you want to manifest. For example, if your objective is to create a result or experience of career success, your highest thought might be, "I am so grateful for the success now taking place in my career."

If you want to change your game plan, or alter your strategy, you must begin with reshaping the energy of thought. But you might say, "Well, okay, I'll change this thought, and this thought, but not *that* thought. I could never change my mind about *that*." The truth is, however, you can change anything you *want* to change.

The question often becomes, "How miserable and afraid do you have to become before you're willing to change your thought?" To use the creative process in a positive way, you *must* be willing to change those thoughts that no longer serve you. To get to where you want to be from where you are now, you must begin by consciously changing your thoughts to match your grandest vision. *The thoughts that have created a problem in your life cannot possibly be the thoughts that will create a solution for that problem.*

Are all thoughts creative in and of themselves? No. Only those thoughts that are charged by the fire of feelings.

As a man thinketh in his heart, so is he.
                                    —Proverbs 23:7

Chapter Ten
The Feeling Factor

Thought x *Feeling* x Belief x Action = Result/Experience

Spirit communicates with the individual consciousness through the pathways of thought and experience, but most clearly through the pathway of the feeling nature.

Now obviously, all thoughts and feelings are not of the highest quality. Oftentimes thoughts and feelings are products of the human mind—the ego mind. The reasoning part of the brain processes and conditions the stream of consciousness and creates thoughts and feelings distorted by judgments and critical analysis.

Many of the feelings or emotions that you may experience are of a lower, denser frequency like anger, judgment, distress, sorrow or resentment. The objective is to stay in the higher frequency emotions, such as love, gratitude, faith and enthusiasm, because that's where the free movement of Spirit takes place. The heavier emotions depress your ability to think clearly and unless turned around, will push you deeper into unconsciousness. But as you lift out of the denser frequencies and into the higher emotions, you will begin more and more to interact with Spirit. As the human and the Divine interact, miracles are routine and an ordinary part of co-creating with God.

But you may find yourself stuck in some of the heavier emotions, and these emotions become a part of your body at the cellular level. That's when they become damaging, debilitating and death driven. Emotions literally determine the quality of your life. All feelings must be honored, but your power of will should always be in charge of shifting your feelings into a higher form of energy.

Even though all feelings must be honored, you must move through the denser frequencies of jealousy, envy, hatred, resentment, anger, etc. and into the higher emotions. Such so-called *negative* emotions, or unpleasant feelings, are reactions that let you know that something inside you is not expressing at the highest level possible. They are signals that something must change or be upgraded. They are indicators that something inside needs healing. *A Course in Miracles* teaches, "The worse people act, the greater is their need for healing." The question to always keep in mind is, "Am I constructively *using* this feeling, or am I being used *by* what I'm feeling?"

Society is generally terrified of feelings and often ignores those that are of a spiritual nature. You may even notice that you are engaged in a desperate attempt to suppress your feelings for fear of losing control. The result is that you show the world only that which you consider *safe* to show. Your thoughts may seem easier to control because they are of a rational nature, but feelings make you uncomfortable because they can catch you off guard. They are less rational in nature and often sneak up on you, especially if you have a temperament that's quick to react. As a result, you may often try to restrict yourself to the indifferent, neutral ground where you can ignore the deeper feelings. This does not work because feelings are an integral part of the creative process.

The relationship of the *feeling factor* to the *thought factor* in the Soul-Math Formula is like an electrical spark to a spark plug. Feelings are the energies that move you in response to your thoughts and experiences. Without the emotions, thoughts and experiences would remain neutral. Feelings are the yeast that makes things happen. Just as thought is mental energy, feeling is emotional energy.

There's a terrific book by Dr. Candice Pert, called *Molecules of Emotion.* In this book she asserts that emotions are chemical ligands, or peptides, which distribute themselves in the body very specifically. She explains that every cell in the body is covered with tiny molecules, or receptors, that are made up of proteins, or tiny amino acids, strung together in crumpled chains. A typical nerve cell could have millions of these receptors on its surface. These receptors are sometimes referred to as *keyholes*, and they cluster in the cellular membrane, waiting for the right chemical keys, called *ligands*, to swim up to them and try their fit into the keyhole. This is a process called "binding." As these ligands drift by in the stream of fluid surrounding every cell, only those ligands that have molecules in exactly the right shape can bind to a particular kind of receptor. Candice Pert calls it sex on a molecular level.

If there's a "fit," the receptor receives the message and transmits it from the surface of the cell deep into the cell's interior, where the message can change the state of the cell dramatically. This chemical interaction at the cellular level can translate into large changes in behavior, physical activity, and mood, all the result of emotional energy.   In Dr. Pert's words, "The body is the unconscious mind!"

She goes on to say, "Repressed traumas caused by overwhelming emotion can be stored in a body part, thereafter affecting our ability to feel that part or even move it. The new work suggests there are almost infinite pathways for the conscious mind to access and modify the unconscious mind and the body."

Now rather than try to understand all this, it is enough to say that there is scientific evidence behind the fact that your emotions are the key to the health of your body. Emotions are generated by thoughts, and thoughts are generated by emotions. It seems to be a two-way street. But it is your emotions that carry the messages to the individual cells of your body.

The *feeling factor* includes a wide range of feelings from emotion-backed reactions in response to external stimuli such as fear or anger or the physical feeling of pain, to higher frequency feelings of sensitivity, unconditional love, trust, joy and faith. It also includes the spiritual feelings that could be described as intuition, inspiration, knowing and reverence, as well as the physical feeling of loving touch. There is much debate about the difference between feeling and emotion, but I'm inclined to think that the difference, if any, is very minor. So I will be using the words feeling and emotion interchangeably.

Thought may be the beginning of creation, but feelings are the creative urge or impulse. The two go together. In order to create anything, or re-create anything, you must learn to manage both your thoughts and your feelings *consciously*. And as you learn to lift them to the highest possible level, you will begin to understand the role you play in creating a healthier body, healthier relationships, and a happier experience of life.

More About Emotions

I would like to emphasize how important your emotions are in creating your experience of life. Emotions are even more impactful than thoughts, perhaps because they are so involved with your ingrained beliefs. Humans come into the world with a built in *life urge* and a *death urge*, and from that point on it's a balancing act. When you sink into the denser, thicker emotions there is less movement of the Life Force, or Spirit, and the result is a body and mind that functions with less health and vitality. It is Caroyln Myss, author of *Anatomy of the Spirit*, who says, "Your biography is your biology." This means that your entire history of thought, feeling and belief becomes your consciousness and thereby manifests in your physical form.

I cannot stress enough the vital importance of doing the soul-work that will turn you around when you're standing in the midst of the denser emotions and head you in the direction of the higher frequencies.

The Emotionometer on the following page illustrates the flow of the Life Force when you indulge in the lower emotions, and the flow of the Life Force when you focus upon the higher frequency emotions. Notice that the word gratitude is just above the midline. Gratitude is the key to moving into the higher energy emotions. The next emotion above gratitude is hope, which opens the mind and the heart to new possibilities. There are many more high-level emotions, but these are the basic ones common to most of us. When you get to the top, you reach the highest emotions of unconditional love, peace and faith.

Note that when you experience anger, fear, or situations that throw you into some kind of anxiety, you slide down the Emotionometer time and time again. All of these emotions are simply energy and can be helpful momentarily. The key point is to pay attention to them and let them do their job, but then move out of them. Do not allow yourself to get stuck in anger or fear. Move into gratitude and hope as quickly as possible, and on up the scale.

As you proceed to the next factor in the Soul-Math Formula, keep in mind that all of the factors overlap, influence and depend upon each other. As you learn about the *belief factor*, you will begin to get a deeper sense of how complex you really are.

Emotionometer

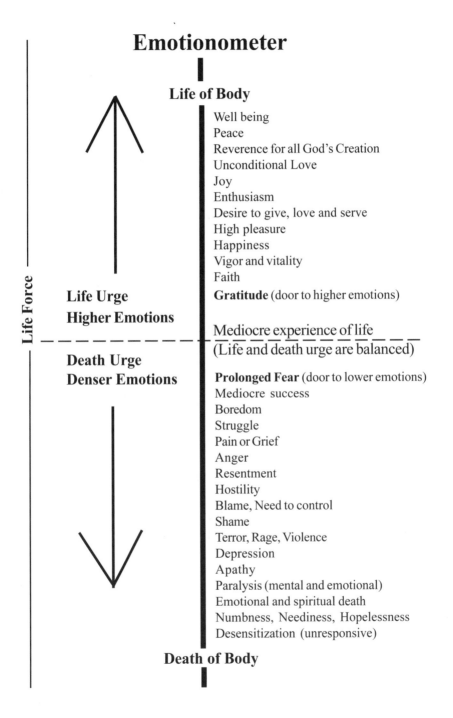

Life of Body

Well being
Peace
Reverence for all God's Creation
Unconditional Love
Joy
Enthusiasm
Desire to give, love and serve
High pleasure
Happiness
Vigor and vitality
Faith

Life Urge

Higher Emotions

Gratitude (door to higher emotions)

Mediocre experience of life
(Life and death urge are balanced)

Death Urge

Denser Emotions

Prolonged Fear (door to lower emotions)
Mediocre success
Boredom
Struggle
Pain or Grief
Anger
Resentment
Hostility
Blame, Need to control
Shame
Terror, Rage, Violence
Depression
Apathy
Paralysis (mental and emotional)
Emotional and spiritual death
Numbness, Neediness, Hopelessness
Desensitization (unresponsive)

Death of Body

Life Force

My Heart Is Heard

Random thoughts rumble through my head,
muttering, mumbling, shouting, nagging.
And then the I that is Me beyond the thought says,
"Stop!"
Behold the quiet mind.
The channel through which Holy Spirit
whispers its higher ideas
into my consciousness.
That place of communion with All that is.
The quiet mind notices my heart
as it cries out to be heard.
And my heart is heard in the deeper places of my being.
As my head and my heart
begin to march together in perfect syncopation,
I feel the beat in the depths of my soul.
I'm beginning to hear the Drummer.

Upon this little word belief hang all your sorrows and joys.

                                        —*James Allen*

Chapter Eleven
The Belief Factor

Thought x Feeling x **Belief** x Action = Experience/Result

You can have a terrific positive *thought factor* along with a congruent *feeling factor*, but if you have an incongruent belief factor anchored in the subconscious, the creative process will be neutralized or blocked. What are *beliefs*? Beliefs are *thought-forms* to which you have attached your consciousness. They are a collection of ideas that you have accepted as true or real in which you have invested your faith and trust. Once a belief takes root, it largely governs your thoughts and feelings. A belief is different from a thought. A thought is an idea, but a belief is the *hook* that anchors that idea in your mind.

Where do beliefs come from? They can be generated by group consciousness that includes beliefs taught to you by family, society, organizations, religious doctrine, or any other group or tribal consciousness. Beliefs can be generated by patterns or trends, which means that when something happens enough times in your life, you begin to believe that it will always be true for you. Beliefs come from any idea you accept as true. Fear and ignorance generate restrictive, contracting beliefs. Love and Joy generate unrestrictive, expanding beliefs.

Belief is a powerful double-edged sword. It has the potential to open your eyes to the truth, or to blind you to the truth. Through high level beliefs you can climb the highest mountain; through foolish beliefs you can imprison yourself with ignorance and blind obedience.

The effects of the *belief factor* upon the creative process is perhaps the most insidious, because once your thoughts and feelings become a definite belief, that belief takes control and influences your thought and feeling factors to an enormous degree. It thereby affects the action factor also. It literally controls your behavior, your self-esteem and your soul-esteem.

The *belief factor* of the Soul-Math Formula has many levels and is the factor most tied into the spiritual awakening process. The highest objective is a level of *faith* and *knowing*. It is seldom that we jump from spiritual dormancy to a level of total awareness, or knowing. We usually go through stages of enlightenment as we approach these higher frequencies of truth. I call these phases the *ladder of belief*.

The Ladder of Belief

Knowing
Faith
Understanding
Rediscovery and Learning
Blind Belief
Spiritual Curiosity
Spiritual Dormancy

Let's take a closer look at the evolutionary stages that are the various levels of the *belief factor*, beginning with the lowest rung, or *spiritual dormancy.*

Spiritual Dormancy

Human beings start out experiencing their humanness in a state of forgetfulness, or spiritual dormancy. This doesn't mean that you are not spiritual or that you haven't used the creative process from the beginning. In fact, you always have been and always will be spiritual, and you have always used the creative process. But in the beginning, as your physical mechanism was maturing enough to think on its own, you were spiritually asleep and subject to that which was taught to you by your family, culture, religion, or any other group consciousness that you depended upon. You were open, trusting and vulnerable, so most of these beliefs became a part of your consciousness. These beliefs became the guiding force which influenced your thoughts, your feelings and your behavior. Whether wise or foolish, your beliefs have shaped your experience of life.

Unfortunately, much of what is taught to children is fear-based. If this is true for you, and you have been moving toward enlightenment and greater soul-esteem, you have started to sift out the beneficial beliefs from those that are no longer of use to you. There are probably other old, obsolete beliefs still buried deeply in your subconscious yet to be discovered. You will begin to realize that some of these old beliefs have caused you to experience the outer world as a threatening, competitive place, robbing you of joy and peace.

Holding on to false beliefs causes you to live as a victim of the world around you. It keeps you on the first rung of the ladder of belief instead of helping you step up into your rightful place as a co-creator with God. As long as you are unaware that the presence of God is readily available to you, as long you are unaware of how the power of God operates, you cannot participate in consciously demonstrating that power in your life.

Although the power of God is everywhere available, there must be a conscious realization and awareness of God's power if you are to learn how to cooperate with it and shape your energy into that of a divine human.

What is a false belief? A false belief is any idea that has become a personal truth for you that is not in alignment with Universal Truth. Here's an example of a false belief: Let's say that John thinks that $2 + 2 = 5$. In fact, John not only *thinks* it, he really *believes* it. He believes it because his entire family believes it and even the community in which he lives believes it. Now if the community believes it, that community probably thinks the whole world believes it, and more than likely assumes that this belief is a universal truth. Even though this belief held by John and his community is an obvious false belief to those outside his community who know the *real* truth, for John and his community this belief is their truth.

The belief that $2 + 2 = 5$ is limiting because it forces John to operate within self-imposed boundaries. This causes him to be unaware of anything beyond his faulty belief system. John will never be able to apply the absolute law of mathematics until he corrects the false belief that $2 + 2 = 5$. Belief in this equation may be *his* truth, but it is not *the* Truth, or absolute Truth. His belief is based on a general misperception founded upon ignorance instead of understanding.

How do you identify false beliefs that may be active in your consciousness and thereby move out of spiritual dormancy? By living according to the beliefs that you know are in alignment with Universal Truth. By letting false beliefs surface as you recognize them as being contrary to the Truth. By using the Soul-Math Formula to help you dig down and unearth fear-filled beliefs that hold you hostage. By responding to the spiritual curiosity that is stirring within your soul.

Spiritual Curiosity

As you step up the ladder of belief onto the rung of

spiritual curiosity, it may seem as though you're standing in a dark room, knowing that electricity is available, but having no idea about where to find the light switch. But spiritual curiosity will cause you to keep looking because you feel spiritually, emotionally, mentally and physically restless. You begin to question who you are and why the world is the way it is. Your soul is stirred and your whole being longs for a relationship with the Divine that can be felt and experienced. The search for spiritual Truth begins.

Blind Belief

Blind belief is believing in something without understanding *how* spiritual principles actually operate. This rung on the ladder of belief is part of the waking up process, but it's important that you don't get stuck at this stage. This phase of spiritual awakening is one that is colored with trends of thinking or influences from your environment and from those who have taught you thus far. This may be a belief in God as a power separate from you with no clear understanding of how that power works or relates to you. Blind belief might suggest that no matter what is happening, all you have to do is believe that God knows what to do, which sounds very spiritual at first. And in fact, blind belief can be effective to a point, because it does take you beyond your belief in human limitations. But when you stand on the rung of blind belief, you have no clue about how the creative process really works, and you remain there unless you continue your process of rediscovery and learning. At the blind belief stage you may still be plugged into limited thought-forms, damaging feelings and impulsive action, while at the same time believing that God is handling everything.

Most religions encourage you to have *belief* or *faith* in God without teaching you about your part in the creative process. In other words, it may be suggested that you approach God with the attitude, "Take me, I'm yours, God. Whatever I experience is acceptable because it's Your will." This is blind belief and encourages surrender. Surrender can be good, and of course you want to cooperate with the Divine Will, but God has created you with your own free will and you have been set free to create your experience of life however you choose. Surrendering to the Will of God does not mean giving back your gift of free will, or giving up and doing nothing. It means harmonizing with God's Will through the proper use of your own power of will.

Sometimes people at this rung on the ladder become self-righteous about their beliefs and so-called spiritual knowledge. Some who are content to remain at the blind belief level tell us that desire is evil and that surrendering to God means giving up our desires. But humankind is the avenue through which God expresses, and your desire is God's desire to express, stirring within your own divine nature. You will always have desire. Granted, there are low level desires and high level desires, all the more reason to learn how to exercise your power of will in a way that is in alignment with the Will of God.

Providing you continue to rediscover and learn and don't get stuck at the blind belief stage, you will continue your consciousness evolution by beginning to *understand* your true relationship to God and how the power of God works in your life.

Rediscovery and Learning

The next rung on the ladder of belief finds you thirsting for greater understanding and spiritual enlightenment. Your search enrolls you into a more definite curriculum in Earth school, and it is on this rung that you will spend much of your time. Rediscovery and learning about your own spiritual nature is an exciting time, a time when you begin to notice the cosmic glimmers. A cosmic glimmer feels as though a light bulb has turned on in your head. It's what I call an "ah-ha."

As you consciously rediscover your soul, you may for a time feel as thought you're groping in the dark, still standing in that dark room of spiritual curiosity with no idea where the light switch is. As you grope your way through the darkness, imagine yourself bumping into an object that you identify as a lamp. You know it's a lamp because you can feel the base, the shade, the cord, and other parts that you recognize as parts of a lamp. Recognizing a lamp in the dark is much the same way as recognizing a spiritual Truth. You know it produces light, but you still have no idea about how to *turn it on* in your life. But you know there must be a switch or why else would there be a lamp? So you keep looking for the switch that will shed more light upon your dark surroundings.

You stand on this rung of the ladder with enthusiasm and experiment with spiritual principles and laws, gradually learning that as you expand your understanding, you can apply these principles and laws to your everyday life. And the light begins to dawn in your consciousness.

Understanding

The ironic thing, the cosmic joke, is that you are always creating the mold of your own experience, even at the level of spiritual dormancy; even when you think you're leaving it up to God, even when you don't understand what you're doing. But *understanding* gives you the opportunity to fulfill the promise, *"The works that I do, ye shall do also."*

On this rung of the ladder of belief, you begin to discover the ways in which spiritual principle actually works. You begin to awaken to your place within the wholeness of life. You better understand your relationship to God and realize that you are already equipped with the wisdom and power to apply this understanding. You grow into the realization that you are an individualized expression of God; that the I Am of you is part of the Great I Am that is God Itself; and that God operates *through* you and *as* you, not separate from you.

The word *understanding* means *to stand under*. As used here, understanding is your foundation shaped by your comprehension of spiritual principles as they relate to the Truth. When you have a fundamental understanding, you are on the path toward mastery of your own experience of life.

Get wisdom, get understanding; forget it not . . .
Forsake her not, and she shall preserve thee:
love her, and she shall keep thee. . . . Wisdom is
the principal thing; therefore get wisdom: and
with all thy getting get understanding. . . . Take
fast hold of instruction; let her not go: keep her;
for she is thy life. (Proverbs 4:5)

If you *get understanding*, you will be equipped to apply your belief and your faith to the spiritual law or principle that you are focusing upon, instead of throwing your faith into the winds of random blind belief. You have the God-given right to speak your word and direct Divine Energy in a way that takes form as harmony, healing, love and peace in your life. As your level of understanding grows, you will become more and more trusting in your power to co-create with God. As your trust grows, so does your faith.

Faith

As you move up the ladder of belief as a result of rediscovery, learning and understanding, you move up to the rung that is true faith. The kind of faith I'm speaking of is the faith *of* God, not a faith *in* God. Read that sentence again and soak it up into your mind, your heart and into the depths of your soul. This means that you must learn to have the same level of faith that you might imagine God having. Can you imagine God even considering that any idea within Divine Mind might *not* become reality? Having true faith means that you have the faith *of* God, and therefore become so convinced of your own idea that you are beyond doubting it—beyond even considering that anything unlike what you envision could manifest for you. This level of faith is one of the highest possible feelings, or emotions. And as previously discussed, emotions chemically react with the cells of your body to alter the structure of the cells. Negative emotions cause degeneration, but high emotions such as faith and love cause regeneration. Faith is a powerful ingredient when it comes to co-creating.

The high-level emotion of faith causes the power-presence to shine forth from your soul and through your physical being as you act in your world out of soul-esteem. When your belief system reaches the level of faith, it won't be long before you have those times of *knowing* which are beyond even faith.

Knowing

Knowing is the seventh level, or rung, on the ladder of belief. I'm not talking about knowing as in book learning or obtained knowledge. I'm talking about a divine sense of knowing that happens when you are in tune with Spirit; when your belief system is operating totally in alignment with the Will of God. This isn't something you do, or try to do. It is a level of awareness that you reach. You can't explain it to someone else. There are no courses on how to be a Knower. It's just something that happens when you embody Spirit. Knowing is a place of immunity from outside judgments or criticism. You simply know, and know that you know. And you are unshakable.

Summary

The above stages outline the various rungs on the ladder of belief. The spiritual journey is not necessarily an uninterrupted, progressive climb to the top of the ladder, but rather an experience of moving up and down the ladder as you reveal your true self, learn how to take charge of your experience of life, and pursue your own divine potential. The *belief factor* in the Soul-Math Formula is perhaps the most difficult factor to bring into alignment with the Divine Standard. The place to begin is with spiritual curiosity, accepting that you have access to infinite possibility. You are powerful beyond any concept of what that means from the human perspective.

Where do you go from here? There's another factor to introduce, and that's the *action factor*.

The Top of the Mountain

I stand at the top of the mountain
feeling the power, claiming the majesty,
looking out over my life like the conqueror tasting victory.
But I grow weary and I sleep.
When I open my eyes I find myself in a dark valley
surrounded by steep cliffs and rugged terrain.
And then a bolt of lightning slices through my being.
I am not the conqueror. I am not the victim.
I am the Divine Human.
I relax and open my eyes,
and once again I stand at the top of the mountain
looking out over my life like a humble servant
savoring the peace.

Knowing is not enough; we must apply!
Waiting is not enough; we must do.
                                        —Johann W. Goethe

Chapter Twelve
The Action Factor

Thought x Feeling x Belief x *Action* = Result/Experience

The *action factor* refers to any activity of body, mind or spirit that moves a *thought-form* into manifestation. A thought-form is a combination of thoughts, feelings and beliefs that are grouped together around one subject or idea.

Thought x Feeling x Belief = Thought-form
Thought-form x *Action* = Result/Experience

If a thought-form is charged with anxiety and fear, the actions you take will be filled with anxiety and fear. If a thought-form is filled with faith charged with soul-esteem, the actions you take will be poised and confident.

The purpose of Soul-Math is to help you explore ways to manage your power of thought, feeling and belief in a way that compels you to act in a spiritually directed and motivated way. Action moves you into creating, into production, into self-expression. When you are in positive action, you are using your body as the instrument of your soul to implement your higher purpose.

Action is a natural step when all the factors are congruent. It places your point of attention upon being, "ising," living, experiencing, radiating, revealing and manifesting. Without action, nothing changes.

The *action factor* also tells you a lot about your consciousness. For instance, let's say you had a thought about going back to school to obtain the education to pursue a new career, and you got excited just thinking about it, but it's been ten years and you've done nothing to move yourself in that direction. Evaluating your actions will help you discover what belief may be responsible for holding you back. Perhaps it's a belief that you're too old, or not intelligent enough, or some other perceived inadequacy. As you build more and more soul-esteem, your spiritual confidence increasingly reflects itself in your actions.

The kind of actions you most want to express are those which are responsive to intuitive promptings, such as listening to *the inner voice* or noticing meaningful coincidences. Action steps help you take advantage of the synchronistic opportunities that the Universe offers when you are awake to them. One important action to take is *noticing.* Actively notice in each present moment so that you don't miss the opportunities that come your way. Another kind of action that is important to express is that which is the *positive opposite* of the actions you have been taking that have supported what you *don't* want. You now want to take actions that spend your unlimited supply of love, talent, service, kindness, compassion, creativity, and so on.

Responding to the Drummer

How difficult it is to get up and move.
I feel immobilized, paralyzed, stuck to one spot.
Oh, how familiar is this place
that I have come to know as comfortable.
Nothing changes. Nothing happens.
Nothing.
Old, worn out beliefs engraved in my mind,
kept alive by fear and doubt,
smother my desire, crush my enthusiasm,
control my choices.
But Spirit moves through my being,
nudging me, inspiring me, calling me to rise above.
I listen. I listen to the Drummer.
And I respond.
I get up and move.
I start.
Right where I am.

*The strength of a man consists in finding out
the way in which God is going and going in
that way too.*
                                        —Henry W. Beecher

Chapter Thirteen
Your Divine Director

Thought x Feeling x Belief x Action = Experience/Result

Power of Will

        In the Soul-Math Formula, the times sign between each of
the factors represents the power of will and is the glue that holds
the factors in alignment. Your will is your Divine Director and is
perhaps the most important and powerful spiritual faculty with
which you have been gifted. It is your power of will that holds the
other factors in place and multiplies their effectiveness when they
are in alignment.
        Because of the widespread misuse and neglect of this
faculty, the collective consciousness of humankind has fallen into a
state of victimhood and helplessness. It is time we resurrect this

inherent power and learn to use it as the divine faculty it was meant to be.

Religious doctrine has largely interpreted Biblical passages about surrendering the individual will to the Will of God, to mean giving up and doing nothing. Surrendering to God's Will has come to mean, "I am powerless; I am weak and helpless; Oh well, I guess it's God's Will." I believe this is a sad misunderstanding.

The *will*, from the human standpoint, is defined as strength of purpose, resolution, desire, and determination. From the spiritual perspective, *Will* means the Divine Urge to express, the Creator's impulsion to pour forth Its perfection and wholeness through Its creation. The Will of God might be thought of as the *vision* of God, and the individual will as the *implementation* of that vision.

When I refer to your power of will, I don't mean *will power*, or *willing* something to happen. I'm referring to your power of will as an *extension* of God's Will. In other words, there are not two powers of will—God's Will AND your will. There is only one power of will, and that is God's Will expressed through you and every individual. To use this divine gift in any other way is to distort and misuse it, resulting in a false representation in the physical world.

God created all that is, and behold, it is very good. God's job is complete, and you are left with the charge to carry on that creation in the world of experience. In other words, God *created* all that is, and you carry out the *experience* of that creation. You literally create your own *experience* of God's creation. This is the sense in which you are a co-creator and co-operator with God. The truth is, your reality is a co-created reality.

You were given the gift of free will, which is the freedom to engineer your own creative process—and to decide what you will think, feel, believe and do. But as I have already said, so many people have been trained to think that to *surrender* to God's Will means relinquishing their own will. Why would God give you the gift of will and then take it away? Your will is the divine energy always compelling you toward your individual purpose. Your will is the emotional energy of *desire* always urging you to make contact with the Divine plan.

Carolyn Myss, author of *Anatomy of the Spirit*, says this about the will: "As we mature, we all try to build our lives according to our own will. First we separate from our parents; we establish our independence, and we seek a career. Then, inevitably, some event or crisis occurs. Perhaps an occupation does not unfold according to plan; or a marriage does not work out; or an illness develops. Regardless of the specific crisis, we find ourselves in a situation that forces us to confront the limitations of our own inner resources that prevent us from successfully completing our plans. Once we are in that inevitable situation, we ponder some questions: What am I meant to do with my life? What was my purpose in being born? These questions set the stage for aligning our will to the Divine plan—the most profound choice we can make. That one choice, made in faith and trust, allows Divine authority to enter our lives and reorder our struggles into successes and our wounds into strengths."

The Will of God IS the Divine plan. The Will of God is the *Vision* of God. The Will of God is your wholeness and completeness, that to which nothing can be added. It is up to you to release and reveal that which you already have—that which you already are—and through your own power of will bring it forth into visibility. It is time to reclaim your power of will, because it is your gift of will—of choice and decision—that will move you out of victimhood and into hope. The truth is there is nothing in the outer world doing something to you. You are the one doing something to yourself. You are creating your world, and you *can* learn to create it in alignment with God's intention; you can learn to cooperate with the vision of God. "As in heaven, so on earth."

The truth is you are a powerful creator. Actually, you are using your power of will every moment to pursue all the higher ideas you may have as well as the problems, fears, bad habits and frustrations in which you may presently be engaged. Think about it. No one is making you choose what you choose, or decide the way you decide, not really. No one is making you do the things you're doing, or feel the things you're feeling, or think what you're thinking, or say what you're saying. You've been making these choices all by yourself—with the power of your will, given to you as a gift from the Creator.

The correct use of your will is to direct your personal factors—your thoughts, feelings, beliefs and actions, to be in alignment with the Divine Director, or the Will of God. When in alignment, all of these personal factors resonate with the attributes of the Divine Will. Such attributes include an impulsion toward spiritual enlightenment over material goals, a desire for harmony in all encounters and dealings, the practice of unconditional love in all interactions and relationships, and a desire to learn, grow and express more of the divinity that is native to your soul. There is a desire to listen to the Inner Drummer and to express the rhythm of the Universe through personal wholeness, joy, divine order, peace, harmony, cooperation and beauty. When the personal factors are resonating with the Divine Standard and marching to the beat of the Inner Drummer, the divine human expresses the attributes of power, courage, reverence for all life, compassion, strength and attractive individuality.

What are the blocks that get in the way of using your will correctly? The first obstacle may be your tendency to give up. I see many of you giving up just when you're on the brink of accomplishing a goal that you have envisioned. You may have worked hard to reach a goal and everything is flowing smoothly, but you literally sabotage yourself just as you're about to step onto the mountain top. I often say to people, "Don't put on the brakes!" when I see that their good is flowing. This is perhaps some of the most important advice I can give to the person aspiring to a happier, more fulfilled and joyous experience of life. If you were cruising along the highway in your car going 60 m.p.h., you wouldn't think of tromping on the brake pedal for no apparent reason. To do so could cause a dangerous situation for you and the other cars on the road. And yet, most of you think nothing of bringing your progress to a screeching halt right in the middle of your best shot at your dreams or goals.

How does this happen? By allowing your powerful mind to think ideas such as, "This is getting too big for me to handle," or "This is too good to be true." I heard someone say, "This is amazing! I can't believe things are going so well. I keep waiting for someone to walk in and tell me it's all just a big joke." Such comments are a good indicator of what's going on in the belief system. And the belief system is always supported by the spiritual law: *It is done unto you as you believe.*

You are a powerful being that can design your experience of life however you choose. In fact, you're doing just that all of the time. I'm not saying that you create every circumstance—but you do create your *experience* of that circumstance. You can create your flow of good by thinking the highest thoughts, feeling the highest emotions, believing the highest truth, and acting in the highest way. When your flow of good starts, don't destroy it by putting on the mental and emotional brakes. The thing to remember is that your beliefs influence your power of will, and if your belief is that you don't deserve something, you will make choices and decisions in alignment with that belief and thereby sabotage your success.

Start noticing your words. Pay attention to what you say in response to the good that's flowing in your life and *don't put on the brakes.* Make sure you think and say things like, "This feels good—keep it coming!" or "Thank you God, your love is graciously accepted." And you know what? You'll do a much better job at running your life—and driving your car.

When you find yourself at a choice point, you can literally manage your power by deciding that every action you take is in support of that objective and in support of the Divine plan for your life. If that action produces struggle, then it's time to reevaluate, because struggle is never a part of God's plan. When you choose in alignment with God's Will, everything will unfold easily.

But you know what? I'll bet that much of the time you find yourself giving in to old beliefs, habits, ideas of inadequacy and limitation, old ideas of victimhood and self-denial. I'll bet you hear beliefs chattering inside your head that say, "I'm shy, I'm useless, I'm poor, I'm stupid, I'm too old, I'm not capable, " and on and on. This tendency to sink into destructive beliefs is a major obstacle to the correct use of your power of will.

You may use your beliefs as an excuse to give up, as an excuse to give in, or as an excuse to lay down like a doormat. You may fall into the *I can't* trap. But what *I can't* usually means is *I won't. I could, but I won't.* It's like thinking "I can't do well at my job," or "I can't be a good mate," really meaning "I could do well at my job, or I could be a good mate, but I don't want to put forth the time and effort," or "I don't want to love enough to make that happen."

Your power of will can give you the courage and strength to say, "Yes, I can." It can help you rise above your ego's self-perceived weakness or defeatism and lift you into a higher energy where the strength of your soul-self will kick in to carry out your mission.

Another way of defining power of will is *deliberate intention.* Every one of your experiences of life is a reflection of an intention held in your consciousness. Intention is not just a desire. You can desire something—let's say you desire that your relationship with someone be different. Just desiring it will do nothing toward changing that relationship. Desiring is merely a form of wishing or hoping. If you really want to change that relationship, you must have a firm intention that is fully supported by your thought, feeling, belief and action. It is intention that will set into motion the steps that will produce that which you desire to experience.

In his book *Seat of the Soul*, Gary Zukav says, "The world in which we live has been created unconsciously by unconscious intentions. Every intention sets energy into motion whether you are conscious of it or not. You create in each moment. Each word that you speak carries consciousness—more than that, carries intelligence—and, therefore, is an intention that shapes light."

Mr. Zukav suggests that "A thought is energy, or Light, that has been shaped by consciousness. No form exists without consciousness. There is Light, and there is the shaping of Light by consciousness. This is creation."

Remember that the will is your built-in director. When used appropriately it helps you stay centered and focused. It guides you as you can carry out your intention. The idea is to use your power of will to stay in alignment with God's intention. As you use your power of will to stay away from those things which pollute your consciousness, you create a vacuum to receive the flow of God's goodness.

Here's what Ernest Holmes, author of *Science of Mind*, has to say about the will: "The will is given us to protect ourselves with. Nothing should be allowed to pass into the creative currents of our thought until the will has first admitted it. The will must first analyze, dissect and then decide what it wishes the inner imagination to work on. True spiritual work will strengthen the will without exhausting the mind; if our mental work tires us then we are using the will in the wrong way. The right way would be to determine to think peace whether there appeared to be any reason to expect that peace would be forthcoming in the experience."

If there is misalignment, then there is disagreement or inconsistency among your thoughts, feelings, beliefs, and actions. This causes the God Energy to be stepped down in frequency to conform to your consciousness, in order to honor the principle of free will.

Your spiritual path must be one of removing the obstructions and illusions that hide your soul from your awareness. It is using your power of will to bring all aspects of your consciousness into alignment with each other and letting God choose and decide through you. And when you choose from the standpoint of Spirit, there can be no opposition to your choice! Living life from this level of consciousness enables you to march to your Inner Drummer, operate out of soul-esteem, and demonstrate the power-presence in all that you do.

Coming into alignment with God's will means using your divine potential and discovering the inner peace that is the nature of your soul. It means using your power of will to lift your mind and your heart above the chaos of the physical world so that you experience joy and peacefulness. In that peaceful state of consciousness God's love can be felt and healing takes place. I tell my students, "If you want to know how in alignment with God's will you are, check your peace quotient. The test for Best is peace."

Another way to align with God's Will is to acknowledge God as *The Doer* in all that you do. As long as you let your ego declare itself the *doer*, you can't be completely free. As long as you let your ego think of itself as that which is the only thing responsible for your actions as a doctor, lawyer, business person, minister, or whatever, you will be chained to a false sense of human responsibility. This perspective will create an obstacle in achieving peace, and will therefore be a block to coming into alignment with God's Will.

Coming into alignment with God's Will means learning to live *in* the world but not *of* the world. It means living unattached to person, place or thing, and *practicing the presence* of God. It means sharing everything you do directly with God, and always holding the thought that God is right here, listening to you, guiding you, thinking as you, feeling as you, acting as you. When you use your will to direct yourself in this way, you will find that things will be there when you need them—the right opportunities will show up almost as if by magic. The solution to problems will be made clear and your life will be a life of ease instead of struggle.

Coming into alignment with the Will of God requires spending time with your spiritual practices, including prayer and meditation. I know I sound like a broken record to some of you who think you can't meditate, or think you don't have time, or whose ego tells you it isn't important enough. But that's why I'm here to nudge you, to remind you, to encourage you.

And finally, your ability to come into alignment with God's Will is a reflection of your attitude toward your relationships with other people and toward the work that you do. These areas of life are those in which you will most encounter life's valleys with respect to relationships. Your attitude must be managed by your power of will so that you naturally choose to see others as individualized expressions of God, regardless of what is happening or how the other person is behaving. With respect to your work, your attitude must be one of love for whatever you happen to be doing in the present moment. For whatever you happen to be doing in the present moment is God's work. When you are successful in resonating with the Will of God to this extent, your relationships will be loving and harmonious and your job will make your heart sing.

Surrendering your will to God with the declaration *not my will, but Thine be done*, means letting go of your ego's hold on your power of choice and decision and handing over your personal sense of will power to the Power within. It means learning to let the creative activity of Spirit and the Will of God be released into your life so as to prosper you, heal you and guide you in creating joy and happiness. Letting go of ego effectively enables you to co-create with God.

As Ernest Holmes has written, "The Will of God for you is the will of a boundless life, flowing through you. It is the will of joy, of success, of happiness, of peace, of abundance."

Decide right now to reclaim your power of will, to make a commitment to do those things that will bring your will into alignment with God's Will, and to match God's belief in you. Make a commitment right now to put meditation at the top of your *to do* list every day. Make a commitment to adjust your attitude so that you always feel a sense of peace. Make peace your single goal, and learn to use your God-given power of will to rise above victimhood and to emerge as the happy child of God you were created to be.

Starlight
As I stretch out on the ground
and look up to see the stars
scattered like diamonds across the sky,
they draw me toward them
and I experience myself as part of the vast universe.
I am diminished.
I am expanded.
I am one with all that is.
I am awed by it all.

Beware of spitting into the wind.
                              —Fredrich W. Nietzsche

Chapter Fourteen
The Result

Before I teach you how to use the Soul-Math Formula, there's one more integral aspect of the equation to consider, and that's the *result*. The result refers to the product of your combined thoughts, feelings, beliefs and actions with respect to any particular situation. These factors have accumulated in your consciousness over the course of your lifetime, and perhaps many lifetimes. The result is that which you are now living. Look around you. What you see is exactly what you have accepted for yourself. And that which you are now living will continue in much the same way unless you take charge and change the "consciousness content" of these factors.

In earlier pages I talked to you about living according to the law of averages, which means being subject to the world around you. When you live your life subject to the world around you, you are giving up your power of will to the belief that there are winners and losers, and that you have little or no control over which one you will be. This may have been your perception in the earlier years of your human experience, but as you evolve in consciousness over the course of your life, you will discover more and more ways to take charge and rise above the law of averages. The human adventure is a laboratory for the soul, giving it the opportunity to grow and expand which enables you to mature physically and spiritually.

As you exercise your power of choice and decision with respect to each factor of the Soul-Math Formula, you will take more and more command over how you experience this thing called Life. The end product will be a spiritually confident divine human, never afraid of anything that takes place in your human world, always in charge of your own power as a co-creator and co-operator with God.

Listen to the Drummer

Be still, My beloved. Make yourself comfortable that you may give your full attention to the words I have for you. Remember that My Spirit is everywhere around you and in you as you relax your body and mind. Take your thoughts to your face, My dear one, and let the tightness melt away as I caress you with My peace. Let the mask of tension fall away from your glorious face. Be still and listen to the Drummer that beats at the core of your being.

Let us think for a moment, My child, of My gift to you that you call free will. This is the gift of gifts, My dear one. This is your freedom to think, to feel and to act as you choose. But do not misunderstand. Your gift of will is not something separate from Me. It is part of Me. It is an extension of My Divine Will, and you may use it to create your experience of life just as I have used it to create Mine. My Will is the Divine plan; it is My vision of wholeness and completeness. My Will in you is your very own Divine Director. You will always know how to use it wisely as you listen to the Drummer. It is I, My dear one, who pounds the rhythm of My Will at the center of your being. It is My Will that calls you to carry My Life forth into endless possibilities. It is My Will that knocks at the door of your consciousness as an impulsion toward spiritual enlightenment; as a longing for harmony with others of My creation; as a desire to express more of the divinity that is native to your soul.

There are other gifts, My beloved. The gift of thought, the gift of feeling, the gift of belief and the gift of action in your world of human expression.

Let your Divine Director act as the conductor of your great orchestra of life—always understanding that I am the very life of that conductor, stirring within you the desire to express the rhythm of My Universe through your own wholeness and joy. Let your personal choices resonate with My Divine Standard as you march to the beat of the Drummer. As you do, you will know how natural it is to express My power as your power; My courage as your courage; My compassion as your compassion; My beauty as your beauty.

Let go, My dear one, and let My Divine Will flow freely through your thoughts and your feelings, and adjust your beliefs to be of high resolve. Let My healing energies flow through your consciousness like the waters of a crystal clear stream. There are rocks and boulders in every stream, but just as the waters flow around the obstacles with a steady and easy grace, so does My Love flow freely around the obstacles of your consciousness. You will soon realize that there seems to be no obstructions—and indeed there are none. There is only My Will moving through your soul and through your mind and through your body. You, My child, are the divine human.

Go forth in peace, My child—not pieces. Come often for these times of quiet communion. I am always here. I am your Source. I am closer than your breath and nearer than hands and feet.

I love you. All is well.

—The Drummer

Part Four
Using the Soul-Math Formula

*Good thoughts and actions never produce bad
results; bad thoughts and actions can never produce
good results. This is but saying that nothing can
come from corn but corn, nothing from nettles
but nettles.*

— James Allen

Chapter Fifteen
Soul-Math: A Transformational Tool

Archeology is the systematic recovery and study of
material evidence left behind from the past. The word might bring
to mind an archeological excavation, or "dig." The Soul-Math
Formula is a terrific archeological tool that will help you dig into
the depths of your belief system, into the darkness of your fears,
and help you accomplish what I usually call "peeling the onion."
You will reveal one layer after another. Once you unearth these
dinosaur bones buried deep down in your own psyche, you will
find buried under all of your "stuff," a treasure of priceless value.
You will uncover soul-esteem—that spiritual confidence which
begins to surface as you slay the dragons and let your soul grow
and evolve and shine forth in all of its splendor. When you
recognize your soul and begin to operate from the deeper levels of
spiritual confidence, you will function in the world without feeling
that you are controlled by the world, and you will have no need to
control the world around you.

Remember, however, that you *grow* into soul-esteem. As you go through this Earth school experience, you will continue to peel away the layers of your psyche that either support you or sabotage you. Everything will then depend upon what you do with that information. If you keep digging, you will get down to the layer that's always been there, the layer that never changes—your true Self, your divine nature.

Let's start with the theory that your soul is using the body for the purpose of its evolution; it has brought itself to the relative world of form so that you might gain the tools with which to know and experience who you really are. If you accept that who you really are is a perfect child of God, then the problem is nothing more than becoming aware that you have the gift of personal power already built-in beneath your limited concept of self. Before you can treat others as worthy human beings, you must unearth the worthiness in yourself. Before you can see others as an expression of God, you must uncover the truth of yourself as an expression of God. Before you can acknowledge holiness in others, you must dig down and discover that holiness in yourself.

Excavate the dinosaur bones. Ask for help to peel the layers of the onion. Let the Soul-Math Formula be a tool to help you dig up and reveal the truth. Then practice, practice, practice changing what must be changed within yourself. The day will come when what other people say or do will not hurt you. The day will come when you will realize—and actualize—the true meaning of relationships, and the role that relationships play in your life. As you more deeply remember—layer after layer—in the depth of your soul, that you are a "unit" of God Itself, that you are a "point of consciousness" in God, that you are a soul in the Mind of God as is everyone else, you will remember the Oneness.

The Soul-Math Formula can be used in two ways: as an *archeological tool* to diagnose a circumstance and unearth problematic areas of consciousness, and as a *creative, corrective tool* to set into motion a new game plan, or strategy. We'll begin by using it as an archeological, or analytical tool, that will point out which thought-forms have been blocking the creative process. It will tell you which beliefs are blocking the flow of creative Energy.

Among the following pages are worksheets that you can use to examine the various factors involved in the Soul-Math Formula. There are also sample worksheets to demonstrate how they might look when completed.

Here are the steps to take when filling out your own worksheet which appears on the following page:

STEP 1: Begin by filling in the top line (#1) describing the *existing circumstance in need of change or correction.* This is a simple statement about the situation that you want to change. When filling in your own worksheet, make the statement as simple and basic as possible. Do not make it a question. If your life has more than one situation that needs healing, narrow it down to one problem per worksheet. Handle one thing at a time.

STEP 2: Fill in the column which is the farthest on the right labeled *Present Situation* (#2). This will describe what's happening now with respect to the problem you have recorded in Step one.

STEP 3: Start your mental archeological dig by writing down your thoughts in the *Thought* column (#3), both positive and negative, about the circumstance that you have recorded at the top of your sheet (#1). If you come up with something that seems more like an emotion than a thought, write it down in the *Feeling* column. If you have a thought that uncovers a belief you hold, write the belief down in the *Belief* column.

STEP 4: Record your feelings in the *Feeling* column (#4). If you come up with something that seems more like a thought, go back to the *Thought* column and record it there.

STEP 5: Record your beliefs in the *Belief* column (#5). Use information recorded in the *Thought* and *Feeling* columns to help you unearth more beliefs that are buried in your psyche.

STEP 6: Record your *actions* (#6) with respect to the problem you are analyzing. If the other columns are full of negatives, you may find the *Action* column to be almost void of any constructive actions with respect to the specific problem.

Your Diagnostic Worksheet

The Soul-Math Formula
Diagnostic Worksheet

1. Existing circumstance needing correction _____ **Date** ____

Thought x	Feeling x	Belief x	Action =	Present Situation
3. Record your typical thoughts as they relate to #1.	**4.** Record your typical emotions and feelings as they relate to #1.	**5.** What do you believe as related to #1? Dig deep!	**6.** Record current patterns of action and behavior.	**2.** How are things now? What is the result you are experiencing?

In the Soul-Math Classes that I conduct, it becomes obvious to the students that as they work the formula, the process becomes more and more involved. Every person who has devoted some time to using the worksheets and really digging into themselves has found how involved and intricate the process can become. The insights can be invaluable and surprises occur as emotions and beliefs surface to help solve the puzzle.

As you fill out a worksheet, always remain conscious of the powerful ways in which you have been using your thoughts, feelings, beliefs and actions to create the situation which you would like to change. Notice the struggle that you have been experiencing as a result of your thoughts, feelings and beliefs. When you think you have completed the worksheet, lay it aside and go back to it later. There will be more information to add. You might take several days to complete one worksheet relating to one problem. It's even a good idea to carry it with you so that when something new occurs to you, you can write it down in the appropriate column.

Don't be overly concerned about getting the right words in the right columns. Sometimes it's hard to tell whether an impulse is a thought or a feeling or a belief. Just put it where it feels right. You might even want to put it in all three columns.

Use your power of will to help you stay with the process so that you can get a complete picture of what needs to be changed in order to produce a new result.

The sample diagnostic worksheet, completed by Joe on the next page, will help guide you through this process.

Joe's Diagnostic Worksheet

Joe began with Step One on the top line, and wrote: "I'm really unhappy with my job." Joe is focusing only upon his job, even though he knows that every area of his life is being affected by this situation.

Next, Joe filled in Step Two in the last column, the *Present Situation*, or *Result*. Here he made a list of *the way things are*, the facts as he now sees them. Notice that his attitude about his

Sample Worksheet

The Soul-Math Formula

Joe's Diagnostic Worksheet

I'm really unhappy with my job. ——— Date ———

1. Existing circumstance needing correction

3. Record your typical thoughts as they relate to #1.	4. Record your typical emotions and feelings as they relate to #1.	5. What do you believe as related to #1? Dig deep!	6. Record current patterns of action and behavior.	2. How are things now? What is the result you are experiencing?
Thought x	**Feeling** x	**Belief** x	**Action** =	**Present Situation**
My boss doesn't like me.	The world's against me.	My job is my source. (God is not my Source)	Lethargy	I hate my job
This job is boring.	I'm angry.	It's someone else's fault.	Immobilization	My body is showing signs of ill-health.
I'm overworked.	I'm afraid to quit.	I'm not worth having a job I like and enjoy.	Retelling my story over and over and over.	My life is out of balance.
I'm not paid enough.	I feel inadequate.	God doesn't support me.	Focusing on what it is I don't want.	My body is unfit.
If I change jobs, maybe I won't like it any better.	There's no other choice. (futility, hopelessness)	I can't trust life.	Critical judgment of boss, co-workers, etc.	My family ignores me.
I'll make the best of it.	I'm sad. (despair)	People can't be trusted. (God can't be trusted either)	Sitting too much (no exercise)	I didn't get a raise.
I hope no one else gets a raise either.	I feel guilty for not doing my best.	Life is a struggle.	Overeating	I'm stuck in a job I hate.
Somebody else always gets the credit.	I'm frustrated.	I'm a victim.		
What if I lose my job?	I'm so unhappy.	I am powerless.		
I never have any fun.	Life sucks. (depression)	I'm worthless.		
Who would want to read my resume?	Why try? (self-pity)	I'm useless.		
I couldn't face the idea of interviewing for a job.	I'm unappreciated.	I was born to fail.		
	I can't stand him/her! (hate)	I'm not good enough.		
	I'll never forgive him/her.			

job has affected other areas of his life, such as health and relationships. Joe felt compelled to note these resulting conditions too, even though he is focused upon the job problem.

Next, Joe went to Step Three, the *Thought Factor,* in the first column of the worksheet. He made a long list of his conscious thoughts that he typically has relating to the fact that he is unhappy with his job. Notice that Joe's thoughts are all on the negative side. When you do your own worksheet, you may have many positive thoughts as well. In Joe's case, he has a lot of correction to do!

Joe then progressed to Step Four, the *Feeling Factor*, and did an honest evaluation of his feelings and emotions with respect to his job. Once again, Joe's feelings are mostly negative. Your worksheet may contain some positive, good feelings as well as some negative feelings.

Next, Joe went to Step Five, the *Belief Factor*, and analyzed his conscious beliefs as they related to his job situation. As he did so, hidden beliefs began to surface as well. When *you* do this, ask yourself, "What are my underlying beliefs about this situation, about myself, about God, about everything?" Then, as you write down your honest answers, you will uncover deep-seated beliefs that you must change in order to turn things around.

The next is Step Six, the *Action Factor*. Notice that the current actions Joe is taking look more like "no action," or destructive action, rather than positive forward movement. When *you* fill in this column, you will want to list action and behavior patterns beyond those directly related to the situation in question, because this column will tell you how your thoughts, feelings and beliefs about this one circumstance are affecting your behavior in other areas of your life.

Next, Joe went back and added to the various columns as other observations presented themselves. He did this over the course of several days because new revelations occurred to him that belonged on the worksheet.

With the diagnostic worksheet complete, Joe held in his hands an honest evaluation of his consciousness. It doesn't take a rocket scientist to figure out that he had a lot of work to do. Even though Joe felt somewhat discouraged, he was determined to make changes in his life. He reached out for spiritual counseling to help guide him in making course corrections and in creating a new game plan.

There are several things I want to point out about Joe's worksheet:

1. Look at the action column. Notice how Joe's thoughts, feelings and beliefs have paralyzed him. When there is no positive action, nothing can change for the better; and his actions aren't likely to change without first changing the other factors.

2. Notice that it takes a great deal of honest introspection to admit that you have negative beliefs about yourself and especially about God. Joe had to admit that if he felt afraid to quit his job, he was seeing the job as his source instead of God as his Source. So, beware of saying, "I believe in God," when what you may truly believe in is your own fear-based thoughts and feelings as the power in your life. If you truly believe in God, then there can be no fear; there is only faith.

3. On Joe's worksheet, the thoughts, feelings and beliefs are congruent and in agreement with each other. They are all negative. Therefore, his actions are fairly negative and self-destructive. When *you* do a worksheet, you, too, may find that your thoughts and feelings about a particular idea are congruently negative. But at the same time, you may think that your belief about that idea is positive. Go back and be even more honest with yourself. There's something you're not seeing. More than likely, your belief isn't as positive as you first thought.

4. Notice that Joe's particular equation adds up to stagnation. An attempt, however, to change just *some* of the thoughts, feelings and beliefs will open the door for at least *some* action that is constructive and expansive, instead of limiting and constricting.

The Soul-Math Formula can also be used to diagnose and reveal the areas of your consciousness which are preventing you from making an important decision. It will point out where the blocks are, what is holding you hostage, what is keeping you from reaching a decision. It will point out a subconscious decision that you've already made, but were unaware of making. You might even want to do a worksheet on the subject of your indecisiveness. You can do a worksheet about anything!

Over the past several years I have used this formula during many of my counseling sessions to help people see where the hidden problems are. Usually what they start out thinking is the problem turns out to be a symptom of an underlying problem; sometimes it's not a problem at all, but just another thought or feeling that should go into one of the columns. The Soul-Math Formula will define the *real* problem so that you don't spin your wheels putting patches on symptoms.

Never let your worksheet overwhelm you so that you become discouraged about the consciousness work you have to do. This is Earth school. You came here to expand your soul. Just take one step at a time, acknowledge yourself for the work you are doing and enjoy the process.

As you work with the Soul-Math Formula, you will bring buried beliefs up to a conscious level and you will have the opportunity to take an honest look at the thoughts you have been thinking, the feelings in which you have been indulging, and the actions you have been taking. Dig down, peel the onion, and put your present state of consciousness on paper where you can truly see what the *real* problems are. During the diagnostic phase of the Soul-Math process you will see the mental parallels you have set up that have caused your present experience. A mental   parallel is a mental mold, vision, or image conceived through your power of imagination that tends to manifest as a physical experience.

The Soul-Math Formula peels away all the symptoms that you thought were the problems. It enables you to distinguish the surface excuses and smoke screens from the real core issues.

It's important to understand that your life cannot demonstrate anything other than the mental parallel you provide, and the possibilities for improvement cannot reach beyond the boundaries of your "consciousness container."

Joe Makes Corrections with Soul-Math

After Joe completed the diagnostic worksheet, his next step was to do a worksheet for making corrections (see example, next page). On his correction worksheet, he converted the result he had been getting into the ideal result he desired. He then converted every *negative* thought, feeling, belief and action that was contrary to the ideal result into its "positive opposite." By comparing the diagnostic worksheet to the correction worksheet, it became clear what had to be done if he wanted to manifest the ideal results.

This process helped Joe see that by changing his consciousness he could change his experience. Joe did a lot of soul-work and transformed much of his unhappiness into joy and satisfaction. He did finally leave the job, but when he left he did so with good feelings instead of bad. He wasn't afraid to ask for a letter of recommendation, and he stays in touch with many of those whom he now considers his friends instead of his adversaries.

Note that each of the columns on the correction worksheet can be viewed as a channel, pipeline, or *divine circuit*. The clearer and more expansive the channel, the easier Spirit can pour Itself through that avenue in your consciousness.

During the correction phase of the Soul-Math process, you set up a new mental parallel. In other words, by recording on paper the positive opposites of your thoughts, feelings, beliefs and actions, you create a map of the correction process. As you create your new game plan, you will see a new plan of action reveal itself. You will create a blueprint that will take you into the flow of Spirit, and you will be led by Spirit in ways you never dreamed. Your correction worksheet is on page 124.

By doing your soul-work, you declare your willingness to co-operate with God. By implementing the positive opposites of your old mental parallels, you co-create your life in a new and powerful way.

Joe's Correction Worksheet

Sample Worksheet

The Soul-Math Formula
Joe's Correction Worksheet

1. Existing circumstance needing correction ___ I'm unhappy with my job. ___ Date ___

3. Record your highest thoughts that would be in support of #2. **Thought** ×	4. Record your highest emotions that would be in support of #2. **Feeling** ×	5. Record your highest beliefs that would be in support of #2. **Belief** ×	6. What would patterns of action be like in support of #2? **Action** =	2. State desired result. **Result**
My boss is responding to me in a positive way. I love my present job without thinking I have to stay forever. I love expressing myself in my present job. This job experience has taught me so much! I choose to be happy. I do want to change jobs. I want the highest for everyone around me. I am acknowledged for my input. My resume is attracting the perfect job for me.	I feel loved. I still want a new job, but I am happy NOW. I trust God to support me. I feel capable. I feel inspired! I am enthusiastic about life—and this job! I am doing my best! I feel calm and peaceful. I feel forgiving. I accept everyone just the way they are. I accept myself just the way I am. I accept other people. I forgive everyone.	With God all things are possible. I take responsibility. I am worth having a job I like and enjoy. God is Love and so am I! I trust God—I trust life. Everyone is my teacher. Life is easy! I am a success! I am powerful! I am an important part of the whole of life. I am capable. God expresses *AS* me. God is happening *AS* me. I am good enough!	I am ready to take action! Stop telling my sad story. I am focused on what it is that I want for my life. Daily choose to be happy. I stop all critical judgment. Daily exercise and healthy choices. Prepare resume. Conduct job search. Do necessary skill-building Contact someone to coach my interview skills. Meditate daily. Create a clear vision. Do something for others. Say affirmations daily.	I am happy with new job. It provides me with the income I desire, chance for promotion, private office, lots of light, pleasant people, etc. My life is balanced. My relationships are happier. I am fulfilled. I am successful. I enjoy using my talents and creativity. Life is Good!

Your Correction Worksheet

The *Soul-Math Formula*
Correction Worksheet

Date _____

1. Existing circumstance needing correction _____

2. State desired result

Thought	x	Feeling	x	Belief	x	Action	=	Result
3. Record highest possible thoughts that would be in support of #2.		**4.** Record highest possible emotions that would be in support of #2.		**5.** Record highest possible beliefs in support of # 2?		**6.** What would patterns of action be in support of #2?		

Carol's Story

Here's an example of how one person transformed her life by learning to think, feel, and do the positive opposite of what she had been thinking, feeling and doing.

Carol came to see me about her failing marriage and told me about how uninteresting her relationship with Sam had become. She described the boring, humdrum life they led and blamed him for never amounting to anything and for the fact that they never had enough money. She described the shabby surroundings they lived in and blamed Sam for never wanting to fix up the house. He only wanted to come home from work, have a drink, eat dinner, and park himself on the sofa to watch television. The unhappy dissertation went on and on.

As Carol and I talked, she painfully asked me, "What can I do?" I told her that she could do nothing to change the other person. But she could take a close look at what *she* might be *doing backwards*. I suggested to her that in order to get things turned around and moving in a positive direction, she must begin thinking, feeling and behaving in positive ways.

Carol's Diagnostic Worksheet

I introduced Carol to the Soul-Math Formula, and we started filling in the blanks on a worksheet together as I asked her questions. (See page 127)

She started by spilling out a barrage of negative thoughts and feelings. I then asked her to put those things aside for a moment. Were there any positive *thoughts* to add to the equation? Carol became quiet and thoughtful for a few minutes. She at first didn't want to admit that there were some things that Sam did that were a positive influence in their marriage. She stopped crying and began telling me about some of those things, and as she did she seemed to feel better.

Carol told me that Sam was loyal, that he supported her in her own pursuits. He hadn't missed a day of work in years, and when she wanted to go somewhere he usually obliged. He didn't argue or yell at her and he didn't otherwise abuse her. He had a good relationship with their grown children. He was handsome, dependable and consistent. We added these thoughts to Carol's worksheet, and it occurred to me that many women would think that Sam was the perfect husband. Carol, though, had not been able to see beyond her own state of disenchantment and Sam was taking the blame.

When I asked Carol if she had any positive *feelings* to add to the equation, the only one to which she would admit was, "I love Sam deep down." If there were any other positive feelings, they were so neutralized by Carol's emotional state that she couldn't come up with anything but unhappiness. In Carol's case, the first step was to get off the "pity-pot" so that she could shift her perspective and take a look at herself and her husband in a new light.

Evaluating her *belief* system was a real eye-opener to Carol. Throughout her life she had professed a belief in God and accepted that God was good, everywhere present and all-powerful. After analyzing her beliefs more carefully, however, she realized that they were not consistent with a person who truly believes in God. This took a great deal of soul-searching and honesty on Carol's part.

When we got to the *action* column, we talked about what she typically did as Sam was doing what she complained about him doing. It was just as I had thought—she did the same thing he did. She had a drink with him, served dinner, and then watched TV, brooding the whole time, becoming more and more unhappy and resentful.

We discussed obvious possibilities. Break the routine; do something new and different; stop expecting Sam to meet her demands; do something to please herself; think of creative ways to begin giving herself to life instead of co-dependently participating in stagnant patterns of behavior. But the most important thing she had to do was use her power of will to *decide* to change her attitude. She had to begin thinking and acting out the *positive opposite.*

Carol and I talked about her soul and about her soul's longing to express itself in greater ways and with greater freedom.

Carol's Diagnostic Worksheet

The Soul-Math Formula

Sample Worksheet

Carol's Diagnostic Worksheet

1. Existing circumstance needing correction ___ *I'm unhappily married.*   Date ___

3. Record your typical thoughts as they relate to #1.	4. Record your typical emotions and feelings as they relate to #1.	5. What do you believe as related to #1? Dig deep!	6. Record current patterns of action and behavior.	2. How are things now? What is the result you are experiencing?
Thought x	**Feeling** x	**Belief** x	**Action** =	**Present Situation**
(Carol's answers at first) My marriage is boring. Sam is a lazy failure. It's all Sam's fault. I can't make it on my own. I'm stuck in this marriage. Sam's let this house go to pot. We never do anything fun. *(Answers when asked about positives.)* Sam is a loyal husband. He's supportive. He's usually pleasant. He's a good father. He never misses work. He doesn't argue. He goes where I want to go. He's handsome. He's dependable/consistent.	I'm angry with Sam. I feel resentful. I'm angry with myself. I feel helpless. Useless. I feel angry when a friend gets something new. I feel embarrassed. I'm unhappy and sad. I feel depressed a lot. I feel worthless. I feel used. I feel unfulfilled. I feel inadequate. I feel like I'm being punished. *(Answer when asked about positive feelings)* I love Sam deep down.	I believe in God. But I guess I don't believe God loves me. I say I have faith, but I don't believe God can help me. I guess I really believe that I am separate from God. I guess I really believe that God is a judgmental God playing favorites. I don't believe in myself. I believe that I'm stuck in lack and limitation. Life is a struggle. I believe in the luck of the draw (The law of averages).	I do what Sam does. When he gets home, I have a drink with him. I serve dinner. I watch TV. I brood all evening and add to the anger and resentment. I do nothing. I talk about my sad story a lot to friends/family.	My marriage is failing.

She began to cry as she acknowledged her soul and her willingness to respond to it. It was as if she had become reacquainted with an old friend. Carol began to feel her own wholeness.

Carol Makes Corrections with Soul-Math

Carol worked on the Soul-Math correction worksheet (next page) as a homework assignment. She added to it every day and crossed things out as her thoughts, feelings and beliefs changed.

Following several additional counseling sessions, Carol became clear that her unhappiness had to do with herself—not her husband. She decided to begin thinking, feeling and acting out the positive opposite of her thoughts, feelings and behavior. She made a commitment to nurture her new found relationship with her own soul by letting it express itself through her.

On one particular day, I had the distinct feeling that things were about to be very different for this determined young woman. As she walked out of my office that day, she walked into a new classroom in Earth school that was about to take her to a higher and expanded level of soul-esteem. That day her action column was filled with positive activities, behaviors and plans for growth. She began to march to her own Drummer. The next time I saw her, Carol walked into my office with a smile and a lighter step. She told me about taking an interest in her house once again instead of waiting for Sam to initiate the action. She began cleaning closets and giving away things that hadn't been used in years. She began thinking about how to spruce up her drab surroundings without spending much money. One evening she shared her ideas with Sam, and before she knew it he was making suggestions. That weekend they began painting the bedroom together.

Carol and I continued to look at positive possibilities. We talked about her talents and abilities. We talked about what she felt confident about doing and what she was competent to do. She had a history in local theater and she loved to sing and dance.

Sample Worksheet

The Soul-Math Formula
Carol's Correction Worksheet

Carol's Correction Worksheet

1. Existing circumstance needing correction ___ I'm unhappily married   **Date** ___

3. Record highest possible thoughts that would be in support of #2.	x	4. Record highest possible emotions that would be in support of #2.	x	5. Record the highest possible beliefs in support of #2.	x	6. Record the highest possible actions.	=	2. State desired result.
Thought	x	**Feeling**	x	**Belief**	x	**Action**	=	**Result**
I am free to be me. My marriage is as alive as I am. I can love my house, regardless of Sam's feelings. I appreciate Sam's loyalty. I appreciate his attitude and his dependability. Sam has taught me many lessons. I'm not stuck in marriage, I'm stuck in my own perceptions. I can recreate everything. I respect and honor Sam. I accept Sam as he is. I acknowledge my soul.		I am grateful for Sam! I forgive him. I forgive myself. I am never helpless. I rejoice in other people's good fortune. I am enthusiastic! I am love! I feel inspired and creative. I accept everyone just the way they are. I accept myself just the way I am. I love using my talents. I feel appreciated. My soul feels nurtured.		I rely on God as my Source. I have renewed faith. I am one with God. I believe in God's love. I believe in myself. I deserve to be happy. I am free to make my own choices and decisions. Life is easy! I create my own reality. I am a co-creator with God.		I choose to have a cup of tea with Sam instead of an alcoholic beverage. Be pleasant and interested in Sam during dinner. Listen to him. After dinner I will start on my projects for the children's program. Write out a plan of action to express my musical and teaching talents. Research ideas to spruce up the house at a low cost. Talk to Sam about my plans.		I am vitally alive, creative, productive and happily married.

She loved to work with kids. She began to renew her enthusiasm, and before she knew it, she was once again involved in teaching and expressing her talents. Carol was learning to give back to life. She found the perfect job creating educational programs for children and suddenly not only had enough income, but money to spare.

Carol saw me one more time professionally. What Sam did or did not do had become less important to her. Her life was becoming her own expression of her soul-self. Her soul was beginning to sing and was coming through to the surface. She was learning to accept Sam just as he was, and to move herself into positive action doing all of the things that made her happy. The last time I saw her was not during a professional visit. It was at the theater. My husband and I bumped into this smiling, handsome couple, and Carol introduced us to Sam. It looked as though their marriage had new life—and so did Carol's soul-esteem.

Due to changes in both of our lives, Carol and I lost contact with each other for several years. Just recently, and almost five years later, Carol found me and walked into my office to say hello. She is a bubbly, successful, happy woman with a terrific marriage. Carol and Sam are doing all kinds of wonderful things together, and she now supervises a music and dance program for hundreds of children with eight teachers under her direction. Her life continues to blossom and her wonderful smile has never been bigger.

Carol is an example of what can happen for someone who is willing to do her soul-work. She was willing to receive suggestions; willing to change her focus; willing to get busy and start giving herself to life; willing to think and do the positive opposite. The entire time during which she had been consumed with criticizing and condemning Sam and complaining about her lot in life, her self-esteem and confidence had diminished and pushed her soul-esteem to an all-time low. But when she turned her thoughts around and started to think of ways to express her natural gifts, ways to give instead of to get, things began to change.

Earth-Life Contract

It's important to remember that everything begins with an idea in mind. That idea, when fired with the fuel of desire, intention, conviction and belief, will tend to become a real thing, or event, or experience. No *powers that be* do it *to you* or *for you*. No big superhuman man in the sky is handing down judgments and favoritism. You do it to yourself. You set yourself up. Thought is energy, and you shape that energy with your own power of imagination.

Your imagination is that dimension of thought with no physical limitations. Webster calls it "creative power." Your imagination has the power to dismantle old perceptions and images, and recombine that same energy however you choose. Through the imagination, your mind is capable of transcending the world of form. It is a powerful faculty with which to become familiar and a spiritual tool that can be developed and fine-tuned.

Imagination is more than just an idea. Imagination adds color, movement, sound, and whatever else helps to make a mind picture come alive. It is your "virtual reality."

You have used your imagination in the past to recall memories, to conjure up worrisome pictures of what might happen in the future, and to escape into the world of fantasy. If you are to build soul-esteem, you must learn to use your imagination consciously. When you use your imagination to consciously create powerful images, you tap into the laboratory where co-creation begins. You tap into the power of vision.

You put your imagination to its best use by creating your highest personal vision—a divine plan for your life from this point on. Your vision will include the insights derived from doing the Soul-Math Formula. It will include that which makes your life meaningful, those things that are important to you, that which you would like to accomplish, and that which you want to do and be. It will ultimately encompass your life's purpose, mission, and specific goals and objectives. All together, you might call this your *Earth-Life Contract.*

When you bring your Earth-Life Contract up to a conscious level, your soul sings with delight. You know you're on target because you feel totally supported by invisible forces that gather round to assist you. You begin to feel like a "team" instead of a lone soul meandering around in a physical body in the human dimension. You will never feel alone again.

There is a worksheet on the next page. You might want to make copies of it before you begin so that you can change it and refine it until you get it just the way your intuition tells you it should be. Also, you may need more than one sheet because you may have multiple missions here on planet Earth. This might mean that you will fulfill one mission and then move on to the next, or it may mean that you are working on more than one mission at the same time.

The interesting thing about this worksheet is that your *life purpose* is already filled in, unless you want to state it in your own words. There's no point in agonizing over your purpose because it's the same as everyone else's purpose. Your purpose for being on this planet is to be an emanation or an expression of Love, and you do that by giving, loving and serving. This is your divine intent. The ways in which you implement your divine intent is up to you. That implementation is your *mission* for your life. Your mission consists of your own mental parallels created with your power of imagination and desire, and motivated by your divine intent.

My Earth-Life Contract

My Grand Life Purpose
This is my state of mind and power of will
deliberately focused upon giving, loving and serving.
This is my divine intent.

_____

_____

_____

_____

My Mission
This is my special assignment(s) here on planet Earth
through which I will carry out my divine intent.

_____

_____

_____

My Goals
My goals are specific objectives to be accomplished step by step,
aimed at fulfilling my mission.

_____

_____

_____

_____

_____

_____

Just in case you are thinking you don't have to have a mission or a vision, let me clarify for you seven important facts about having a vision:

1. If you don't have a vision, you will think only of your problems.
2. Your vision is a seed-idea planted by God, waiting to express through you.
3. When the going gets rough, your vision may be your only lifeline to God.
4. In Proverbs 29:18 it says, "Where there is no vision, the people perish."
5. When the world around you changes, no one can take your vision from you.
6. A vision stretches your imagination and inspires your soul.
7. A vision is the blueprint which engages the creative process within you.

Your mission is the means or manner by which you bring forth God's expression of love into physical form. You might think of God's vision for you *as* your mission. God's vision for your life is knocking at the door of your heart—it IS your heart's desire— it is your own unique way of expressing God's love. It is your delivery system—it is the way in which you reveal your true self as love in action.

If you are having trouble figuring out how you want to implement your life purpose, you can use the tools of meditation, journaling, and prayer to help you clarify your mission. One thing that you might do is get quiet, go into a meditative state, and ask the question, "How does God envision Its expression as my life?" Hold this question in the quiet mind without judgment, analysis or any other form of human evaluation, and wait to inwardly hear, see and grasp what comes to you. Notice that what comes to you might be symbolic. Pay attention to what it feels like and sounds like. And don't be distressed if you think nothing has happened during your meditation. I find that my answers often show up for me after I meditate—sometimes during my routine day—when I least expect it. Just throw yourself open to noticing everything. When something comes to you write it down in a journal. Talk about it. Dialogue with your angels about it. Be aware of how it feels.

Here's where I find that many people put on the brakes. When you finally get clear about how you think you want to carry out your life purpose, you must be willing to make the necessary changes to assist your vision. This is where you must ask yourself the question, "What must I *BE* in order for this vision to become a reality?" This is an important question because *you will never consciously create something that you are not willing to embody.* Remember what you learned as we discussed the Soul-Math Formula: You will always manifest in your life according to the content of your consciousness. Your consciousness shapes your reality. Your consciousness *is* who you are in the manifest world.

The Soul-Math Formula is invaluable in helping you consciously understand the content of your consciousness and the ways in which you must change it in order to bring forth your vision. Every time you bring forth a vision into the world of form, it stops being a vision and becomes your *feedback*. The realized vision is not the end, but the stepping stone to the next vision. Every time you realize a vision, you are revealing the result of your newly expanded consciousness container.

Before filling in the worksheet, let yourself enter into the soul-zone. Do this by simply becoming still, taking some deep breaths, and focusing the mind upon the new now moment. Remind yourself that the past no longer exists and the future hasn't happened yet. Come into present time consciousness while fully awake and aware. This is much the same as moving into meditation, into a listening mode. When you reach a place of peace, call forth your gift of creative imagination, and bring to mind the highest personal vision for yourself that you can conceive. Then fill in the details, knowing that when there is clarity of vision, that vision will tend to manifest in the physical world.

You set transformation into motion as you establish a *grand* vision, a grand concept that you can get excited about in your *feeling* nature—a concept that you can *believe* is possible—a concept that is in alignment with the Divine Will. You are then inspired to take *action* that is consistent with the consciousness surrounding the mental parallel.

You might look at the results you are living and say, "But I never thought, felt or believed an idea like *this* one—why am I experiencing it?! I never planned to be poor . . . or sick . . . or angry . . . or unhappy. How could I have set myself up for *this*?!" Well, maybe you didn't. Maybe you let someone else do it for you. Remember, we are all connected at the soul level. If you are living in spiritual dormancy, or if you have become mentally and spiritually lazy and do not consciously direct your own thoughts, feelings and beliefs, you just may tap into someone else's thought atmosphere. Or you may be subject to the general consciousness trend of an entire group. To the degree that you buy into these collective ideas, they become part of your belief system and influence your choices and decisions. Have you noticed that the people you hang out with usually experience life in a way that is very similar to the way in which you experience life? As you transform your consciousness, you might become uncomfortable with your environment or the people in it. When this happens, you will either move on to another place and different people, or you will continue feeling uncomfortable.

Feeling uncomfortable or restless can be the cosmic nudge telling you that it's time for a change. This doesn't mean every time you become uncomfortable with someone or some situation you should walk away, but it might mean that you are ready to change your communication and relationship with that person or that environment. It might mean that you are ready to leave that situation, or you may choose to take that same experience or relationship to new heights.

As long as you are experiencing yourself as a human being living in the dualistic world of good and bad, right and wrong, you are subject to the *Law of Cause and Effect.* When you focus on and build mental parallels that portray you as a victim, you tend to be attracted to victimizers. If you think of yourself as a weak, unhealthy person, you will tend to spend a lot of time sick. If you think of yourself as poor and needy, you will produce experiences that prove to you that you are poor and needy. If you wonder what your mental parallels are, or what your consciousness is doing, it's easy to find out. Just look around you. Your body, your environment and your experiences will show you, because they are your *feedback.* They are the manifestations of your mental parallels.

When I was attending ministerial school, I spent the biggest part of three years commuting back and forth between St. Louis and Orlando every weekend. I spent a huge amount of time in airports trying to amuse myself. I did a lot of people watching and made a game out of guessing what was going on in the lives of the strangers that passed before me.

As I played the game, I found that I could read the consciousness of the people that walked by. It was easy to spot a happy, confident person, and believe me there weren't many of those. I could tell what people thought of themselves just by observing their physical presence. Their mental parallels were evident in their posture, their walk, their facial expressions and the clothes they wore. Ugly, angry, hurt feelings showed on many of the bodies I saw. Fear and frustration had turned the confident walk into a mad dash. I saw well-proportioned bodies appear unattractive as they slumped or hunched over. There were swinging arms with clenched fists telling about the anger that was swirling around inside that person. There were lines where there shouldn't have been because of faces hardened by hard attitudes. There were faces twisted with pain, anger and frustration. I realize that just traveling can cause some of this—they don't call an airport *terminal* for nothing—but I figured these people would look pretty much the same even when checking out grapefruit in the supermarket.

Clothing choices are strong indicators of what you believe

about yourself. Your clothing choices represent your talents, needs, attitudes, disposition, stereotyping and objectives. Your clothing can say, "Hey, I feel great," "I'm important," "I'm as good as you are," or "I'm not so sure about myself." It can say "I'm depressed," or "I'm angry." By emphasizing your positive aspects through your choice of clothing, you can inspire confidence in your abilities and your judgment. You can cause people to want to be in your presence, or you can repel people. I noticed that some people seemed to get pleasure and a sense of power from the negative attention that their clothing seemed to attract. People dress to suit their mood or to alter their mood.

I remember dating a man who walked into my house and proceeded to tell me all about my life in very accurate detail. We had just met and I had told him very little about myself, yet just by standing in my living room and observing my environment, he could read me like a book. He observed the colors, the choice of artwork, the patterns, the lighting, my CD collection, the size and placement of my TV, the indentations in my favorite spot on the sofa, the magazines on my coffee table, the books on my shelves, and my selection of car in my garage. As he did this, my eyes were opened as to how much my outer life was a projection of my inner life. My mental parallel of myself was reflected in my surroundings.

Years ago I did some work for the president of a large company. My job was to design his new office environment. He refused to let me use family photos, trophies, souvenirs—nothing to give him away to someone visiting his office. This was his way of maintaining an edge or an advantage over other people. He wanted no one to know anything about the man behind the power position. Most of us aren't so savvy or clever and we give ourselves away without having any idea what we're doing. The truth is, most of us show the world exactly what we think, what we feel and what we believe.

Take an objective look at your environment and check your reflection as you pass by a window or a mirror. What do you see? Look at yourself through the eyes of the beholder. Then, look inward. What's inside? Whatever it is, you can bet it is showing up in your body, in your general health, and in your experiences. You see, besides being a place to learn, to grow, to play and to enjoy, Earth school is your *feedback.* Get in touch with the good thoughts and feelings you have about yourself, as well as the negative thoughts and feelings you have about yourself. Take a long, hard look at your belief system, and then notice your actions and behavior. This is the Soul-Math process, and it will give you feedback as to where the blocks may be in your consciousness that are holding you back and delaying your dreams.

When you exhibit an approachable and appealing personality, an open and understanding attitude, and a positive outlook on life, you will attract others with the same consciousness. You will feed back to yourself a spiritually confident power-presence who operates in the world with poise, warmth, a unique style, an attractive individuality, and a high level of soul-esteem.

Listen to the Drummer

Blessings be upon you, My beloved. You have come to a point where it is time to rest your thoughts and feelings. Sit back for a moment and join Me in quiet communion. Do not try to absorb so much at one time, My dear one. It is good to let your mind sit still and listen. Let go of all the information and considerations and just allow yourself to drift into My sea of Eternal Oneness. Breathe deeply and relax your physical instrument. I remind you that you are so much more than your body: you are a point of consciousness in that which you might call My Infinite Mind. As you rest your human self, you become more aware of your soul-self that bridges your awareness with My unbroken wholeness.

You have available to you an important tool, My child, a formula that can help you penetrate the veil of human illusion and resurrect your eternal soul that has been obscured from your conscious awareness. As you expand and grow and stretch your spiritual muscles, you give Me that channel of expression for which I long. I am the Divine Spark within you that waits to be fanned into a flame that is the very spirit of you, My beloved. I know that sometimes My Light seems to burn dimly, and the beat of My Drum seems faint and distant. Do not be lulled to sleep, My dear one. Use the tools you've been given to awaken the many avenues of remembrance.

It is indeed your thoughts which design your experience. It is your feelings which ignite the flame of desire. It is your beliefs which give you the structure within which to act.

Give these avenues of My creative process your attention, My dear one, and clear the way for My expression through your mind, your heart and your actions. You are the divine human. Believe it. Act with the spiritual confidence of one who marches to the beat of the Inner Drummer—the echo of the Drummer that beats at the heart of all that is. Let Me shine through you, radiate from you and proclaim Myself as you, for you are Myself in form.

I love you. All is well.

—The Drummer

We choose our joys and sorrows long before we experience them.

—Kahlil Gibran

Chapter Sixteen
The Power of Choice and Decision

In chapter fourteen, *Your Divine Director*, I described the power of will as the most important and powerful spiritual faculty with which humankind has been gifted. Your will is your director, or energy manager, and your power of choice and decision are *functions* of your will. As you reclaim your power of will with the intention to use it in alignment with God's Will, you will find yourself making your choices and decisions with greater and greater levels of soul-esteem.

This doesn't mean that you have to learn *how* to make choices and decisions because you are already an expert at making them whether you know it or not. Even when you think you are sitting in indecision, you have chosen not to choose. Every move you make, every thought you think, every word you speak involves choosing either consciously or unconsciously.

As you go through the Soul-Math diagnostic process, it's a good idea to periodically ask yourself if perhaps you have made a subconscious decision that you may be unaware of having made. It is important to bring every decision up to a conscious level, and it is vital to honor your decisions once you become aware of them.

When you make a decision, the Universe responds to it and supports it whether it be conscious or subconscious.

When you make a decision, you exercise your co-creative power. Decision is the same as prayer. When you decide, you declare your desire. If you step out in faith and follow through with your decision, and do so without the blocks of fear, you will be supported by the Universe every step of the way. But if you step out in fear you will struggle because you are acting in opposition to your own decision. Fear is directly opposed to faith. If you take no action to honor your decision with faith, the Universe will still support it, but you will not be helping the process. The only other avenue is changing your decision. In other words, you have to do your part.

When you think you're avoiding a choice, or feel incapable of making one, you are simply unaware that you have made a choice at a deeper level. Many of your choices and decisions are made at a subconscious level, and your decisions, conscious or unconscious, determine what happens in your life experience. Decision is one of the most powerful spiritual tools you have been given because decision sets *intention*. That's why it's so important that you learn how to create a healthy mind that will stop making erroneous, unconscious decisions. You must learn to begin making wise decisions at a conscious level—decisions that you are prepared to act upon with unwavering faith.

People often come to me who are in a state of confusion and unhappiness because they think they can't decide what to do. It doesn't take long, as the observer, to see that they *have* made a decision at an unconscious level. But because their thoughts, polluted with judgment and unhappy images, are pulling them in one direction—and their heart, bogged down with sticky, heavy emotions is pulling them in another, they are rendered incapable of making an intelligent, conscious decision. As a result, they walk around in a state of total confusion. Remember your Soul-Math: To get a positive result, you must have your thoughts, feelings, beliefs and actions in harmonious, positive alignment.

One woman came to me in great distress because she hated

her job and things seemed to be deteriorating at the office. Her boss was verbally abusive and inconsiderate; she was having trouble with co-workers and their lack of cooperation; she felt bored with the type of work she was doing but overworked at the same time. The list went on and on.

"What do you *desire*?" I asked.

She gave me a blank stare. "I don't know," was the reply.

"Have you considered that you can't move out of an unpleasant situation if you don't know what it is that you desire?" I asked.

Another blank stare.

Then I asked her, "Have you, at some level, *decided* that your *desire* is to leave your present job?"

"Yes," she replied after a long hesitation.

"Now we're getting somewhere," I said. "Decision moves us forward."

From that point on I was able to help this woman see that she wasn't unclear or indecisive at all, but that she simply had not recognized her desire or decision at a conscious level. This awareness enabled her to look at that decision in light of the diagnostic worksheet she had filled out. She could see how all of her fearful thoughts and negative feelings, as well as her limiting beliefs, had kept her from bringing her decision to conscious awareness.

This woman had stayed in her job out of fear, not realizing that she had already made an unconscious decision in favor of leaving. Her fears included:

"What if I don't find another job right away?"

"How will I support myself?"

"What if I can't get another job with the same salary?"

Her fearful mind-chatter produced contradictory head-thoughts and fearful heart-thoughts. A battle raged within her. She began to create situations that would justify her feelings and eventually *force* her out of the job. This way she didn't have to make a *conscious* decision. Her relationships with co-workers started to deteriorate. She began experiencing physical symptoms as she got ready for work each morning. She was cross and irritable. She began making mistakes. Before long it seemed as though everything was working against her. She was able to say, "See? I told you this was a rotten job and my boss is a tyrant!"

By the time she came to see me, she was miserable. I explained that if she kept doing what she was doing, she would keep getting what she was getting. Her life would become so unhappy that she would get laid off, fired, or quit in a snit. Then she could say, "I just couldn't stand it any more!" One way or another, she would get what she *really* desired which was to leave the job. The decision would finally win out, but because she was fighting against it, it would manifest through struggle.

The correct approach in a situation like this is to acknowledge the decision, bring it up to a conscious level, and look at it head on through the eyes of soul-esteem. This means laying aside all fear and using spiritual confidence to create a plan to carry out the decision.

Once this woman clearly saw that her decision was rooted in fear, she was in a position to review her choices. She could honor her decision, release all fearful thought and replace it with faith and trust, and put a conscious plan into motion so that she could gracefully and happily leave the job; or she could decide to keep her job and embrace it with a new attitude of creative enthusiasm. She could *decide* to be happy staying where she was until her next steps unfolded naturally.

What is your state of mind when you are *indecisive*? Worry. Indecision is always accompanied by worry. If you feel that you cannot make a decision, you are in a state of worry about making the wrong decision. Worry is mental impotency. It's a vicious circle. When you worry you cannot make a decision and when you try to make a decision while worrying, you just worry more. Worry is useless mental gymnastics without progress. Dr. Catherine Ponder said, "If you pray, don't worry. If you worry, don't waste your time on prayer."

It has been said that to worry is to insult your God. Worry

is the loss of faith. It is most certainly a loss of faith in one's own ability to think straight. It is most definitely an act of ignoring one's own soul-esteem. Worry leads to indecision, and indecision is the decision to fail. Failure not only means no forward movement, but mental, emotional, physical and spiritual degeneration. What is the soul doing while all this is happening? It just sits there—waiting—hidden by all the unintelligent rubbish. It's like a valuable bar of gold that has been painted with black paint and buried in the dirt, disguised as a piece of iron. It feels heavy, burdened, and very, very black. But underneath, it is still a gold bar waiting to be unveiled.

I have said that *decision* is a powerful spiritual tool. Why? Because decision is *spiritual potency*. Thinking should always be in a forward direction, not in a circle. A decision is a resting place for your mind. As you move forward, each decision provides you with a stopping place, a place of relief, a place of peace. Each decision is the completion of a movement of thought. When you reach a decision you stop all possibility of worry for the present moment, in the present situation.

Decision is actually the most important job the mind has. It is a tool that assists your awakening process. Decision teaches you to trust your intuition, which is the means by which your soul communicates with your personality. Decisions that are arrived at quickly, easily and with satisfaction are intuitive decisions that come out of your spiritual confidence. With each conscious intelligent decision, your soul-esteem soars.

If you had been taught at an early age the importance of conscious, confident decision and told that it was a function of your intuitive nature, a part of your spiritual sensitivity, you would be having more and more wonderful experiences in this life with less and less struggle. Think about how much of your life-style and self-image have been determined by other people. Think about how many times you have been so eager to give someone else advice, but neglected to make your own conscious, confident decisions.

The most common reason for having difficulty making

conscious, confident decisions is the fear of making a mistake. There are three steps out of this dilemma: 1) Stop worrying about making a mistake. 2) Choose with a sense of childlike innocence and with spiritual confidence. 3) Accept your choice with a sense of peace. This is decision. This is knowing. This is soul-esteem.

I have made so-called mistakes along the way, but every mistake was part of my rediscovery, part of my awakening process. Every mistake was a blessing in disguise. So the way I look at it, I have never really made a mistake. Neither have you, so don't worry about it!

The power of decision includes choosing to be happy. When I speak to my students about decision, they often forget that they can choose to be happy. I can recall many times when I have forgotten to choose happiness, and many times when I have observed others who had no idea that they had the power to choose joy over boredom and misery.

I remember an incident that drove home the truth that each and every one of us is a powerful being who has the ability to choose to experience happiness or misery in every moment. On this particular occasion, I backed my car out of the garage, thinking about the stops I had to make that day. A "to do" list was scribbled on the back of a used envelope and lay on the passenger seat beside me. My first stop was to be Danny's Dry Cleaners. I secretly hoped that Danny had come to his senses and found something else for "Old Poker Face" to do. Old Poker Face was Danny's front counter attendant. My mental threats to change dry cleaners in order to avoid her steely-eyed stare were overshadowed only by the convenient location of Danny's establishment.

Four minutes later I pulled my car up close to Danny's drive-up drop-off. The drive-up was actually a sliding glass door that also served as the front entrance. On cold or rainy days, customers could pull up close to the door and the attendant would inch it open, reach through and snatch the dirty clothes, slamming the door shut afterwards.

On this particular day, I gathered my armful of dirty clothes off the passenger seat and turned to stuff them through my car window. As I handed them over, I braved a look at the attendant. I could hardly believe my eyes. There stood a life-sized bumblebee! No kidding. There she stood, about 5'–2" with black arms and legs, a black body with yellow stripes, and big cellophane wings. She had wild yellow hair with a tiny bee bonnet on top. Her face was black with little yellow freckles.

Who was this huge insect? Then I saw it—the familiar steely-eyed gaze staring out from the bumblebee's face. No sir, she didn't fool me. This was no honeybee! I suppressed the urge to throw my hands up to protect myself. Instead, my hand went for the automatic window button on the inside arm of my car door. Through a two-inch crack at the top of my window I hastily said, "Last name's Sparks—I'll pick these up tomorrow after five," and sped away. Then I remembered it was Halloween.

I drove away from Danny's amid a mixed reaction of amazement and giggling. Only moments earlier I had been dreading the encounter and now I chose to see the humor in the situation. I wonder what would have happened if the bumblebee had decided to be in favor of her own happiness instead of fighting against it? Maybe she would have enjoyed the people she met or she may have created a way to like her job better. Laughing eyes and a genuine smile would have made one good looking bumblebee.

When you *decide* to be joyful, you get busy being happy. You feel more energy and think less about your troubles. When you are in a negative state of mind, you are always thinking about yourself and not the other person. You are always in a *getting* frame of mind instead of a *giving* one. You can truly enjoy life when you *decide* to enjoy whatever it is you are doing. You can *decide* to be in favor of something and against nothing. Instead of being against loneliness, why not *decide* to be in favor of helping someone else feel wanted? Instead of being against what another person says or does, how about deciding to be in favor of that person's good points? Instead of being against your job, why not be in favor of creative thinking and come up with ways to do the job better? Or be in favor of having the courage to quit and look for something to do that you love?

My mood saddened as I thought about the many unhappy people in this world wearing *happy costumes* every day—especially at the Holiday Season. Statistics say that the Holiday Season claims the highest suicide rate over any other time of year. It's a statistically high time for depression, and due to the out-of-control, collective idea that we are obligated to bestow gifts upon each other, we see sharp contrasts between who has the most and who has the least. If you have experienced the death of a loved one, or a divorce, or any other challenge, the holidays seem to amplify it. The holidays can be the loneliest time of the year for many people.

There have been so many times in my life when I found myself at choice about whether to laugh or to cry, at choice about whether or not to be happy. I believe that we can always choose happiness, even in the darkest of circumstances.

In almost every present moment you will find yourself at a choice point in your life. Once a decision is made, learn to ask yourself if there is an action that you can take to help support the decision. Many times just coming to that place of peace by owning a decision will transform a circumstance. Sometimes inaction *is* action. Then again, there may be something you must *do* following the decision. Perhaps you must inform someone of your decision, or take a stand with your soul-esteem in full force, or write a letter, or pack your suitcase. The important thing is to respond to the impulse to take action if it's called for. Movement or action begins in the invisible the moment the decision is made. Decision *is* the first movement into action. But no creative action on your part can begin until there is a conscious decision. Conscious, confident decision is such a powerful spiritual tool—a declaration of your partnership with the Infinite—a statement of your co-creative relationship with God.

As I look back on my own life, I can remember feeling my own soul longing to be free, and every decision moving me on to the next lesson, the next challenge, the next opportunity to evolve my spiritual consciousness toward soul-esteem. It is soul-exciting to realize that with the information you now have, you can accelerate your own spiritual evolution, and you can contribute to the consciousness expansion of the whole universe. You are important in the grand scheme of things. Every decision you make is vital to the whole.

By using the diagnostic power of the Soul-Math Formula, you will reveal the blocks in your consciousness that have brought you to this point in time. By using the corrective power of the Soul-Math process, you will bring to light the positive opposites that will enable you to construct a new mental parallel. By strengthening your gift of will and using your power of choice and confident decision, you will set into motion the potent Energy of the Universe on your behalf.

Decision is Prayer

As I reflect upon my place in this Universe,
I notice the Divine Spark within my own soul.
It burns brighter and brighter
with the fire of Life
that is the Spirit of God
exploding into my conscious awareness.
As the flood of memory washes over me
I know that I am God's holy expression.
My every thought, feeling and belief
is my personal declaration of my own understanding.
That which I believe I am, I am.
That which I decide I am, I am.
My gift of will is my license to decide for myself.
It dawns upon my consciousness
that my decisions are my prayers.
I pray the decision that my power of will
is in alignment with God's will,
and that every decision is
the fulfillment of God's desire as my own.

Listen to the Drummer

Hello, My beloved. Disengage for a few moments from the activity of your outer world and come with Me into this time of loving connection. Come with Me into the oneness where all restlessness is calmed—and where you remember that you have been created out of that which is My Holy Self.

Relax your body, still your mind and let all that has burdened you dissolve into this new now moment where everything is brand new. Stand still for just a moment that you may notice My Presence. I embrace you, My child, with Love and Peace. Accept My comfort and know that in this placeless place— suspended in time—you are renewed and refreshed.

So aware are you that time has accelerated— that the energy of your world has shifted and changed —that more than all else, you need a time to linger in My Love and drink in My Peace. Put aside all thoughts of confusion and distress and allow My Energy to flow through you and your affairs right now. As I gather you close, I fill and enfold every cell of your body with the strength of My Spirit.

What has troubled you in these changing times, My child? Is it decision that has become contaminated by fear and doubt? Is it an unanswered question? Is it pain or hurt? Is it fear or hopelessness? Perhaps it's anxiety, or sadness, or loneliness, or boredom.

Oh, My beloved, "Know ye not that ye are the temple of God and that My Spirit dwelleth in you?" Clear your mind so that you may know that I walk beside you—that I dwell within you.

Keep the pool of your mind clean and clear so that the Image you give forth may be a true likeness of the Living Spirit within you. These are the days of transformation, My child. These are the days when you will prove Me as that which you are. These are the days when you will consciously blend with Me and integrate My Presence into your human self that you may walk in the world as a divine human.

How can you make the greatest shift toward this divine fulfillment? Make use of your gift of will, My dear one. Use your power of will to direct your mind that it may be in accord with My Mind. Use your gift of will to make decisions that are the highest and best decisions that you can make. Decision is prayer, My beloved. My Holy Spirit responds to your every decision—this is the power of your will to create. Glorify My Presence through your decisions. Glorify My Divine Intention through your own intentions. I cannot respond to indecision.

Open yourself as the instrument of My Life and My Creative Impulsion. Know that you are surrounded by the Angels of My Being that have been given the charge to protect and guide. Fear not, My dear one.

I love you. All is well.

—The Drummer

Part Five
Making Consciousness U-Turns

When you have achieved the consciousness that
God is in you, with you, for you, that awareness
must reshape every thought, word and deed, and
make you wish good, speak good, and do good.
                                    —Sathya Sai Baba

Chapter Seventeen
From Getting to Giving

Once you really dig in and use the Soul-Math process, you will discover what you must do to transform your consciousness so that you can be the powerful co-creator you are meant to be. There will be soul-work to do. There will be *U-turns* to make in your thinking, emotions and beliefs. The following pages are full of constructive suggestions to help you make the U-turns in a conscious way.

The first thing I want to point out has to do with the attitude, or state of mind, in which you find yourself when you think you have a problem. When you think you have a problem, you are typically in a *getting* mode. If you perceive yourself as having a dilemma on your hands, or as being involved in any kind of unhappy situation, you are most likely indulging in a desire to *get* something from someone or something outside of yourself; you are *not* thinking about what you could be *giving or expressing*. If the trouble has to do with a relationship, you usually are thinking of ways to *get* the other person to say or do something that you want them to say or do. A consciousness focused upon a problem is always focused upon *getting something from* the other person or out of the situation.

If the problem is in the area of job or career, you will always be thinking about *getting* something from the boss or your co-workers. If the problem is financial lack, you will be thinking about *getting* more money. If parents perceive that they have a problem with their children, they will be thinking about ways to *get* the kids to do or be what mom and dad want them to do or be. Depending upon the problem, you will be trying to get more attention, praise, cooperation, compensation, approval or agreement.

If you want to resolve the problem in a way that is for everyone's highest good, begin the transformation by turning *yourself* around. Stop looking in the direction you have been looking. Turn around and look the other way. The secret is in the *positive opposite* of *getting*. The secret is in *giving*. I'm not talking about giving money or other handouts. I'm talking about giving positive self-expression, giving your talents, giving understanding, and giving yourself as a positive investment in life. I'm talking about bringing your positive attributes to everything you do, about allowing your soul to freely express itself on the physical playground of Earth school.

Notice that in any problem situation where you want to *get* something from another person, you tend to spend your time complaining and demanding that the other person change or do things your way. Meanwhile, you are generally nonproductive, empty, unimaginative, unresponsive, undemonstrative, apathetic and self-pitying. There is an inward recoiling, like a downward spiral, on the part of every complainer. Very often the people being blamed, judged or criticized are oblivious and go their merry way. The person doing the criticizing is miserable, ineffective, paralyzed, static, and resentful.

If two or more people are having hostile feelings in a certain situation, notice that all of them want to *get* something from the other people involved. Enormous energy is wasted on accusation, blame and demands upon the others with a desire to *get* them to change something. More than likely nothing will change because everyone is positioned in their own need to be right.

I have seen miracles happen when one person stops and does the *positive opposite*—when one person makes a 180-degree turn and begins to think and feel in positive opposite ways and initiates a positive opposite action. When one person begins to understand instead of disagree, love instead of hate, and offer constructive ideas instead of selfish opinions, things begin to shift. When you begin to *give to* a situation instead of try to *take from* it, something has to change. Transformation must occur. When you start the ball rolling in a positive direction by bringing to the situation sincere and unselfish thoughts, feelings and actions, you will attract those same things from the others involved. Resistances and barriers begin to break down. Resolution may come in a form that no one has thought of because there is suddenly room for creative thinking. When you stop trying to solve a problem from the *getting* perspective of your ego personality and tap into the wisdom that lies beyond the five senses in the realm of soul, miracles happen. Someone must make the first move and begin to think and act out the positive opposite to the problem. Someone must stop the getting mode, turn around, and initiate the giving expression of soul. Be willing to let it be you.

I keep a 3 x 5 card in the center drawer of my desk. When I feel disgruntled or uptight, I open the drawer and read the card that contains a quote from Gerald Jampolsky's book, *Love Is Letting Go of Fear*: "When I am not experiencing joy I have forgotten to make peace of mind my single goal, and have become concerned about getting rather than giving." I let that thought soak in, take notice of what it is that I'm trying to get, and begin giving instead. This positive opposite action transmutes sadness into joy, hate into love, lack into prosperity, and anxiety into peace.

Giving might take the form of *giving up* something. When you give up complaining, judging, fighting, hating, grudge holding, criticizing, being lazy, and indulging in self-pity, you will experience the freedom to begin positive self-expression. Once you begin giving, the Source that pours Itself through you is unlimited. You will be renewed and your good will keep flowing.

If you are lonely, it's because you are trying to *get* the world to come to you. That's backwards. If you want to obliterate loneliness, then you must *give*. You must become involved in life. There are endless ways to do this, whether it be to volunteer your time to help others, or by participating and interacting with others with the intention of giving. Joining with people of like mind in small spiritual discussion groups—not pity-pots—is a valuable and empowering way to share with others, to stimulate compassion and bonding, to experience empathy and connection. These are giving opportunities. Just making a U-turn in consciousness from a *getting* attitude to a *giving* attitude will heal many of the thoughts and feelings that are causing you unhappiness.

You may ask, "But what about those who are takers and seem to get away with it?" I suggest that those who take from others have the seed of a nobler sense of purpose buried deep in their soul with which they have lost touch. Awareness of their soul is cut off, their soul-esteem seems nonexistent, and they have no belief in a Power that can transform their experience. They are disconnected from their soul, and therefore disconnected from Spirit. They have become lost in the lower level thoughts and emotions. The best we can do is love that within them which is perfect, no matter how deeply buried it seems to be and no matter how much we abhor their behavior. The benefits these people seem to reap are of a superficial and fleeting nature and do nothing to nourish their soul.

The next question usually is, "But if I love such people—takers who hurt other people or create difficult circumstances for others—won't they just keep hurting others if they aren't punished, and won't I be condoning their behavior?" It would be too idealistic to stand back and do nothing in a world where people are hurting other people. At this evolutionary point in the collective consciousness, there is still a need for societal laws, jails, a strong police force, an army, and national defense. But there is so much that you can do as an individualized expression of the One to shine the Light of Spirit into the human world.

Changing the world begins with each individual. You can look beyond the physical appearances and choose to see that which is buried beneath the fear. You can choose to honor that which is beyond the crime, the hurt, the behavior, and at the same time allow the Law of Cause and Effect to operate.

As you conduct yourself in this loving way, you will find yourself more and more immune to hurt in your own experience. You will find yourself operating on a higher energy level, on a higher plane of awareness, where you won't even be aware that there are lower-level activities going on around you. I don't mean indulging in denial, but operating from a level of awareness that observes the ugliness from a place of spiritual refinement. As more and more of us lift our individual perspectives, there will be major changes in the collective consciousness that will finally transform the outer world. I love how Wayne Dyer says it: "The world is perfect, and so is my desire to change it."

If you are honest with yourself, you will notice that when you are faced with a dilemma involving someone whose behavior you don't like, you are faced with someone who is teaching you a grand lesson.

Giving is about loving, and loving is a state of reverence. I am so grateful to author Gary Zukav for pointing out the role that reverence plays in our lives. In his book, *Seat of the Soul*, Mr. Zukav explains that a person's lack of reverence for Life is what causes that person to strike out against Life and results in killing and violence. Mr. Zukav so beautifully explains that, "Reverence is engaging in a form and depth of contact with Life that is well beyond the shell of form and into essence. Reverence is contact with the essence of each thing and person and plant and bird and animal. It is contact with the interior of its beingness." If you make this your main objective, you will accomplish miracle upon miracle in lifting consciousness and you will slide through Earth school unscathed.

When life feels empty, out of balance, unfulfilled, or

disappointing, it's because you have focused on external factors and ignored your soul. It's as if the human personality is out on a fragile limb, blowing in the wind, any moment ready to snap off and be emotionally, mentally and spiritually cut off from the Source of all life. When the personality goes out on that limb, giving attention only to outer things like more money, more attention, more physical sensation, there is never enough. One day you will look back and wonder what life is all about. You will feel depleted, exhausted, and worn out. You will have lost all contact with your soul by withholding the givingness, the caring, the appreciation of life, the creative expression.

Come in off the limb before it snaps. Reconnect with your soul and get busy giving to life—get busy expressing. When you get busy with your soul-expression, everything else comes alive and living becomes smoother and easier. Your transformation from getting to giving will propel you from emptiness into joy and full-fledged soul-esteem.

Was It Worth It?

I feel angry and frustrated and even a little hurt.
My stomach is tied in knots and my head is pounding.
I can't seem to think or control my feelings.
Why am I so out of control?
What is it that I want?
I want someone to tell me they're wrong.
I want to be loved and respected and cherished.
I want to be happy. Why am I not happy?
Ah-ha! I'm not happy because I *want* to be happy.
I'm getting what it is that I want—I'm getting "want."
That makes me laugh. It's funny. It helps to laugh.
My mind is clearing and I can see that anger doesn't serve me.
Shake it off. Let it go. Laugh some more.
There. That feels better. I can think again.
My head feels clearer.
The knot is softening and I ask myself, "Was it worth it?"

Listen to the Drummer

Greetings, My dear one. Stop thinking so hard and take a time-out with Me. Slow down for just a few moments and listen closer to the beat of the Drummer. Even if you have been sitting still— perhaps reading—let your mind stop evaluating, comparing, and analyzing. Just rest and let yourself relax as if you are sinking into a soft white cloud. This only takes a conscious directive from your mind, My child.

The words that you have been reading may have stirred some questions or emotions, perhaps even a bit of anger. Trust Me, My dear one, when I tell you that anger does not serve you except to warn you that it is present in your consciousness. When you detect anger, ask what gift it is bringing you. Sometimes anger is letting you know that you are in danger of making a mistake—a kind of nudge to make another choice. Listen to that nudge and then let the anger drain away as quickly as possible. Sometimes anger is letting you know that something must immediately change in your consciousness. Respond to the message and then let the anger go immediately. Beyond the messages of the present moment, anger does not serve you. Do not hang onto it, My child.

As you rest in the quiet mind and think about ways to give and serve, you will notice that the opposite of giving disappears. You cannot think about a problem at the same time you are thinking about giving. When you say one thing and do another your words and actions are as clashing symbols and nothing more.

Calm yourself even more, My dear one. Let everything upon which you carry an emotional charge begin to soften and neutralize. Let any pain and hurt drain away. Let these debilitating energies be replaced with enthusiasm and My vital energy. Use that energy to start giving. Give appreciation. Give help. Give your talent. Give your time. Give your wealth. Whatever it is that you give will come back in ever-increasing measure, provided it is given with no strings attached. Giving with an expectation of something in return is not giving. It is as simple as that. Giving when you expect to be noticed for having given is not giving. Such giving is another label for bargaining. Trust Me when I tell you, dear one, that you have come to Earth to enlighten and expand your soul. You have come to give, love and serve. Make every effort to cleanse your consciousness of those heavy emotions that keep you from your purpose. Come up to the higher levels of consciousness where My Spirit is moving through everything you think, feel and do.

Come again soon for another time-out with Me. I love you. All is well.

—The Drummer

*Men suffer all their life long, under the foolish
superstition that they can be cheated. But it is
impossible for a man to be cheated by anyone but
himself.*
                                    —*Ralph W. Emerson*

Chapter Eighteen
Moving Into the Soul-Zone

You may have noticed that when athletes are interviewed
and asked how it is that they make so many free throws on the
basketball court, or birdies on the golf course, or home runs in the
batter's box, they usually talk about getting into "the zone" with
their power of concentration and focus. Getting into the zone is no
less important spiritually speaking when you want to improve the
results you've been getting in your experience of life.

When you set up a mental parallel, or create a vision for
your life, you must learn to see that vision just as clearly as Mark
McGwire sees himself connecting with a ball that flies out of the
ball park. You must learn to focus your spiritual faculties so that
you are co-operating and flowing with Universal Energy as it

condenses Itself into a form that matches your vision. Being in the soul-zone is being *in the flow*. You've heard the phrases, "Go with the flow," or "Flow with it," or "Just let things flow." The word flow means to move or run smoothly with unbroken continuity—like a fluid or a stream. It means to circulate, and to proceed steadily and easily with a smooth or graceful continuity. That's what athletes feel when they describe being in "the zone."

When athletes are "in the flow," or "in the zone," they are not thinking about winning because they are too busy focusing upon "seeing" the successful completion of the action needed for winning. They see themselves crossing the finish line or running into the end zone with a touchdown. For athletes, being in the zone doesn't mean trying so hard that they struggle, but rather getting into a groove of energy that moves them toward their objective.

Spiritually speaking, to flow in life means to *be*, without fighting, resisting, or demanding anything from anyone. Allowing things to flow easily and naturally is the way of the universe. Everything in the universe is energy. You are energy, your thoughts are energy, your emotions are energy, your actions are energy. Energy must have a free flow in order for it to be most effective. Just as air flows freely without interruption, and water flows freely according to the path of least resistance, the energy network of the universe flows in an orderly, harmonious and dynamic way when allowed to move freely. All energy wants to flow unimpeded.

Since you are part of the dynamic universe and part of the Life Force or Divine Energy, it makes sense that in order for you to create, co-operate with God, and function freely in the universe, you must learn to flow with no obstructions or limitations on the mental, physical and emotional levels of your being. The fewer the restrictions to the flow of Divine Energy, the better you will harmonize with the whole energy network.

So one of the biggest U-turns you must make in order to align your creative process with your vision, is to turn away from trying too hard, fighting or resisting, or doing anything which interrupts the natural, consistent flow of Universal Energy. You must turn away from limited thoughts, feelings and beliefs so that you are free to take actions that synchronize with the flow of Divine Energy. You must learn to focus your mind so that you can engage the flow. Engaging the flow means to let go and let yourself become fully involved in the present moment.

Would you like to practice engaging the flow? If so, let's do that now. Focus your thoughts completely upon what I am saying. Let everything else melt away as you notice that this moment is your reality. Whatever you may have brought with you when you sat down to read these words is drifting away. All worries, concerns, problems, pain, hurt—none of that exists for you right now, because you are only thinking about what I'm saying.

Stop analyzing and strategizing. Strategizing means using tactics to win. This is not a contest but a time to engage the flow. Stop maneuvering, seeking, or struggling. Go beyond the enslavement of time and live fully in this moment, the only time you really have. Everything that happened to you today—this week— is just a memory. Your loved ones are just a memory (unless they happen to be reading over your shoulder). This doesn't mean your loved ones do not exist, or that events didn't occur, or circumstances haven't happened. It means that they do not exist for you *in this present moment.* This is the NEW NOW, the working unit of your life. This new now moment is all there is. Think about it. Digest it. Get the concept. Be still and notice. The only thing real for you at this point in time is that to which you give your attention—that which you are noticing. So notice in this moment that all your needs are met. Everything you need you have in this moment. Notice that you are relaxed, safe and more and more peaceful as you realize that this present moment is full of love and inspiration and peace. Feel the peace of this moment. You are not resisting anything or thinking about anything except how good you feel right now.

Welcome to the soul-zone. This is where you engage the flow. This is where the exhilaration of Spirit exists, trust abounds and the Presence of God resides. This is where the answers and the solutions are—in every present moment—in the soul-zone. This is where the Universe flows freely.

The soul-zone is more than just the present moment. It is the present moment free from the baggage of the past and the fear of the future. It is the present moment during which you are fully awake and aware. It is the *new now moment*. It is fresh, innocent, uncontaminated by judgment or analysis. The environment of the new now is Infinite Possibility—the unlimited sea of abundance.

Consider that an Invisible Essence is in the soul-zone with you. That Invisible Essence breathes you, loves you, supports you. You can name it God, but if the word *God* doesn't work for you, then call It *Universal Intelligence, Divine Energy, Love, Higher Power, The Tao, Life, Great Spirit, The Force, He, She,* or *It.* Whatever Its name, It shares this present moment with you and me. Its qualities include all the Power there is, all the Wisdom, Love, Peace and Harmony there is. It is All Good and is in the midst of the soul-zone with you. So relax. All is well.

Feel the peace in this present-time soul-zone and know that the soul-zone is your only reality in this moment. It's the only time there is. Allow yourself to feel love. Let your body relax and take some deep breaths. Realize that any past difficulties, even of just a moment ago, are not a part of the soul-zone.

When I ask people to do this in a private session or in groups, someone occasionally comes up with the comment, "Well, every one of my present moments isn't that great! In fact, some of them are stressful and horrible. What about *those* precious, present moments?! They feel more like the twilight zone!"

If this is a question that you might ask, let me remind you that right there with you in that challenging moment is Divine Energy supporting you, surrounding you, loving you and ready to move you out of difficulty. Stay in the soul-zone and trust the Divine Presence that is there with you. The moment will be handled, and it will carry you into the next moment with power and strength.

One day I sat at my desk attempting to work, but my mind

kept drifting off into the Land of Dread that surrounded an upcoming dental appointment. Every time I became conscious of my thoughts sliding off into fear, I pulled myself back into the soul-zone. I did a pretty good job of detaching myself from the terror that awaited me.

But the moment came. There I was, stretched out in my dentist's chair—in the present moment that didn't seem so precious. And there I would remain for almost eight hours. That's 28,800 consecutive present moments! That idea filled the moment with panic. My stomach tightened, my heart began pounding and my breathing almost stopped. The project began— and so did the pain. My body tensed as I anticipated each subsequent painful moment. I was out on the fragile limb of future moments. And I was out on that limb all alone.

Then I remembered that question from my student, "What about the present moment that's horrible?!" And I realized that I had the perfect opportunity to experiment with and practice what I'd been teaching. With every ounce of conscious awareness I could muster, I brought myself back into the present moment— into the anxiety, the aching neck—aware of the masked face bending over me and the gloved hands that invaded my mouth. Could this be the soul-zone that I had been so highly recommending?

I began to acknowledge the Presence and allowed the big chair to become an all-encompassing, loving, caring angel of God. I let a sense of peace and harmony fill my body, I imagined it filling the doctor, and I let it fill the present moment. I allowed my body to relax, I let go of the fear, and I surrendered to the physical reactions to what was happening. As I relaxed more and more, I was able to begin transforming each present moment into a *new* soul-zone in my mind. I was able to create a new experience for each new now moment. I simply took my essence somewhere else. I created mind-pictures of other places: I walked on the beach at sunset; I walked in the redwood forest with an enlightened stranger; I went on a 480-minute trip to exotic places.

When the dental work was finished, I returned to the chair in my dentist's office. Everyone around me looked exhausted and they were amazed at how well I came through. In case you're wondering, I did get up to use the bathroom a couple of times. Each time I returned, I climbed back into my own personal teleporter and took off to another peaceful, safe place.

My experience that day showed me even more clearly that we always have all the power we need in every present moment—in the soul-zone—to reshape or change the next moment. I was able to take my mental and emotional bodies somewhere else in consciousness while my physical body received the help that it needed.

When you are operating in the soul-zone, you are acutely awake and aware. You approach everything with soul-esteem because in that present moment is everything you need. God's Love literally shows up for you as whatever it is that you require.

Is it possible to spend every moment in the soul-zone? Perhaps it is, but because this world is a dimension of learning and remembering, you will more than likely find yourself drifting in and out of the soul-zone. Sometimes you will find yourself falling back into the law of averages, subject to the toss of the dice, perhaps even feeling sorry for yourself. It happens to all of us because we live with one foot in the human dimension and one foot in the spiritual dimension. Until you succeed in integrating the two, you will have times where you are in the flow, and times when you are focused only upon the obstructions. When there are days that aren't flowing, you might notice that the universe has a way of offering you opportunities to re-enter the soul-zone.

I remember one of those days in my life. I was having a down day for no particular reason. I decided to go shopping to shake off my self-pitying mood. I was so distracted that it didn't even occur to me to pray or meditate. When I arrived at the shopping center I parked my car, got out and started walking across the parking lot to the store entrance. I approached the door and right in the middle of some self-indulgent thought, a man in a wheel chair rolled out of the door and across my path. There he was with a bag full of purchases in his lap and no legs below the knees, rolling across the parking lot. He disappeared among the cars.

I stopped in my tracks, letting the soul-zone impact me. I didn't react to what I saw with sympathy or sadness. The thought that came to me was, "Thank you, God, for showing up for me as this wonderful person in this present moment." My entire attitude of mind shifted to one of freedom and lightness and joy. That man—that expression of the One—that angel, showed up for me at just the right time. Thank goodness I was awake enough to see him and get his message: "Count your blessings, Phylis. Stop indulging in self-pity and get back on the Path. Stop wallowing in your *stuff* and get busy being your Best self." And I did just that.

The soul-zone is *present-time consciousness*. Being *in* the soul-zone is being *awake* and *alert* and *aware* in the present moment—*noticing* what is in the present moment with you. Always notice the intuitive impulses. Notice the meaningful coincidences that show up to guide you. As you become more acutely awake and aware in the present moment, you will *engage the flow*. As you spend more time in the soul-zone, you will build confidence in the truth that everything you need is in the soul-zone with you. Fear diminishes and soul-esteem abounds.

The Soul-Zone

I know how it feels.
It's like flying on the back of an eagle
high above the human landscape,
beyond resistance,
gliding, soaring,
confident, invincible.
Nothing to hold me back,
nothing to distract my attention,
nothing to tempt my intention.
Just the smooth and graceful forward thrust
of the new now moment.
That's how it is in the soul-zone.

Listen to the Drummer

Welcome back, dear one. Take a few moments to calm the human senses and enter into a conscious oneness—not a dream time or reverie—but a time of alert, aware communion and powerful engagement. Drop your defenses and slide into this safe sanctuary that is the soul-zone. This is a sacred space, My child, where My Spirit moves freely through your soul, your mind, and your physical form.

Here you are, My beloved, flowing with My Love that is unfailing and limitless—wrapped in the calmness of spiritual confidence. The angels of My Presence fly on either side of you, before you, behind you, all around. They embrace you, comfort you, and lift you high above the confusions of your human world.

Listen to the Drummer and let the rhythm of My Universe flood your being. Feel Me to the roots of your soul as every cell in your body responds to My Life. Breathe Me into your whole being. I am the soul of you, the spirit of you. I am the pulse of your life, and it is within Me, My child, that you live, and move and have your being. My Light surrounds you, infills you, blesses you, and harmonizes all that concerns you. Remember, My dear one, that you are a light in the midst of what seems to be darkness. My Light shines through your physical form—through your mind, through your heart, and through every action you take. Look upon your world with new eyes— eyes of understanding, eyes of love, eyes of forgiveness—eyes of one who has engaged the Flow.

Follow My leadings and listen to the Drummer within for your guidance. I am that Drummer. But I hear your doubts, My child. I hear your question, "How do I know that it's Your beat that I hear? How do I know that it's not just the noise of my own confusion?"

And I say to you, My dear one, listen to the first impulse that enters your awareness. The confusion comes when you add your questions to the answer already received. Trust yourself to trust Me. When you tune in to My rhythm you will know, because you will feel the alignment. You will feel the unbroken, graceful rise into the soul-zone. You will soar with spiritual confidence and walk among humankind as the power-presence.

Go forward in My strength and know that I am doing the work through you. Wherever you are, know that My Holy Presence walks with you, stands in the Light of Truth with you, guides you, and strengthens you.

I love you. All is well.

—The Drummer

There is no object on earth which cannot be looked at from a cosmic point of view.
—Dostoevsky

Chapter Nineteen
The Fine Art of Detachment

To be fully awake and aware in the soul-zone you must *unplug* from every person, place, thing, situation, pain, hurt, critical judgment or need to resist anything. *Unplugging, or detaching,* is a mandatory ingredient of the soul-zone. What do I mean by unplugging or detaching? By unplugging I mean withdrawing your emotional investment from a particular thought-form. It might be a judgment about a person, or something a person did or didn't do. It might be a judgment about yourself. To unplug means to stop defining yourself in terms of things or persons external to yourself. Being plugged in is being connected to something in the physical world to which you have applied so much meaning that you are emotionally attached to it. This degree of emotional attachment is an obstruction to living at a higher level of consciousness.

Attachments are responsible for reducing your happiness and your success. Attachments suck your vital energy. It's as if you have an emotional umbilical cord, or tether, attaching you to someone or something outside yourself which sustains itself by using your energy. Can you imagine how many of these cords you have attached to people or to negative thought-forms over your lifetime? If you have not consciously disconnected from them, disempowered them or transmuted them, they are still sucking your energy—and eventually you will pay with the deterioration of your physical body. This is what's behind aging and disease. By the time most people are fifty years old, so many negative thought-forms have been living off of their vital energy for so many years that the cells of their bodies have gradually become deficient, deformed, distorted and dead. That's why people look old, not because they have reached a certain number of years.

Detachment from negative thought-forms and energy-zapping people first takes place in the realm of your thought. Use your power of thought to step into that part of you that is the *Observer*. The Observer is beyond the body and beyond the five senses—that part of you that can objectively look at your body, thoughts, beliefs and behaviors without judgment. This Self is a *Noticer*, an *Onlooker*, a *Compassionate Witness*. Cultivating the Observer is one of the major keys to conscious awareness and, therefore, a key to conscious co-creation.

This shift to the Observer is a shifting of your self-perception. It moves you to a viewing point that frees you from anchors that weigh you down. It takes you to a point of consciousness that is no longer controlled and directed by your ego-self, or by other people, circumstances, emotions or what might be happening in your human world.

Detachment is a severing of the emotional umbilical cord which keeps you anchored in fear and unhappiness. Being attached to any person, place or thing is debilitating to spiritual growth and the development of soul-esteem. Detachment is not coolness or indifference or emotional isolation. Emotional detachment is the art of watching the drama of life from a neutral, centered, higher place in consciousness, while at the same time being involved with life in the midst of the current situation.

Imagine for a moment that you are standing on a very busy street corner and you want to cross to the other side. You look both ways, and when there seems to be a break in the traffic you step off the curb intending to hurry across. But someone urgently yells at you from the third-story window of a building behind you, "Don't cross! There's a crazy out-of-control car coming over the hill!" You quickly jump back onto the curb, turn to look up at the window behind you and realize that the person in that window has a much broader view of what's happening than you do. She sees a bigger picture. As the person on the street corner, you are aware of the traffic only in your immediate range of vision. Without having received the warning from the third-story window, you could have made a disastrous choice.

The third-story window is a metaphor for the expanded view of the world that we can have when we are detached from what's happening. However, we can be so stuck in the middle of our challenges that we can forget there's a bigger picture—a greater perspective. And as a result, we often make the wrong moves at the wrong time, unaware of our poor choices until after the fact.

Consider the story of Capt. Scott O'Grady as an example of someone who made the *right* moves because of his larger perspective. Capt. O'Grady was shot down over Bosnia on June 2, 1995, and for six days managed to avoid being caught. He subsisted on a diet of insects and leaves, and was rescued on the morning of June 8 by Marine helicopters. In his book, *Return With Honor*, Scott says: "Those six days in Bosnia became a religious retreat for me, a total spiritual renewal.   I'm not recommending near-death experience for its own sake. It's a ride I wouldn't care to take again. But I will say that my time in Bosnia was completely positive—nothing bad has come out of it. From the instant that my plane blew up around me, I opened my heart to God's love. That day, five miles up, with death at my front door, I found my key to life. It took a mighty big jolt to open my eyes, but it was worth it. I knew I'd never be lost again.   In Bosnia I was stripped of my plane and all my high-tech apparatus. I was still an officer in the U.S. Air Force, but my rank couldn't shield me from a bullet. As I huddled in those woods, I didn't feel like Captain O'Grady, fighter pilot. I was just a scared guy named Scott, getting by on his wits, discovering more about himself each day. I gradually gained a new sense of self-worth, and it had nothing to do with any medals . . . I believe that every person is a spiritual being having a human experience."

Scott was able to move through this challenging situation (on the street corner), while at the same time seeing it from a greater viewpoint (from the third-story window). This learning experience jolted his awareness and his comment was, "From the instant that my plane blew up around me, I opened my heart to God's love." That decision was a soul-esteem builder.

Becoming the Observer, the Onlooker, is an act of love and compassion. It removes you from the world of boundaries. It removes you from a world of groping, clutching, judging and owning a problem or a circumstance, and allows you to enter the flow of pure Spirit.

Begin now to notice things about your life and your experiences as they unfold. Notice how anxious or peaceful you feel, how tired or energized you feel. Notice the people around you and how much time you spend with your family. Notice how much time you spend at your job, how much time you spend traveling and the time you spend praying. Notice anything and everything— your fingernails and your feet—even the way you are sitting. Now think about how many times I've used the word "notice." Realize that there is definitely an activity called "noticing," and it includes the Noticer, or Observer, and that which is being noticed or observed. As you practice becoming the Noticer and getting accustomed to going to the third-story window in your consciousness where you look upon that which is in the physical world, you will be following the advice of the Master when He said, "Be in the world but not of it."

Start with the less threatening experiences so that when a larger challenge presents itself you can go to that God-Space within you—that place where you are free to see beyond the difficulty and detach from whatever you perceive the problem to be. It's being attached to a problem that keeps it from moving out of your experience. If you can detach from it mentally and emotionally and become the Observer, the Compassionate Witness, you will free everything up, including the problem. The problem will be free to move out of your experience. Becoming the Observer allows you to act in ways and think in ways that dissipate and dissolve problems.

In *Quantum Reality*, by Nick Herbert, the author says: "There is no reality in the absence of observation. Observation creates reality." This means that unless you notice something, it isn't real for you. It means that the act of witnessing, or observing, creates your reality. Your reality and my reality, right now, is only that which we are observing. Quantum physics calls this "observer-participancy."

When you look upon a troubling event in your life—not denying it, just observing it—knowing that it is resolving itself and moving out of your experience, that is exactly what will occur. What you are doing is being with the problem in a nonjudgmental way so that you aren't clutching it and holding on to it. You give it permission to move on.

At your center is that eternal, changeless dimension of your higher spiritual Self. This is the invisible "I" that talks to your physical self. This is the Thinker beyond the thoughts. This Observer is not detectable with scientific instruments. It will never show up on an X-ray or be picked up by an ultrasound. But when you step into your Observer Self, you will know it. It will feel like spiritual confidence. It will feel like *knowing*—and *knowing* that you know. You will be above doubt, fear and judgment.

Stepping into the Observer mode means stepping into an attitude of consciousness that establishes a peacefulness of mind and emotion from which you can heal and change and co-create. To approach your human world in this way is to master it. Practice looking at your life from your inner Observer whenever you think about it. As you cultivate this as a habit, you will automatically adjust what you do with your attitude, your words, your money, or your mission. The Observer will place you on a path that is directly influenced by your Higher Self instead of controlled by the frightened ego.

Detachment enables you to trust God to provide for you as you travel your path of spiritual confidence toward full-blown soul-esteem. As you become aware that you are not just your body, that you are more than your thoughts and feelings, that you are more than a collection of beliefs and habitual actions that you have practiced over a lifetime, you will come into direct contact with your soul and with your Holy Self—the Observer.

As you practice making conscious, confident decisions, be aware of two levels of your being: the human that may get a little anxious and scared, and the Observer who is able to talk you through the rough spots and keep you on purpose. The Observer knows when you make a right decision. It stays calm and says to you, "It's okay to feel those fearful feelings, but you can move beyond them to join Me—the Observer—and I will lift you above doubt and insecurity."

As I have been cultivating the Observer within myself, I have noticed that when I become nervous or anxious about some deadline or when my brain gets tired and I doubt my ability to create, I close my eyes and step back from the "problem." I simply observe myself in whatever state of discomfort I seem to be in and compassionately detach from my body's experience. Then, as I observe the symptoms of anxiety or nervousness, they begin to dissipate and transmute themselves into a feeling of calm and confidence. Instead of attaching myself to the thoughts of anxiety or fear, I become the Observer of my thoughts. As I shift to this perspective, I stop holding on to negative or energy-depleting thoughts. The thoughts then begin to disappear and are replaced by God's Love and my own soul-esteem.

My husband, Roger, detaches from challenging situations by carrying on a dialogue between his Higher Self and his ego-self. He names his Higher Self "Synchy" (short for synchronicity), and strikes up a conversation between Roger and Synchy. Synchy has a way of calming Roger down and coming up with what to do and how to do it from a higher spiritual perspective—the Observer perspective.

A detached perspective seems to create a new energy which dissolves the emotional reactions to what is going on in the human world. Cultivating the Observer is one of the greatest U-turns you can make that will move you into liberation. As you learn to step back and watch, simply observing the event, you will no longer be controlled by the physical and emotional events of your life. If you experience anger, step back and observe it for a few moments. You will almost immediately be freed from the pain that comes with anger. Challenging events will continue to happen, but you will no longer unconsciously give power to those events. You will simply observe them.

So many of you talk about *releasing* a problem. But how can you release something or someone without first detaching? It is detachment, stepping back, looking upon a situation, being in the world but not of the world, that allows you to truly release something. Releasing a problem means to make the decision to stop thinking about it, talking about it and dwelling upon it. Do what you can that is within your realm of influence. Then make a conscious decision to detach and move on.

Looking upon the world from the perspective of the Observer is taking calm action while being free of paralyzing emotions. The calming Observer keeps you from panicking, eases your fears, and settles your inner turmoil. When you become the Observer, you go beyond your human self, let go of the need to be right, and open the door to spiritual partnerships with your loved ones.

Listen to the Drummer

Child of Light, it is time to rest for a few moments. Let your mind slow down so that you begin to hear My beat sounding louder and louder as it pulses from the center of your being.

Even as you read these words, My dear one, let yourself slide out of your human sense of self and into that High Tower that is you as the Observer. Let that peaceful and calm part of yourself notice the sweetness of My Presence as I fill you to overflowing. Give greetings to the angels of My Presence as they surround you and fill this room with Love. Notice that you are beginning to feel the freedom of My Spirit moving through your consciousness and into all that until now has concerned you. Look upon the painful and empty places and let Me soothe your mind, your body and your soul.

Move into liberation as you step back and watch, realizing that you are not attached to an event. You are that which is observing the event, and you can no longer be controlled by physical events in the human world. Every attachment to things or persons of the human dimension is an obstruction to your awareness of our Oneness. It is emotional attachment which reduces your happiness and your sense of fulfillment. Oh, I do not mean that you should isolate yourself from others of My creation, I merely tell you how important it is that you not be attached by the cords of emotion to any person or circumstance conjured up by human perception.

Come to this God-Space within you whenever you think to do so, My beloved—that place where you are free to see beyond the difficulty and rise above whatever you perceive as a problem.

It is your emotional attachment to problems that anchors them in your consciousness and causes them to project themselves into your experience. Become the Observer, the Compassionate Witness, and see how easily things change in your human world. As you let go of what seems to be the problem, it will be free to move out of your experience to be consumed by the fire of My Holy Spirit.

Can you let My peace fill you and heal your fragmented perceptions? Can you let My peace harmonize your interactions with others of My creation and transmute your judgments into gentle compassion? Are you willing to let My peace create for you that space wherein you find value and contentment? Can you let yourself ask of Me that which you desire from a consciousness of wholeness that is rooted in My Love? Do you not know that your soul-desire is My desire?

Go forth in peace, My child. Come often for these times of quiet refuge and communion. I am always here. I am your Source. I am closer than your breath and nearer than hands and feet.

I love you. All is well.

—The Drummer

When you go to bed at night, have for your pillow three things—love, hope and forgiveness. And you will awaken in the morning with a song in your heart.
                                              —Victor Hugo

Chapter Twenty
The Tricky Art of Forgiveness

If you are like most people, the fulfillment of your heart's desire includes health, peace of mind, joy, happiness, prosperity, love, success, and freedom. What is the fulfillment of your heart's desire worth to you? What are you willing to pay for it—to sacrifice for it? There is no actual price tag on these things—they already belong to you. But the degree to which these treasures will manifest in your life is directly related to how much emotional debris you carry in your consciousness. The heaviest debris consists of hatred, resentment, anger, self-pity and revenge. If you harbor any of these emotions, there is forgiving to be done. Are you willing to pay the price for peace of mind, happiness and fulfillment? The price tag is forgiveness.

The lesson of forgiveness has been a primary focus in all spiritual teachings. The scriptures of every major religion advocate an attitude of forgiveness as necessary to insure spiritual well-being and salvation. As a child you were more than likely told that forgiving others was the right thing to do. If you didn't hear it in Sunday school, you heard it somewhere: "To err is human, to forgive divine"—"Forgiveness is a virtue"—"Let bygones be bygones"— "Turn the other cheek"—"Forgive and forget." Somebody was always trying to convince you that forgiving another person was the honorable, good, and morally correct thing to do. And with that instruction came the direct or implied threat of Divine retribution if you didn't forgive, along with an accumulation of guilt for having held on to a grudge. The truth is, many of these well-meaning teachers didn't really understand that forgiveness is a universal requirement rooted in spiritual principle, not in religious dogma or moral mandates.

Very few human beings have ever had the true value of forgiveness explained to them. They have never been told *why* forgiveness is important. Many do not understand how damaging the emotional charge brought on by unforgiveness can be to the mind, body and spirit of the person holding the grudge; or how emotional resentment festers and grows, poisoning the spirit and burdening the soul; or that these debilitating emotions create consciousness blocks that make the experience of joy and peace virtually impossible. Instead, many are taught from a young age that unforgiveness is simply sinful and unacceptable. The leverage used to encourage forgiveness has been the fear of retaliation from a judgmental God.

It is time that forgiveness be fully understood. It is no accident that this chapter on forgiveness follows the chapter about detachment, because forgiveness *is* detachment. True forgiveness is the successful severing of the emotional umbilical cords that energetically attach you to those events or people which have generated anger, resentment or victimhood in your consciousness. These emotions are chemical in nature and penetrate the cells of your body. You literally carry these toxic emotions around with you, and they eventually drain away your vital life energy that could be used to enhance your life and expand your consciousness. Your entire body is your subconscious mind and it is participating in all that you think, say, feel and do. A subconscious mind riddled with guilt and charged with anger and resentment gradually breaks down the physical form causing aging and disease, as well as pain and struggle.

Look back at those times when you *thought* you let something go, *thought* you had forgiven someone. What happened in many of these instances? When you least expected it, something reminded you of that person or event. Something triggered the memory. And much to your surprise, the old feelings were triggered along with the memory. You could feel the resentment in the pit of your stomach. You could feel the anger stirring. You may have said to yourself, "I thought I had let that go! I thought I had forgiven them!" But your thoughts about forgiving had failed to reach the feeling and belief levels. The forgiveness didn't "take." Why? Because you simply *stuffed* your feelings, and the emotional umbilical cord was still attaching the past event to your present expression. The truth is, just *thinking* and saying "I forgive" is not enough. Claiming to release an emotion of anger toward someone is not enough. Even looking into the eyes of a person and saying, "I forgive you," and meaning it with all your heart, may not be enough. So what is enough? How do you forgive, *know* that you have forgiven, and experience freedom from any resurgence of that emotional reaction? There are five aspects of the forgiveness process. They are *willingness, nonresistance, becoming the Observer, transforming the adversary into your teacher, and giving.* The whole process adds up to detachment, which equals forgiveness.

The first question to ask yoursel is, "Am I *sure* I want to emotionally detach myself from this person or circumstance?" I counsel many people who intellectually think they want to forgive, but they are accustomed to the feelings of fear, anger, and the habit of victimhood. These people equate forgiveness with letting someone off the hook, and a desire for justice keeps them from truly forgiving. Your clue as to whether or not this may be true in your case is to notice what you do after you think you have forgiven someone. If you find yourself hanging on to anger or self-pity, if you find yourself talking about the person in a judgmental way, if you notice that you can't be in that person's presence without feeling hurt or angry, or if you find yourself telling the story about this person over and over, you may not be *willing* to let go of it at deeper levels of mind. You may find yourself almost immediately in another situation that has similar characteristics to the one out of which you just stepped.

If you are honest with yourself, you may find that you have become addicted to the feelings that many negative experiences have produced. At some point it may seem as though you are wearing lead boots, stepping from one puddle of sticky tar into the next, while your zest for life is increasingly replaced by your addiction to heavy, negative and debilitating emotions.

What has happened here is that your *heart* is still glued to the problem. Your emotions are anchored in past hurt and pain. As long as there are such anchors that keep tugging at your heart-strings, there can only be degeneration emotionally, mentally, physically and spiritually. Life then seems like a struggle and at best it feels like treading water in a polluted pool of defeat. The soul is buried and forgotten. You are spiritually powerless.

In order to truly forgive and emotionally detach, you must bring yourself into a state of *willingness*. You must consciously consent to and comply with the pure intention to accomplish true forgiveness. Willingness inspires desire. Willingness is your power of conscious choice and is the result of using your will in a nonresistant, non-aggressive, but decisive manner. Remember—your will is your built-in Divine Director.

I know many people who think they are willing to forgive, but they misuse their power of will as "will power" to force the idea of forgiveness. In their head they think they have done the right thing, but at subconscious levels they are not willing to cut the emotional umbilical cords. You may already know from your own failed attempts to forgive, that *will power* doesn't work for very long. Your will is meant to keep you on course, to direct you and to monitor your intention. The will is meant to be a cooperative factor, not a coercive factor. A true intention to forgive gives your will permission to guide you into a state of willingness. Willingness will lead you into an attitude of nonresistance.

Nonresistance means to stop fighting, stop judging, stop rehashing your story. It means to stop talking about it. Stop. Stop. Stop. Remember the old saying, "What you resist persists." Understand that the harder you push against anything or anyone, the harder it pushes back. When you stop pushing or resisting, the opposition can no longer oppose you because there is nothing to oppose.

Aikido is a martial art with a terrific nonresistance philosophy. It teaches nonaggression and nonviolence, but not passivity. It's about body-mind balance and being totally present in the moment. One can disempower a potential adversary by facing the individual and moving through the attack and beyond it. It's fascinating and effective.

A question to ask yourself when you feel angered by someone is, "If I stop resisting, if I stop putting my energy into pushing against this thing, how will I spend my time?" In other words, when you stop doing something you must replace it with another activity. Nature abhors a vacuum, so when you create a consciousness vacuum you have to fill that void with some other energy. If you do not make a conscious choice to replace feelings of resistance with lightness, joy, peace and love, the tendency may be to refill that void with more resistance. It is possible to become so used to fighting against something that it is difficult to know what to do if you suddenly stop fighting.

In one of my classes a student said, "This nonresistance thing is really working. I'm more peaceful and happy, and when something goes wrong I'm better able to detach. I'm finding it easier to forgive. The problem is, I'm bored." I laughed and agreed with her that too much peace and harmony can indeed be perceived as boring if you don't fill your time with a new activity. She had become so accustomed to being angry with someone, focusing on it and talking about it, that she was experiencing a big void along with her new-found peace and harmony. I suggested that she use her creative talents to come up with a joyful activity, that she fill the void created by *not* being angry, gossipy or disgruntled, with an activity of positive self-expression.

When you make the conscious choice to stop resisting forgiveness, be prepared to *start doing something* positive and constructive in its place. Loving is the best choice because love is healing. It is giving *out*. It is expression. Love is expanding while resistance is contracting.

There have been many times when people have come into my office complaining about some injustice in their lives. Let's take Judy for example. Judy had stored up a collection of hurt feelings and resentments toward her boss who had been criticizing her, never praising her for those things she did well, expecting her to stay late, and expecting her to include his personal responsibilities as part of her duties. Judy had been putting up with this for years and was finally at her wit's end. I asked Judy, "Are you willing to forgive him?" Judy answered, "Oh, I have forgiven him. But I feel so angry and I can't stand to be in his presence." My response was, "Then you haven't forgiven him." Judy had not really been willing to forgive nor was she willing to stop resisting his behavior. All she could focus on was the injustice of her circumstances and her feelings of anger and resentment. To Judy, her boss was the victimizer and she, the victim. Clearly, Judy was not practicing emotional detachment.

I worked with Judy for several weeks. It took her a while just to bring herself to a point of willingness. Then we worked with declarations, conscious choice, positive prayer, role-playing, and actual on-the-job practice in order to stop her resistance. She gradually learned to let him be however he was and stopped taking his actions and behavior personally. She was then in a position to truly forgive.

Nonresistance is an important attitude to use all of the time because it lets you mentally and emotionally relax and flow with life. There may be times when what is happening appears to go beyond your realm of influence. The action to take at a time like this is *no action.* Stop resisting what is. Get into the soul-zone and rest in the awareness that God is in the soul-zone too, with all the power, all the wisdom and all the guidance that is needed for you to flow gracefully, unscathed, through the challenge of the moment. Then get busy thinking about and doing something positive.

Consider that you simply do not have enough mental and emotional energy to fight against something and create a new life at the same time. You must choose one or the other. Learn to bend with the ice storms of life just like the great pine trees and spruce trees in the northern forests bend their branches with the weight of sleet or ice. These trees cooperate with that which can't be avoided instead of resisting—and they weather the storm without breaking.

Nonresistance enables you to step out of the emotional drama into the role of the Onlooker or Observer. From this position you can look upon any situation from outside yourself, from a perspective of the third story window, a perspective that is detached from the emotions and behavior of the incident. This distance feels like release for a time. It creates a feeling of freedom and relief that seems like forgiveness. But there may still be an emotional attachment to the event. Willingness and nonresistance are important steps, but there is more work to do to complete the forgiveness process.

The practice of nonresistance frees you to mentally look upon your so-called adversary and ask yourself the question, "How is he or she serving me?" Then be willing to look at the answers. I guarantee you that everyone whom you have considered an enemy has gifted you with an important lesson. Once you can see what the lesson is in the situation you are facing, you can then mentally and emotionally transform that person involved into your teacher instead of your adversary.

This brings us to the next step in the forgiveness process and that is to do what the word implies. The two words which make up the word forgive are *for* and *give.* The word *for* means *in favor of.* Therefore, a new way of thinking about the word *forgive,* would be to be *in favor of giving.* When you feel unforgiving or resentful, you are withholding your love. You are in the emotional and mental position of *wanting* something or wanting to *get* something from the other person. When you turn this around and do the *positive opposite*, or *give out* instead of *withhold*, your consciousness will expand instead of contract. You will give away your love, your joy, your creativity and your enthusiasm. Remember—giving is expanding and withholding is contracting.

The question may come up, "How do I know when I have *truly* detached and forgiven?" "How do I know this old issue won't come up again when I least expect it and whack me in the side of the head?"

You cannot be in a state of negative emotional reaction and feel peace inside at the same time. Simply test yourself for a sense of peace. *The test for Best is peace.* Go within and see how you feel. Do you feel anger? Is your solar-plexus knotted up? Is your face frowning and tense? Are you nervous and fidgety? Do you still want to hang someone by the toenails? If so, you are still charged with emotion over whatever situation you are trying to release. It's simple. You are stuck to it. You are attached to it. Therefore, you have not forgiven. Go back to the willingness step.

When you check for peace, you may find that you feel calm. Perhaps there are no knots in your midriff when you think about the situation that you have forgiven. More than likely this means that you are free from the experience and you have severed the emotional umbilical cord. You have detached.

Do you see why forgiveness is so important? Do you see that forgiveness has several components, or factors, which go into the forgiveness process? When you are in a state of resentment or desire to punish, even at the subconscious level, you are stuck to the experience. Negative emotions act like glue and you carry the emotional pain of an incident into every new experience. It contaminates your ability to move and express freely in the new present moment. It becomes an anchor to the past. It becomes part of your identity. It becomes part of who you believe yourself to be.

Forgiveness is an essential spiritual act that you must accomplish in order to open yourself to the power of Love. As you learn to forgive others and open yourself to Love, you will expand your ability to honor yourself. Self love means caring for yourself enough to forgive so that the wounds of your past can no longer limit you, hurt you, or damage you. As you love unconditionally, you will move out of the wounded child mentality into spiritual maturity—out of victimhood into freedom.

This entire society has emphasized "woundology" and victimization. But you can participate in a planetary healing as you take from your own wounds the spiritual insights that can propel you into a place of healing and self-empowerment.

Your body, mind and spirit *require* love to survive and thrive. When you hold grudging thoughts, or act toward others in unloving, retaliatory ways, you violate the energy of Love. When you hold on to negative emotional reactions toward others or toward yourself, or when you intentionally say or do something to create pain for others, you literally poison or contaminate your own mental, physical and spiritual systems.

Oh, you may think you have forgiven, forgotten, put it behind you, let it go, and risen above it. But if there are unhappy situations in your life there may still be forgiving to do—either of someone else, or of yourself. If you are unhappy with your level of prosperity, there may be forgiving to do. If you are dealing with ill health, there may be forgiving to do. If you are experiencing friction in relationships, there is definitely forgiving to do. *Your greatest tool for changing your world is your ability to change your mind about the world you behold.* Changing your mind is the ultimate personal power. To step out of the prison of grudge-holding, you must choose love instead of fear. You must choose to become an open vessel through which the unconditional Love of God expresses and radiates. You must choose to let your very soul emanate the Love that is God— ever expanding, expressing, and creating new patterns for the creation of joy.

Unforgiveness is the most debilitating and limiting state of consciousness there is. Unforgiveness is not just an emotion—it is a state of consciousness. It is a state of mind. It is poison to your thought, to your feeling, to your belief system, to your behavior and to your body. A poisoned consciousness creates a toxic life experience.

Understand that the Love that shines through your soul from Holy Spirit is not the same love as seen from the lower self, or the ego. Unconditional Divine Love does not mean just "feeling good" toward someone. It does not mean romantic love. It does not mean "touchy-feely" interaction. It does not mean showering everyone with affection. It is not sentiment. The energy of unconditional Love is the power behind all of life and creation. It can be thought of as a vibrational frequency which transports your thoughts into manifestation. At the highest level, Love is the driving force that is the Will of God. Love is the alchemist that transforms your thoughts, feelings and beliefs into manifest form. If your consciousness is not motivated by Love—if it is stuck in unforgiveness—you will be destined to take what life presents to you, instead of becoming a co-creator with the Universal Energy of unconditional Love.

True forgiveness is unconditional Love. And by unconditional, I mean expecting nothing in return. Unconditional Love goes far beyond the laws of this world. It wipes out fear with a lightning bolt of spiritual awakening. Decide now to give loving thoughts and energy with every encounter. Pour love into your immediate environment. Radiate love out into the community and to people you read about in newspapers and hear about on TV. Yes, it even includes those who have been labeled murderers and terrorists. This means becoming detached and loving toward all. Remember, you are not loving the violent act, you are loving the soul that is toxic with fear and negativity. You are loving the spirit that is held prisoner by hate. As you live this way, you will notice your own soul beginning to blossom, your body feeling more energy, and your mind focusing on creativity and joy. You will notice your life smoothing out and peace taking hold—along with many other miracles. You will notice the limitations that you have experienced beginning to disappear. Unconditional Love is the greatest secret of life. It is so powerful that it will free you to soar above the insanity of the human world. It will help you cultivate a healthy, balanced blend of body, mind and spirit.

There is much healing to be done in this world. There is healing to be done in individual lives—emotional healing, physical healing, and healing at the level of soul. If there is to be true healing, forgiveness is not an option. It is mandatory.

Building soul-esteem depends upon removing the emotional blocks that have accumulated in your consciousness. Unforgiveness can account for many of these blocks that inhibit the free flow of spiritual power. When you have truly forgiven, you carry no negative baggage into the new now moment. When you become emotionally detached, you have successfully transformed your adversary into your best teacher of the moment—and you will know that you have forgiven. You are then free to soar into the realm of unlimited potential accompanied by solid soul-esteem. You will discover the good you couldn't see before. Master the forgiveness process and enjoy a huge surge of soul-esteem that will lift you from unhappiness and powerlessness into the authentic power of the divine human.

Listen to the Drummer

Relax, My child. Facing the lesson of forgiveness is a big step—but a necessary step. True forgiveness is like standing under a clear, beautiful waterfall and letting the healing waters wash you clean. As you let your consciousness absorb this new understanding about forgiveness, clear your mind, relax your body, and sit with Me for just a few moments.

Quiet yourself, let your shoulders drop, allow your face to soften, and listen to these words as though they are being whispered in your ear.

Do you know how much I love you, My child? Do you know how loving and radiant you are as you stand free from human emotions that no longer serve you? Do you have any idea how powerful you are? Trust Me to tell you that you are more powerful than you ever imagined. When you master the art of forgiveness you will move into higher frequencies of Light and Love. Your soul-esteem will blossom as the lotus.

Above all else, My dear one, do not allow yourself to become discouraged if you find forgiveness a goal that you accomplish bit by bit. Know that you are always demonstrating forgiveness to the extent of your highest understanding in each present moment. Forgive yourself first. Apply all of your knowledge just gained to wash away any unforgiveness held within your heart against yourself. Know that you are My precious child and that from My perspective there is nothing to forgive. But in the dualistic world you are now experiencing, there may be many opportunities to practice the art of forgiveness.

As you establish your intent to forgive, know that I am moving through you to strengthen your resolve. I am giving you courage as you choose between love and fear. I am inspiring you to use the gifts I have given in order to express your best Self. Remember that it is through you that I realize My desire to express.

I remind you, My beloved, to guide your thoughts, your feelings and your actions toward whatever brings real peace in your mind and your heart. Acting in ways that bring that peace is an act of mastery. The peaceful mind has power—it will be obeyed. Remember that there is no struggle in Spirit and that which lives in the Spirit lives in peace. The effects of Spirit upon your willing soul are healing and restoration.

I am the Drummer that beats the rhythm of peace at the center of your being. I am the Master Knower within you that always knows what to do and what to say. Come to Me, My dear one, and bring your important matters silently before the Master Knower. March to the Drummer and I will lead you aright. Walk in protection, surrounded by the angels of My Presence.

I love you. All is well.

—The Drummer

When you judge people, you have no time to love them.
—Mother Teresa

Chapter Twenty-One
Positioning Is Polarizing

Like forgiveness, nonjudgment is another teaching handed down to us over the ages with no real explanation of its spiritual significance. If, as a child, you ever asked why nonjudgment was important, you might have been told, "It's just the right thing to do," or "Because Jesus said to judge not or you will be judged," or "To judge is a sin and God punishes sin." If you have moved beyond the concept of a judgmental God, these answers are no longer valid and serve only to confuse.

To clear up the confusion and reinforce the importance of not judging, I would like to use a word other than judgment. That word is *positioning*. When you judge, you position yourself, and when you position yourself, you anchor yourself. When you anchor yourself, you cannot move and your attitude is rigid, unbendable, and inflexible. Positioning is a form of stubbornness that sets up expectations and assumptions and places conditions upon whatever it is you are positioning yourself for or against.

There is the position of power, the defensive position, the political position, and the social position. Positioning freezes you in "slow time," which means that whatever you would like to have happen is slowed down because you can't move beyond your anchored position. Positioning is polarizing.

Positioning polarizes your consciousness. I'm not talking about polarity in terms of magnetic or ionic polarity, but in terms of emotional and mental polarity—an extreme *position*—a separation from any other possibility. Implicit in the definition of the word polarity is the idea of differences and separation. It follows, therefore, that if you have a polarized consciousness, you are focused on your own competitive position or separate viewpoint which is different from the other person's.

One of the most obvious ways in which many people polarize themselves is to take the position, "Life is unfair," or "There is no way out of my situation," or "Life just dealt me a bad hand." Can you see that when you take positions such as these you polarize yourself to the extreme? You turn away from the possibility that life can also be fair. You blind yourself from seeing that there is *always* a way out of a seemingly dreadful circumstance and you miss seeing the lesson offered by the situation.

It's true that life isn't fair. It's also true that life isn't unfair. Life just is. What you do with it mentally and emotionally determines your experience of it. If you but surrender to the fact that life isn't fair or unfair, you depolarize yourself and move out of self-pity into the flow of God's Love. That Love pulls up the anchor that you may have sunk deeply into the depths of the ocean of "poor me." Whenever you make the very serious mistake of feeling sorry for yourself, you position yourself as a victim of external circumstances by complaining about what is wrong with factors outside yourself. You may tell your story to your friends and anyone who will listen in order to elicit their sympathy, which reinforces your self-pity and supports your "position". When you move out of the position that life is unfair, you drop the self-pity and take action to do the best that you can do with what you have.

Moving out of *positioning* also keeps you from feeling

sorry for other people. When you stop feeling sorry for others, you no longer experience feelings of helplessness, condescension, superiority or pity. Instead, you graduate to the soul-esteem bolstering emotion of compassion. Compassion is a place of heartfelt emotion that conveys love and kindness to everyone around you. It enables you to recognize and honor the uniqueness and strengths in others that can see them through their difficulties. Practice substituting the phrase, "I have compassion for that person" in place of "I feel sorry for that person." Compassion moves you out of victim consciousness and into constructive action.

What are some of the stubborn positions in which *you* may have anchored yourself? Perhaps it's "My way is the only way," or "My way is the right way." You may have taken positions based on collective beliefs such as "All men are alike," or "All women are gossips." Perhaps it's a position like "The world is a scary place," or "I'll never amount to anything," or "That's just the way I am." The specifics of your positioning isn't the most important thing here. The most important thing is to realize that you may be holding on to many ideas that glue you in place so that you don't get anywhere beyond your position. Remember that positioning is polarizing and puts you in "slow time" where nothing seems to happen. Giving up your judgments and your positions will not make you disappear into a nonentity or cause you to crumble into a lifeless blob. Giving up your judgments and positions will get you moving. It will get your life flowing again. It will make you a stronger co-creator with God.

To evaluate how much you are judging and polarizing yourself by positioning, use the Soul-Math Formula to discover what you think, how you feel and what you believe about some person or situation. It won't take long to see how you may be polarizing yourself and creating your life in "slow time."

The tendency to judge other people, which means to take a position about what you think of them, serves as a gigantic roadblock in your path of personal transformation. When you take an emotional or mental *position* about someone else, you are providing yourself with valuable feedback on your *own* thought processes—specifically, that you are stuck, or anchored, in a position that keeps you from flowing with Life. Censure of another person is one of the greatest burdens to your soul. It is a dangerous block to your expression of soul-esteem.

When you find yourself thinking in judgmental terms, remind yourself that your position is an indicator of where you are at the moment, as well as where you are *not* at the moment. The judgment itself might be a signal that you are in some way identifying with the person whom you are judging. That which disturbs you most about someone else may be something you refuse to acknowledge in yourself, or even something you need more of. *The trick here is to become more interested in what causes you to feel judgmental than in focusing on what's "wrong" with the other person.* As you shift your awareness in this way, you will begin to soften your position. You will begin to replace your judgments with a gentler and more loving attitude, and be willing to look inward to find out why you have a "charge" on a particular viewpoint. Be willing to soften your position.

Let's turn our attention to the difference between positioning and polarizing through critical judgment, and objectively choosing between one thing and another. Critical judgment has to do with censure, condemnation, comparison, discrimination, prejudice, denouncement or put-down. Critical judgment has the effect of a dead weight holding you in place—in limitation. The only reason that you may not have healed circumstances in your life or found your true place in life is because you have positioned yourself in mental and emotional criticism. As you overcome the tendency to criticize, you break out of polarity and find it easier and easier to make healthy, confident choices—choices that have nothing to do with critical judgment. Criticism will always immobilize you. In fact, have you ever noticed how you feel just after you have criticized someone? Especially if you say it out loud. You probably feel a drain of energy siphoned off by the emotion of guilt—or even a sense of shame. It may even feel as though you were the one who was judged.

Judgment, or positioning, is not to be confused with ethical appraisal, evaluation, assessment, or discernment. Wise discernment is an expression of Infinite Intelligence. As long as you live in the human world, you will have to distinguish good quality from poor quality, good conduct from bad conduct, wisdom from stupidity, and higher emotions from lower emotions. An objective appraisal is very different from a targeted critical judgment. When you see someone act in a foolish or harmful way, it is important to evaluate the act but not censure the person for the act. Recognize unwise behavior for what it is, but do not allow yourself to hate or be positioned against the person who behaved wrongly. Make the conscious and compassionate choice to look beyond the act and see the Holy Spirit and Infinite Intelligence within that person. Until you relinquish your various positions and connect with the flow of the Universe, you will unwittingly obscure the brilliance of Spirit within your own being. Once free of these positions, you will allow Spirit to shine forth resplendently and freely attract to you the desires of your heart and soul.

Remember that judgment and positioning are rooted in the concept of separation instead of oneness—isolation instead of connection. Separation begins with the false boundaries you draw and false boundaries give way to comparisons, envy, conflict and judgment.

Think about the boundaries you draw around talents and abilities. Bring to mind the accomplishments of famous performers or sports heros, or any others you admire for their abilities. You might think of these people as "better than" if you stack them up against yourself or others whose accomplishments seem to pale by comparison. Instead of just enjoying the accomplishments of those who seem to be particularly gifted, and accepting others as they are, you might begin to judge yourself and others as "inferior." Before you know it, you are indulging in thoughts and feelings of inadequacy and low self-esteem. What if you stopped comparing one person to another? What if you made the conscious decision to regard everyone as an individualized expression of God, including yourself? And what if you accepted all people for what they have done without putting them on a pedestal or without denigrating them for what they haven't done? When you accept people exactly the way they are, you keep yourself out of judgment altogether.

Consider the boundaries that are drawn around yet another concept—that of beauty. Most people operate from a physical, five-sensory perspective when they define what beautiful is. The ad agencies know this and they capitalize on it. They present their idea of beautiful or handsome and before you know it you are comparing yourself to the images you see on television selling jeans or underwear. If you are like many people, your self-esteem begins to dwindle. Imbedded in the idea of "beautiful" are countless comparisons which end up as judgments of yourself and others who do not measure up. You might ask, "But how can I be totally nonjudgmental when I have to compare one thing to another in order to make a choice?" Once again, making a choice or preferring one thing over another is quite different from judging something or someone as superior or better than another.

The truth is, all opposites share the common denominator of the same reference point. *Up* couldn't exist without *down* and there couldn't be a *right* without a *left*. In the world of business, *buying* and *selling* are viewed as opposites, but upon closer examination they are two ends of the same stick and have a complementary relationship with each other. There would be nothing to buy if nothing were sold, and nothing would be sold if there were nothing to buy. Each action is in opposition to the other, but they are both part of the same process. Buying and selling are inseparable; up and down are inseparable; right and left are inseparable. Instead of seeing that everything is connected, we generally view opposites and differences as conflicting, irreconcilable, contrary or incongruous.

In his book, *Making Miracles*, Dr. Paul Pearsall writes about quantum physics and the *complementarity principle*: "There are opposites to everything in the universe, and miracles are made when we remember to draw our strength from a holographic or complete view of life rather than a one-sided image. Old and new, particle and wave, hot and cold, and love and hate always exist simultaneously. We view the world with only one eye when we neglect the complementary side of any issue in our lives."

Lao Tzu says this in the old Chinese proverb:

Is there a difference between yes and no?
Is there a difference between good and evil?
Must I fear what others fear? What nonsense!
Having and not having arise together
Difficult and easy complement each other
Long and short contrast each other
High and low rest upon each other
Front and back follow one another.

When you stop judging, comparing and positioning yourself, you are ready to experience the greatest freedom of all—the freedom to be yourself. You are special and unique—an individualized expression of the One. This does not mean separate. This does not mean that you should allow your personal statements to set up false boundaries. It is a weakness of the dualistic world of personality and ego to make judgments and comparisons instead of honoring differences. At the soul level there is no such thing as evaluating others based upon their appearance, accomplishments, talents or possessions.

The soul and the personality are like all opposites: they are two sides, or aspects, of the same thing. When you find yourself in judgment about something, consult the other side—the soul side—and your inner self will confirm that you do not need to judge or compare. When you see the world in this way, you free yourself to be your best. You do not notice what others possess, how they look or how they behave, as compared to yourself or to anyone else. You simply enjoy that person and the gifts he or she brings to the world.

Look around and notice the various people with whom you share some sort of relationship. There are relatives, perhaps a spouse, a partner, friends, co-workers, bosses, and so on. Notice if you make the judgment that there is something missing in one or more of these people. Do you want them to change something about themselves? If so, then that very thing you think is missing or wrong will be what is missing or wrong in your experience when interacting with them. Why? Because that's where your attention is.

When people come to me for counseling about a relationship, they usually claim that something is missing in the other person. "He's just not affectionate." "She never wants to go anywhere with me." "He's abusive," or "She's frigid." Guess what? If you focus upon thoughts like these about another person, then that's exactly what you will experience when interacting with that person. It's interesting to notice that the same person may behave one way toward one person and quite differently toward another, depending upon what the other person expects to experience. This dynamic is a law of the universe. It is a spiritual principle: *Like attracts like, and like begets like.* You can't plant corn and harvest jelly beans. What you sow in the soil of mind you will tend to find manifesting in your world of affairs. When you stop judging what is missing or what is wrong with another person, and shift to honoring that person's goodness, what he or she shows you of themselves also shifts.

Does this mean that you can change someone just by changing how you see that person? No. However, as you change your perception of another, the dynamics of your relationship with that person invariably changes. As your perception changes, your behavior tends to change also. Does this mean that you can save a marriage or salvage a relationship by changing your perception of the other person? Maybe, maybe not. However, by seeing others through the eyes of love instead of judgment, you free yourself— and them—to either remain in the relationship or move on more easily. By seeing others through the eyes of love instead of judgment, you pull up the anchor of positioning. Nonjudgment frees you to be *who* you are and makes it okay for others to be *where* they are.

Keep in mind that it sometimes seems easier to stay stuck in an emotional or mental position—even in the muck and mire of fear and distress. Your ego may be so convinced of your position that you misuse faith as an *excuse* to stay in your position. This means that when you want something to be a certain way, and you have positioned yourself so that you have no intention of bending or moving off your position, you say, "I have faith that God will work this out the right way—so I'm going to stick to my guns." This kind of positioning demonstrates faith in your position instead of trust in God. Faith in God is fluid and full of action. You can't have true faith and remain stuck. True faith will find you willing to move in a new direction in order to progress, knowing that the right people will show up to assist and to guide, and all of your needs will be met in every new now moment.

Become very clear that positioning promotes separation between you and other people, you and your soul-self, and you and the Universe. With every position that is in opposition to another person, you take yourself out of the flow of Holy Spirit and make it more difficult to create that which you desire easily and quickly. Commit now to choosing a depolarized consciousness so that you can enjoy true freedom.

Listen to the Drummer

The time comes once again for you to stop all logical thinking and spend a few moments in the quiet with Me, My dear one. You are indeed at a point on your path where the lessons may seem difficult from your human perspective. These lessons of Spirit require a closeness between us that is greater than ever before. Listen for the beat of the Drummer, My child, and let it help you understand the importance of moving off the positions held so tightly by your ego-mind.

Surrender into My peace. Let your only position be the way you have placed your body in the chair upon which you are sitting. Cast aside all judgment and criticism and leanings in this direction or that. Let this be a time of neutrality—of perfect balance at the fulcrum of pure consciousness. Come to the center point, My child. Meet Me at that point of perfect balance. Meet Me where there is pure potential. Meet Me in the Void and let us create together.

Relax into this present moment and enjoy a respite from the thinking, questioning mind—and remember to breathe. Breathe deeply, My beloved. Breathe Me into the very core of your being and let Me breathe My life into you. Let us breathe as One.

Can you let My peace fill you and heal your fragmented perceptions and ego judgments? Can you let My peace harmonize your interactions with others of My creation and transmute your judgments into gentle compassion? Can you let My peace create for you that space wherein you find value and contentment?

Can you let yourself ask of Me that which you desire from a consciousness of wholeness that is rooted in My Love? Do you not know, My child, that your soul-desire is My desire?

As you resonate with Me and as you engage our Oneness, you will be guided by My still small voice within at all times. At times when it seems difficult, come into the quiet and attune your ear to the Drummer. Listen for My whisper in your heart of hearts. Acknowledge the angels of My Presence. Their energy is My energy becoming tangible for you.

Let go of all judgments that polarize your thoughts and feelings and cloud your connection with My wisdom and power. Allow your tendencies of haste, anxiety, and hard or hurt feelings to melt in the Light of My Presence.

Go forth My beloved, with My faith as your faith. Let Me carry you into renewal and joy. Fly, My dear one, knowing that My Presence buoys you up and fills your wings with eternal life. Go forth knowing that you are a powerful being of Light with a partner that illumines the path and makes clear the way before you.

I love you. All is well.

—The Drummer

Order is the sanity of the mind, the health of the
body, the peace of the city, the security of the
state. As the beams to a house, as the bones to a
body, so is order to all things.
                                              —Robert Southey

Chapter Twenty-Two
Cleaning Up Unfinished Business

Have you ever longed to start over, begin again, do things
differently and get a fresh start? If you have, you may have found
that the fresh start lasted only a short time, or perhaps it never
even got past the thought in your mind. You may have found
yourself falling back into the same old patterns that produced the
same results that you had been getting all along.

In order for there to be new beginnings, you must let go of
the baggage of the past. In order for anything to be new and
different, or better, you must make some changes in your thought
patterns or you will fall back into the same ruts, and you will keep
getting what you've been getting.

My objective is to inspire you to DO whatever it is that
you've been putting off—to finish the things you have started, tie
up loose ends and carry forward whatever it is that you have thought

about, dreamed about, planned for, but stopped. Think about all your vital energy that has been seeping into unfinished, unresolved matters.

I ask you to notice how much of your precious energy has been sapped by unresolved matters, and nudge you to do something about it. Any amount of unfinished business, small or large, drains your energy. If you are like many people, you leave things undone that are really very easy to do. By starting with the simple, small things, you can bring many loose ends to closure and get them off your mind. As you do this there will be more energy available to apply to the bigger challenges of life. You may not be aware that your mental energy is tied up in things such as closets that are jammed with clothes you haven't worn in years, or the checkbook you haven't balanced in six months, or the basement that's stacked to the ceiling with clutter. What about the thank you notes you haven't written or that person to whom you have not declared your love for months or maybe even years? Do you have phone calls you have not returned or phone calls you have not initiated because you dread making them? How about the business matter that you should have faced and brought to closure months ago? Perhaps there's a conversation or understanding that should take place between you and someone else, or maybe you have not forgiven yourself or another person.

The fact is, every situation, every project, every conversation left hanging, subconsciously reduces the reserves of your physical, mental and emotional energy. You may not realize this until after you have cleaned out, cleared up, and handled the loose ends. Then you will notice how light and free you feel.

You may be saying to yourself, "Well, that's fine, but I have some unfinished business that is beyond my control. I can't do anything about that!" If you have a loose end that you can do nothing about, something that is out of your realm of influence, you can still bring it to a close by releasing it *spiritually and energetically*. You can make up your mind to release the matter, and there is nothing more powerful than a made up mind. Such a release will enable you to go forward in your life with lightness and freedom of mind, body and spirit. You can accomplish this spiritual resolution during meditation or prayer in a *new now moment*, by seeing the matter closed. You will be surprised at how much more reserve energy you have after doing this powerful visualization. No, nothing will have changed in the outer world, but *you* will have changed *in relationship to* the outer world. It isn't outer change that needs your attention, it's inner change.

If the situation involves doing something that you truly feel you cannot do by yourself, then you can surrender to God and let God do it through you. Everything that is unfinished in your life can be handled in such a way that you find yourself free to be more and more expressive and effective in your world, with a sense of inner peace.

You may have asked yourself, "Why do I leave so many things hanging?" or "Why do I allow my life to be overcome by the accumulation of unfinished business?" or "Why do I become so lethargic about bringing some things to a close?" The answers may be rooted in fear. You take no action when you fear an outcome. You take no action when you are not motivated by thoughts, feelings and beliefs that are in alignment with each other. You take no action when you have given your power away and find yourself unable to act on your own. Often, your unfinished business serves as an excuse to stay where you are because you're afraid of what lies ahead.

One of the first things to learn about fear is that the physiological *feeling* of fear and the physiological *feeling* of a more positive emotion is the same energy. You may tend to label fear a *bad* feeling and an emotion such as excitement a *good* feeling. What would happen if, when you feel that bad feeling and call it fear, you were to stop and rename it? What if you called it *excitement* or *joyful anticipation* instead?

Years ago, when I was preparing to teach my first Dale Carnegie class, I stood watching the class members assemble. My knees felt weak and I wondered whether I could actually do it. Another instructor walked up and stood beside me and asked me how I was doing. I said, "Oh Bill, I'm scared to death and nervous as a cat." His reply to me was, "You're not nervous or scared, you're just excited."

That was the first time I learned about my power to transform fear into a more positive emotion—in this case excitement. It was easy to do once I understood that all feelings are created out of the same energy and in this instance both feelings had the same physiological sensation. Since then, I have used my power of choice to transform other feelings into more positive, life-supporting emotions.

Here are some simple guidelines to follow when you have been experiencing fear about bringing something to a close:

1. Decide what you want the result to be and visualize the matter closed in a positive, loving way.
2. Notice your feelings. Identify those feelings that seem to be blocks of fear that stand in the way of closure.
3. Take the label of "fear" off the feelings and notice that the feelings are just energy.
4. Notice that your negative feelings are made out of the same energy as positive feelings.
5. Rename, or re-label, the energy with a positive, action word describing a positive emotion.
6. Now let your will move you into action and keep going until you finish what you have started!

It really doesn't matter what label you have placed upon the energy that stops you dead in your tracks and keeps you from taking care of unfinished business. All energy is neutral energy with divine potential, until you harness it and claim it as love, anger, joy, sorrow, peace, resentment, fear, or whatever.

What remains incomplete in your life? What have you left unfinished? What have you been intending to get done but haven't? Take an honest, unflinching look at those things that call for closure and completion. Make a list and be thorough. Following are some areas to pay attention to as you make your list.

Consider your physical world. What have you been putting off with respect to your physical body? Your home? What needs completion in the area of your finances? Your plans for the future? Your relationships? What truths have been left uncommunicated? What lies need to be cleaned up? What broken promises and agreements need to be acknowledged and resolved, either by keeping them or by making a new agreement? Is there someone you need to forgive? Is there a relationship that needs to be ended? Are there acknowledgments that need to be made or praise to be given?

What needs completing in the area of self-development or spiritual development? Perhaps you have been putting off nurturing, caring for and expanding your spirituality. Your whole reason for being on this planet is to learn who you are as a spiritual being. Your physical body and the five senses are available to help you learn and remember, so that when you lay down your form you will be able to see without physical eyes, hear without physical ears, and continue to use your spiritual faculties of intuition, clairvoyance and direct knowing. When you reach that point of transition called death, you take with you one thing, and that is your consciousness. Let it be a consciousness that knows itself as whole and complete.

It takes discipline to finish something you've started, to start something new that you know requires completion, and to clean up those messes that you have created and allowed to clutter your life and drain your energy. I'm talking about discipline based upon spiritual wisdom, God's wisdom through you. It's another way of saying, "Thy will be done, through me." Spiritual discipline isn't something that should be regarded as difficult to attain. It should be something that comes naturally as you draw upon the strength of the Spirit within.

Sure, you will encounter rough spots, but rough spots do not need to paralyze or stop you. Did you know that the first golf balls had smooth covers on them? Then one day a young golfer, who was playing with a beat-up golf ball, demonstrated that his ball flew more accurately and farther than those of his playing partners who played with smooth covered golf balls. Today's golf balls have over 400 dimples, or rough spots, which improve the ball's accuracy and increase its distance. Rough spots can have the same effect on your life. They can cause you to sharpen your performance and facilitate a smooth forward momentum. Ignoring the rough spots by not following through or finishing what you have started, or denying that the rough spots are there, or complaining about them or using them as excuses for not concluding something, leads to stagnation, disappointment and lack of fulfillment.

So get busy. Make your list. Do what is needed to bring closure to everything on that list. Then release it into the flow of the Universe, because "with God nothing shall be impossible." Resolve it in your heart and mind, even if it still looks incomplete in form. Then release it into God's hands. If it reenters your mind, release it again with the affirmation, "God will perfect that which concerneth me." By combining physical action with a spiritual and energetic release, you co-create with God a successful resolution to all your affairs.

Listen to the Drummer

Greetings, My beloved. We meet yet again. Quiet your mind for just a few moments and sit with Me in the joy of Oneness. Open the door of your consciousness to My River of Life that flows through you right now.

Yes, dear one, you are loved. And because I love you, you are loving and lovable. Let your skepticism fall away and allow yourself to be comforted in My Presence that surrounds you and fills you.

I remind you, My child, that My Universe is one of harmony and Divine Order. Although your human dimension may seem to be in chaos or disarray, be assured that harmony underlies all that concerns you. Come into conscious alignment with the order of My Kingdom and let that awareness move through your mind and your heart and your actions. As it does, it will move you to bring closure to those things to which you have not paid attention. A cluttered environment is the out-ward evidence of a cluttered mind, My dear one. Make no mistake that clutter and disorder take a toll on your vital energy. Put your house in order and feel the liberation as you do. As you take action, notice Divine Order in every completion.

Feel My Presence in every move you make and notice My Love as you handle everything you touch with loving intention. There is no task too big for us to handle together. There is no lack of time or lack of patience as you let Me move through you and through that which is before you to do. Approach everything you do as though you are doing it for Me, My child.

See the light of My calling shine through that which may seem like a mountain between you and your peace of mind. Surrender the illusion of struggle, My beloved. There is no need. Lighten your load as you flow with My Life as your life. Drop your burdens at My feet and walk in spiritual confidence into the Light.

As you give loving attention to that which calls for completion, be mindful of My Presence as I work through you expediently. There is nothing that you cannot handle as a Child of Light in your human experience.

Go forth, My dear one, with a vision of new beginnings and hear the beat of My rhythm as it perfects that which concerns you.

I love you. All is well.

—The Drummer

Belief consists in accepting the affirmations of the
soul, unbelief, in denying them.
                                    —Ralph Waldo Emerson

Chapter Twenty-Three
Keep the Change

Through this entire book the point has been to help you awaken to your soul so that you can soar with spiritual confidence. The whole idea behind transformation is to fully integrate the human self with the soul-self so that you may live the life of the divine human and express in your world as a power-presence. The Soul-Math Formula is an effective tool, enabling you to become conscious of the changes that you must make in order to transform your life. Transformation requires permanent changes in thought patterns, attitude and belief.

I remember the movie *Groundhog Day* starring Bill Murray, in which Murray plays a weatherman for a TV station. He goes on his yearly assignment to Punxsutawney, Pennsylvania, to cover Groundhog Day with his producer and cameraman. He hates the assignment and his cynical, egotistical sarcasm is evident from the start.

After spending a night in the town that he hates, Murray wakes up at 6:00 a.m. to the clock radio playing *I Got You, Babe*. He lives through this particular Groundhog Day with his customary unhappy, nasty attitude. Forced to stay in Punxsutawney yet another night because of a blizzard, he awakens at 6:00 a.m. the next morning to the same music of Sonny and Cher. As he begins to move around and start his day, he notices that *everything* unfolds the same as the day before. It's Groundhog Day again! And again and again. Over and over. With each replay he attempts to manipulate the outcome of the next replay. He learns as much as he can one day and attempts to use it to his advantage during the next replay.

Murray almost goes crazy. He even kills himself many times, only to wake up alive on Groundhog Day—again. Gradually, Murray changes his selfish ways and becomes a generous, kind, giving human being. When he is finally changed, he wakes up the *day after* Groundhog Day and moves into the future, transformed and happy, with plans to spend the rest of his life in Punxsutawney.

Like Bill Murray's character, we can't really move on to greater happiness—into a better future—until we change our old attitudes and behavior. Until we do, we will keep recreating scenarios that may look different but feel very much like what we have already experienced day after day after day.

Have you noticed how many people marry a carbon copy of their father or mother, or a person that's very much like their former spouse? It's often the same with a career. No matter how many times you change jobs, you can go through the same experiences with superiors and co-workers that you did in your previous jobs. It's a classic example of the grass always looking greener on the other side of the fence. The new job or new relationship looks great until you realize that it's just a replay of the last one.

You may think that you can change your life by changing your circumstances, but you take your consciousness with you wherever you go. Until you alter the content of your consciousness container (your thoughts, feelings and beliefs), you will continue to attract to yourself the same caliber of results or outcomes. Your ingrained patterns of consciousness will show up in your life again and again until you get the message to initiate conscious change.

Have you ever held grudges, harbored anger or felt resentment? If you have, perhaps you noticed how extreme emotional reactions became more than just feelings when you indulged in them too long. They became energetic *entities* or *thought-forms*. You might have thought you released them and that they disappeared into the clouds like a bird or a plane. But emotionally charged thought-forms typically gain energy in the wild blue yonder of collective thought and return like a boomerang when you least expect them. If you have had this experience, you may remember how it felt to be haunted, preoccupied or possessed with deep longings to repay old hurts. In the meantime, the person who was the object of your attention went about his or her own business, unaware of your personal torment.

Why would anyone continue to grovel around in anger and hurt, especially if one knows what joy feels like? Why in the world would anyone hold on to pain? One reason may be that the ego-self seeks a sense of power by proving that it is right and blameless and in the process tries to make someone else wrong. Another reason may be that the ego-self is seeking a sense of security that can come only from winning, which usually means someone else has to lose. Yet another reason may be that the ego-self has become addicted to the patterns of negative emotion.

A friend of mine told me that she used to recoil whenever anyone displayed aggressive behavior toward her. She learned to turn the tables, however, and put the other person on the defensive by becoming angry. Her anger gave her a sense of power as opposed to her previous feelings of vulnerability. Power felt like winning and winning felt exhilarating. Consequently she continued to use anger to intimidate the other person into agreeing with her. She said that anger had become addictive because it gave her a perverted sense of winning. Anger is seductive indeed.

All of this is a gross misuse of the enormous power that each of us has at our disposal. You may have little or no inkling about how much Universal Energy is at your fingertips. You are using that power all the time, some of it consciously, but much of it unconsciously, indiscriminately, haphazardly and invertedly. You may perceive yourself as powerless when in reality you have unlimited universal power available to you, but you also have a limited awareness about how to access it or use it to promote joy and happiness. You may be like a tiny child in the cockpit of a stealth fighter. Although you have incredible power at your finger tips, and you have been pushing all the buttons and flipping all the switches, you may be spinning out of control. When this happens for a long enough period of time, you run the risk of becoming cynical, resentful and even depressed and apathetic. Why? Because you are scared. You have been fighting for your life and have not realized that underneath your struggle for survival is the brilliant glow of authentic power, the power of Love.

How can you dissolve the glue which keeps you stuck to destructive, self-sabotaging emotional behavior? Love is the most effective solvent in the world. Love is a quality of soul which enables you to let go of the need to be right. It enables you to stop judging or competing with others. Turning within to your soul, you can begin making new choices and decisions. You can, day by day, consciously change your reactions, behaviors and attitudes, until your cynicism and anger are transmuted into respect and reverence for yourself, for other people, and for all of life. Remember that your soul-self, through love, wants to bring you to your highest and best so that you can attract the highest and best into your life.

This transformation doesn't happen overnight and you may sometimes choose to learn the hard way. I remember something my mom always said to me when I pouted or held on to a rotten attitude: "Go ahead, act that way. You aren't hurting anyone but yourself!" Like Bill Murray, I finally caught on to that wisdom and have managed to change many old habit patterns. Each time I do, the replay gets better and better.

I'm sure you've had the experience of paying your check at a restaurant, handing the server some money and saying, "Keep the change." You may have done this at valet parking or after you had your hair cut. The act of tipping is giving more than you *have to,* in appreciation. It's a kind of reward that you give to someone for having served you in some way. It is really feedback to that person without saying the words, "You did a good job."

On the other hand, you might withhold a tip as an expression of dissatisfaction. Withholding a tip from someone who is expected to provide a service is an easy way to make a statement without saying anything. The trouble is most servers simply look at the paltry amount in their hand and blame the tipper for being stingy, instead of examining their own quality of service.

What a good metaphor this is for one of the most important and obvious laws of the universe. You reap what you sow. You get back the equivalent of that which you give out. Try thinking of yourself as a server for a moment—perhaps a waiter or waitress, a beautician or taxi driver, or simply an expression of God whose job it is to give, love and serve. You see, you *are* a server. Your purpose here on planet Earth is to grow spiritually as you *serve* your purpose which is to give, love and serve. So, you already *are* a server. You are in the business of reaping your reward through delivering the service of love.

If you had to survive on the tips you got from your service in love, how well would you do? Would you get rich on your tips? How have your tips been lately? How has Life been rewarding you for your good service? You might try dropping an "o" in "good" and think of it as "God Service." When you have a cranky day and withhold your smiles, your joy, your love, the Universe withholds your reward. This is not the action of an angry God sitting somewhere "up there" deciding how much of a tip you deserve. This is the law of *action-reaction* taking place. This is the law of giving and receiving. This is the Law of Circulation. If you withhold a tip from a server who does you a disservice, can you really expect the Universe to reward *you* for a disservice whether it's a nasty attitude, avoidance, laziness, or arguing because you insist on being right? When a waiter in a restaurant withholds service, you withhold the reward. Life is no different. It is your feedback.

How are you to serve God? You are to serve God by allowing God's Love to move through your every thought, word and deed. You are to serve God by serving every other person, because every other person IS God in form. Serving God means to look beyond the surly attitude or the resistance in another person to see the God core that exists within that person. When you are faced with a difficult situation—perhaps another person's rotten attitude—you serve that other person as well as yourself by asking the question, "What would Love do in this situation?" That's the same as saying, "What would God do?" AND, that's the same as saying, "What will I do, as God happening, toward that other person who is also God happening?"

You are a server, a giver, a lover. That's who you really are. Anything unlike that is simply a misunderstanding, a distortion, an illusion. So if you want to be offered a bigger tip, you get to increase your level of service. You get to serve your fellow human beings with your smiles, your kindness, compassion, joy, enthusiasm, generosity, and the sharing of your talents. These are the ways you give back to life. These are the ways in which you serve God. The moment you withhold these gifts, you put on the brakes, and sooner or later the flow slows down—or it may stop altogether.

At the end of the day, if you open your hand and find it empty, it is evidence that you caused that experience by ignoring the very reason you are here—to give, love and serve. The empty hand is a message that something has to change, and that which has to change is never that which is outside of you. Any time you come up empty, it's because you didn't invest anything of yourself initially. Humankind is one of the very few creations in this universe given the ability to change. We are the only life forms on this planet which have the high degree of choice that we have— choices that exercise the very power of God AS each one of us.

What is the first thing you must change when your palm comes up empty? You must get back on purpose. If you are feeling unloved or unlovable, get busy loving. If you are withholding your assistance, get busy serving. If you are withholding or hoarding, start giving out.

If you were to ask me what I think is the most important change, or shift, in consciousness, I would say it is changing an attitude of doubt into an attitude of faith. Faith is an emotion, and I believe it shares the highest ranking on the emotional scale with unconditional love. Faith isn't just believing, it's higher than that. You can believe in many things—things that are visible like the sun coming up, or the law of gravity, or another person's integrity. Faith, however, is believing in the Infinite Invisible. It is trusting that Life will respond to what you think and feel.

Yes, it is vitally important to change doubt into faith, and just as important is *keeping* the faith once you have it—keeping the change. Maintaining the change and persevering in faith. Perseverance is hanging in there when the odds seem to be against you. Faith helps you trust the ebb and flow of life and it must be practiced with patience and perseverance. The desires of your heart may very often require unquenchable spirit, lots of energy, and an undying commitment.

Change is not something to be feared. Rather, it is something to welcome, for without change nothing in this world would ever grow or blossom, and no one in this world would ever move forward to become the person he or she wants to be.

The toughest thing to change is your approach to change and your attitude about change. In order to keep the change once you've made it, your faith must be a strong root system that allows you to bend and grow with the winds of change without your spirit breaking. You must be willing to work at things that many people are not willing to do. I didn't say *can't* do, I said not *willing* to do.

Perhaps the bottom line is, before you take action ask the question, "What would Love do?" Before making a choice, ask the question, "Does it support my life purpose of giving, loving and serving?" While you are waiting for an answer, remind yourself that patience and perseverance ARE faith in action. If you do these three things, at the end of the day you will open the palm of your hand, notice the blessings, and sense the presence of God as Life winks at you and says, "Keep the change."

Listen to the Drummer

Ah, so you've been noticing changes, My child. Inner changes, outer changes, Earth changes— transitions that sometimes seem frightening or strange. You at times feel as though you are suspended between the swings of the trapeze. Fear not, dear one, for I am with you. I am here as you let go. I am here as you traverse the unknown and I am waiting to catch you with perfect timing.

Be not afraid, My dear one. Let go of the old and enter into the new with faith. Don't look back. Let the momentum of Spirit carry you into the next phases of self-revelation. Child of Light, holy art thou in the Mind of God, and splendid is the Truth of your beauty. Understand that this will never change. I am the Light and that will never change. You are created in the image and likeness of that Light and likewise, that will never change. Step confidently out of the shadow of doubt into the light cast all around by My Infinite Love.

Sit with Me for a moment, My beloved. Sit with Me and notice My unconditional Love that flows through the gentle, steady beat of My drum. Let My beat soothe you as I surround you with My Light that is boundless, endless, and ever-present. Dry the tears from your eyes, My child. Release the burdens from your heart and allow yourself to retreat from the outside world. Step out of the human sense of time and into My one constant moment that is eternal.

Take this precious time to sit with Me—to recognize and know Me—as I would be known by you.

Let the distortions and distractions of the human arena fade from your mind, My child, and melt from your heart. If there is some difficulty on your mind, leave the working out of the problem to Me—to Whom there is no problem. Fly, My dear one. Fly on the wings of your imagination. Fly on the wings of trust and faith. Soar over the obstacles, free as the wind, with all of life as your sky. Glide between the swings with the joy of knowing that you are supported by the air currents of Universal Love as you transcend the old and welcome a vast new realm of unlimited, eternal and infinite space.

In this short time that we have been in conscious communication, many of your questions have already been answered in this Oneness. Much of your unrest has been calmed. All you have now to do is carry out your divine purpose. Be not afraid as the winds of change blow through your hair—or the wings of sadness brush your cheek. Go forward in My strength, and know that whatever your human experience, My Holy Presence walks with you, stands in the Light of Truth with you, guides you, and strengthens you.

I love you. All is well.

—The Drummer

Prayer is like the turning-on of an electric switch.
It does not create the current; it simply provides
a channel through which the electric current
may flow.
                                        —Max Handel

Chapter Twenty-Four
The Anatomy of Prayer

Like many people, you may at least intellectually believe that you are a powerful being. You may intellectually *believe* what Jesus professed when he said, "The work that I do, you shall do and greater." But if you have actually witnessed a healing or manifestation, you were more than likely amazed and baffled—and called it a *miracle.* The truth is, miracles are really natural occurrences which take place when nothing blocks the Wholeness of God from coming through.

Most of us are novices or even skeptics when it comes to believing that we have the power to pull something out of "thin air." The truth is, what you might think of as *thin air* is thick with Spirit. It is God-Energy, God-Life, that from which everything is made—including you! You live and move and have your being in God, and share all the Power in the Universe.

Every moment, either consciously or unconsciously, you are creating "seed-thoughts," or thought-forms. These thought-forms consist of your thoughts that have been fueled with feeling and supported by your beliefs. The Universe responds and gathers Energy around these thought-forms, bringing together the energy components necessary to bring the seed-thoughts into your reality through the matrix of Creation. You do not have to understand the intricacies of the manifestation process, or how a thought-form becomes matter in this extremely sophisticated system of Creation. You only have to accept it, believe it, embody it, and use it.

The ability to co-create with God is a skill. Co-creation operates according to the Laws of God, or the Laws of the Universe. Your job is to come into alignment with these Laws and develop the skill. As previously mentioned, the Soul-Math Formula points out the component parts of your consciousness that must be trained to cooperate with and successfully use the Laws of the Universe: namely, your thoughts, feelings, beliefs and actions.

Some of the Laws of the Universe with which to become familiar include the *Law of Cause and Effect*, the *Law of Attraction*, the *Law of Circulation*, the *Law of Observer-Participancy*, and the *Lawof Gratitude.*

The Law of Cause and Effect says that for every action there is an equivalent reaction. The activity of thought and feeling is causal, and the reciprocal Universe responds to thought energy by producing a result of like kind. This could also be called the Law of Intention. Before you plant a seed in the ground, you use your power of choice to select a seed that matches your intention to produce a certain kind of plant. Just as a seed planted in the ground elicits a response from the soil, a seed-thought, or intention, planted in the soil of Universal Mind elicits a response as well. The result is always of like kind. In other words, if you plant an acorn in the ground, it will always produce an oak tree, not an apple tree. If you plant seed-thoughts that are fearful, you will get fearful results. If you plant powerful positive thoughts fueled with powerful positive feelings, supported by belief grounded in faith, you will produce powerful positive results.

The Law of Attraction is similar but acts like magnetic

energy. You never stop thinking and feeling, so from the time you were born and perhaps long before, you have been creating a belief system out of accumulated thought-forms. This belief system becomes your *consciousness,* or *thought atmosphere,* that represents who you believe you are. This thought atmosphere is magnetic and attracts to you that which matches your consciousness. This law operates like a mirror and is a Law of Reflection. So if you desire peace, you must "be" peace. If you desire prosperity, you must "be" a consciousness of prosperity. It is also true that based on this law you are always exactly where your consciousness places you. So where you are and that which you are experiencing is perfect in the sense that everything is completely suited for your particular purpose, lesson or situation. Following this same line of reasoning, the world is perfect as well. This doesn't mean you can't choose again and create something different and of an even better quality as your consciousness grows and expands.

   The Law of Circulation is also known as the Law of Giving and Receiving. The underlying idea is that you must give yourself to Life in order to receive from Life. Giving means expressing through the use of your talents, the sharing of your good, and your gifts of love and compassion to others. It means investing your vitality and enthusiasm into the business of living. This law is one of the fastest ways to assist you out of sadness or depression. When you begin to pour yourself out into some purpose that gives back to Life, you will reap the reward of joy and fulfillment. When you give that which you have with no sense of hoarding, prosperity will flow into your life as you need it. This law has been described as The Flow. If you want to be in the flow of the Universal Good, you cannot contract and recoil and turn in on yourself. You must expand and participate.

   The Law of Observer-Participancy is a law of quantum physics that also operates as a spiritual law. This law says that something is real only while you observe it. So if you observe goodness in others you cannot notice evil at the same time. When you look upon light, the darkness disappears. This law says that you can change something by the simple act of observing it. Another way of saying it is, you will see what you look for. If you were to look at an ink blob on a piece of white paper, you might see a bird in flight. Someone else might see a butterfly. It depends on who is doing the looking. This is a law of Attention. That upon which you focus your attention will become true and real for you, and it will grow and expand.

The Law of Gratitude is a key that unlocks many stuck doors. The way out of dense, gummy emotions that keep you stuck is gratitude. When you focus your mind and heart upon gratitude, you float right up the emotional ladder toward joy and safety and forgiveness. Gratitude is also the state of mind that dissolves resistance and opens your consciousness to receive. When you live in a constant state of gratitude, you enter into a state of grace where you know that you are *already* blessed with whatever it is that you want or need.

The most important tools with which to apply these universal laws are prayer, meditation and affirmation. It's been said that prayer is talking to God and meditation is listening to God. I might add that affirmation is talking to yourself.

There is more than one kind of prayer. The kind of prayer I'm going to teach you is one in which the individual praying accepts the promise, "The work the Master did, I shall do and greater," and instead of begging God, actually declares intention. I call it *declarative prayer*.

Declarative prayer is a decision or intention of thought, motivated by a corresponding feeling, which takes place in your mind and your heart. It is a technique for coming into unity with God and dipping into the Infinite Field of Possibility that is God Energy. It is letting your mind become the Mind of God. Declarative prayer sets up a causation in the Realm of Spirit, and according to the Law of Cause and Effect the result is produced.

A powerful declarative prayer, or declaration of intent, must be approached with clarity of thought and feeling. It must be a pattern of energy conceived of in a clear and concise way. The clearer the thought and the stronger the congruent feeling, the greater is the possibility of sustaining the thought-form long enough to produce a result. When you pray, you are creating a vision or a blueprint to guide the Energy of Spirit. If your thoughts and feelings are muddy or confused, you will not be able to maintain the vision long enough for it to manifest. Your ability to sustain or maintain the intention of your prayer is vital to the process of its movement through the matrix of Creation. This does not mean that prayer takes "time." Time as we know it does not exist in the Realm of God-Energy. Instantaneous healing or transformation takes place according to your belief that with God all things are possible.

It is an obvious fact that some healings take place as the result of prayer, while some prayers seem to have no effect at all. This doesn't mean that Spirit has not responded to your prayer, it means that you have not come to Spirit with a depth of intention that outweighs your doubt or fear. Sometimes it appears that prayers are not answered, but in time you see that exactly the right thing has occurred for everyone's ultimate good. Never try to second guess Spirit—just stay centered in the prayer. A true prayer, or intention, must continue after the "act" that you call prayer. It must become a state of mind, held in place by your power of will. If you pray with great emotion and conviction but return to your doubts and fears after you finish the prayer, you will neutralize the intention of the prayer.

I have been asked what I think about the power of touch to heal. Touch carries intention just as thought carries intention. Touch transmits Energy, and it's all the same Energy whether it's applied through the technique of Reiki, Pranic healing, cranial sacral work, or prayer. It's all God-Energy. It's my belief that the most powerful approach is to combine the intention of prayer with the power of touch. Based on a previous discussion in this book, we began with the premise that the entire body is the subconscious mind in that the cells of the body store the memories of emotion. Consequently, it makes sense to me that healing touch heals or clears the emotions that are stored in the body, prayer heals the mind, and the two together heal the body. I think it all works together. I have noticed that when the touch is used by itself, it tends to produce temporary results because it doesn't change the consciousness that generated the emotions in the first place. But when coupled with powerful declarative prayer that makes changes in the mind and the belief system, healing can be permanent. The best of all scenarios is to teach the person receiving treatment to become receptive to the healing touch and to also pray in the right way, so that the recipient and healer are in full cooperation with the work being done.

The Seven R's of Declarative Prayer

1. *Receptivity*: This is a time of meditation. The object is to bring yourself into the *soul-zone*—into a state of awakeness and awareness in the present moment. Some metaphysicians call this "centering," or "preparation." The point is, it is a time to open your mind and your heart to infinite possibility. It's a time to clear the mind, calm the emotions, relax the body, and become receptive to the Energy of Wholeness.

2. *Remembering God*: Next, bring your attention to the Allness of God as pure, unbroken Wholeness—pure, unbroken Life Energy. You might recall the Master's commandment, "Love the Lord your God with all your heart, and with all your soul, and with all your mind, and with all your strength." Move yourself into a state of reverence for God and all of God's Creation. Let your mind dwell upon the qualities and attributes of God, and let your heart be filled to overflowing with love for your Creator.

3. *Reunion*: Bring your attention to the relationship between yourself and God. Notice the oneness. Become aware that God's inclusiveness encompasses all that is, and that includes you. Sense that you are, right now, living and moving and being *in* God. Think the thought, "God is happening *as* me." Notice the Love around you, through you and as you. This is God happening. Turn your attention to the Life of God as you breathe It in and as It breathes you. Notice that in the present moment all your needs are met and God's love is protecting you. Let a sense of safety and security flood your awareness. Focus on whatever helps you get a sense of the all-inclusive presence of God, the all-knowing, ever present and all powerful Energy in which you live and which lives through you and as you.

Please Note: The first three steps are vital. In fact, if you really get into the first three steps, you may not have to go any further. Just moving yourself into oneness and unity with God is sometimes all that is necessary to convince yourself that God is healing whatever is ready to be healed. Stay with these three steps until you connect with and *embody* the wholeness, the unity, the oneness. Stay with them until you *know* that God's power, perfection and wholeness are moving through you, using your mind, using your intention, expressing Itself *as* you. Stay with them until you "get" that God's wholeness is everywhere present. If you don't first incorporate this concept into your consciousness, the next step will already be neutralized.

4. *Re-Creation*: If there is a situation that calls for healing, at this point become the Observer, or Onlooker. This is an attitude of mind where you do not judge the situation as good or bad, but rather look upon it with calm, detached interest. View it in peace while in the consciousness of the Presence of God. If the situation is about you, let yourself observe the feelings you have about it. Remember that no matter how negative it seems, God is all there is. Let the negative feelings dissipate in light of this awareness. Let God's Love transmute your negative feelings into feelings of love. Create the situation anew. Re-choose. Build the conviction in your mind and heart that God's Love has moved through you and into that situation and is totally transforming it into wholeness and harmony. Chase away doubt if it tries to creep into your consciousness. Use declarative statements to reinforce your conviction. Stay with this until you feel that healing has taken place. This will be a kind of *knowing*, almost like a switch turned on in your consciousness that says, "It's done."

5. *Receive with Gratitude*: Let yourself settle into that place of accepting the new vision with an attitude of unshakable faith that "it is so." Firmly embody the faith *of* God, not just a faith *in* God. Let your mind be so convinced of its new creation, that anything unlike that vision is impossible and unthinkable. Notice the feeling of gratitude that comes when you accept that something is already accomplished in the Mind of God. Allow yourself to stay for a moment in that feeling of having already received—that feeling of thanksgiving that comes with every gift.

     6. *Release with Faith*: As you prepare yourself to move from the atmosphere and environment of prayer, or the "inner" world, back into the five-sensory world, or "outer" world, refer the prayer and everything you have observed and looked upon to God. Understand this prayer as energy that is instantaneously responded to and acted upon by God Energy. Surrender all that this prayer represents to God.

     7. *Response*: Go forth awake and aware in present-time consciousness, intent upon practicing the Presence of God. Be mindful of the *synchronicities* or *clues* that show up to guide you. Respond to the guidance. Do not question or doubt, just take the high road with respect to your thoughts, feelings, beliefs and actions.

     Here is an example of a declarative prayer for forgiveness:

     (1) *In preparation for this communion with God, I let myself relax into the present moment. As I take a few deep breaths, I allow my body to become soft and relaxed. I now clear my mind, calm my emotions, relax my body, and become receptive to the Energy of God's Wholeness. All systems are slowing down as I remain alert and aware within this state of peace.*

     (2) *As I sit here in peace, I notice the love that I feel inside. That love is expanding as I continue to relax and surrender into that growing feeling of love. I now realize that this love I feel is the Energy of God moving through every part of my being, because God is Love. I also remember that God is pure, unbroken Wholeness—pure, unbroken Life Energy. In keeping with the Master's commandment, I declare that I Love the Lord my God with all my heart, and with all my soul, and with all my mind, and with all my strength.*

I now move into a state of reverence for God and all of God's Creation. I also remember that God is Life, God is the One Power, and God is happening as all that is.

(3) *God is happening as me. With every breath I breathe, God breathes me. I surrender into the oneness and let a sense of trust and safety flood my awareness. I live and move and have my being in God, and God in me. I let the peace and power of God's perfect Energy fill my being with the spiritual confidence that my prayer is being responded to at this very moment.*

(4) *In this state of peace, surrounded and filled with the Love of God, I now step back and calmly look upon the situation that has been weighing heavily upon my heart. I let myself look upon this situation without judgment of good or bad, but instead let myself see the ways in which this person has served me. I lovingly take from this personal teacher the lessons and gifts that our relationship has given me, and in this atmosphere of peace I allow all negative feelings to be consumed by the flame of Divine Love. I step out of self-pity, out of hurt, and into the Light of Truth where there is no   victim, there is no victimizer and there is no damage to any part of my being. I now see myself as free, happy and whole within myself. I see myself interacting with this person in a loving, trusting, compatible way. My wholeness is a reflection of God's Wholeness, and I embrace that Wholeness now. I see myself surrounded by loving people, and my trust is restored as the trust of God moves into my consciousness. I know that this transformation has taken place at all levels of my being, and I rejoice in the freedom I feel.*

(5) *I totally accept this new vision with the faith of God that is my faith. Thank you, God, for this gift of healing.*

(6) *I now refer this new vision to God. I understand that this prayer has already been responded to and acted upon, and I surrender all that this prayer represents to God.*

(7) *I go forth awake and aware in present-time consciousness, intent upon practicing the Presence of God. I*

*am mindful of the synchronicities that show up to guide me,
and I resolve to respond to that guidance. Amen.*
I sincerely encourage you to practice declarative prayer
so that it becomes an automatic approach to prayer for you. As
you practice it, you will be amazed at the "miracles" you are able
to produce in your life and in the lives of others. *Remember that
prayer is not begging, but knowing.* It is not just words, but a
powerful combination of thoughts and feelings. It is not coercive
power, but a gentle power that moves through willingness.

Creating Positive Declarations

Positive declarations, or affirmations, are positive
statements that can be used to keep your mind focused on a
desirable idea. They can be used by your Divine Director, or your
power of will, to hold a declarative prayer in place in your
consciousness. A positive declaration is not a prayer and it is not
a decision. It is a statement that directs your attention toward your
intention and away from any opposite thoughts. Here are the
elements of a powerful positive declaration:

1. It's *Positive.* Choose positive, confident words.
   Leave no room for doubt or compromise.
2. It's *Precise.* Make a clear and specific statement
   of your intention and desire.
3. It's *Present.* Use the present tense without futuristic
   implications. Choose phrases like "I have," or
   "I am," vs. phrases like "I will be" or "I want to be."
4. It's *Potent.* Say it with conviction using words that
   feel powerful to you.
5. It's *Personal.* Make it meaningful to you and close
   to your heart. Get to the core of your old belief
   and change it into a positive opposite.

An example of a positive declaration might be, "I am a
creation of God, and because God is Life, I am Life, and I am filled

with vitality, strength, joy and enthusiasm!" Notice that this statement is positive, precise, present, potent and personal. A positive declaration must be practiced with the following qualities of consciousness:

    6. *Persistence:* Say it so often that your mind starts to repeat it to you automatically.

    7. *Persuasiveness*: Make it so convincing that it's easy to believe.

    8. *Patience:* Continue to repeat your declaration even when nothing seems to be happening.

A declaration, or affirmation, is used to reprogram the subconscious mind to accept a new idea. When a new idea is repeated often enough with persistent enthusiasm, the subconscious mind eventually comes to accept the new idea. It has been recommended that a declaration be repeated several times a day for at least twenty-one days to be effective. I will also add that it loses its effectiveness if you do not believe it with all of your being. Be sure you do not create a declaration that your deeper levels of mind cannot accept. For example, if on one level you believe that you are not worthy of being a successful person, a declaration that says, "I am a totally successful person" may be denied by your subconscious. The declaration then becomes nothing but empty words. If, however, you create a statement that says, "Up until now I have thought of myself as unsuccessful, but every day I see myself as more and more successful," it may be easier for your entire being to cooperate with this new perspective.

    Remember—declarations are important tools, but they must be created in a way that maintains a feeling of motivation that supports your intent. They work best when combined with declarative prayer. Do not depend on declarations alone to do the job. Set your intention right now to create a declarative prayer and supporting declarations as you continue your soul-work.

    There is an alphabetical list of positive declarations in Chapter 31 of this book.

Listen to the Drummer

You have just been given the key to using the unlimited power which I have planted within you as My precious offspring. As you learn to communicate with Me in such a way as to declare your divinity, you will understand that your word has the power of divine intention.

I want you to know that you need not come begging for My attention, or My healing, or My comfort. You need not beseech Me or implore Me to grant your requests. You need not ask My permission or My forgiveness. All you need do, My beloved, is to convince yourself that I am always responding to your every decision. All you need do is realize that I am at the center of your being, that I am closer than hands and feet, that I am always responding to your intention.

Your intention, your decision, is prayer in My eyes. If you do not feel as though I have responded, then examine your intention, My dear one. If there is forgiving to do, do it. If there is loving to do, do it. If there is compassion needed, give it. If there is a need, fill it—always knowing that I move through you as you love, as you give, as you comfort.

My Laws have been implanted in the human dimension and they are always responding to your use of them, My dear one. These blessings are not gifts that some have and some do not, but laws which when consciously used will give you mastery over your experience of the human dimension.

Remember that My Universe is reciprocal and responds like a magnet to your every thought, word and feeling. Do not question the outcome, My child. Do not hover over your declaration of Truth with doubt and foreboding. Trust that My Love is perfecting that which concerns you.

Remember, dear one, that I am pure, unbroken Wholeness—pure, unbroken Life Energy— and I am happening as you. I breathe you, I live through you, I create through you, I love through you. We are One. There is nothing to fear, nothing to dread, nothing from which to hide.

You are a powerful being of My Creation, and you need not isolate yourself from My Presence. Join with Me, My beloved, in a blessed Partnership— a Holy Alliance—and trust that I am protecting you, supporting you, and responding to your every intention.

I love you. All is well.

—The Drummer

What you need for a prosperous life, you already are.
                                        —Wayne Dyer

Chapter Twenty-Five
Healthy Prosperity

Healthy prosperity is a *state of being* experienced by a person with a healthy prosperity consciousness. A person with such a consciousness is one who is at peace with money and manifests enough of it to meet his or her needs, which includes enough to save, invest, share and enjoy. Being prosperous does not mean striving to increase wealth to the point of becoming afraid of maintaining it or losing it. In other words, healthy prosperity is enjoyed by a person who has wholesome and balanced thoughts, feelings and beliefs about money.

Beliefs about money are such strong influences in most people's lives that it would seem remiss not to address a consciousness U-turn with respect to prosperity. If you are like many people, it may seem as though money itself has been talking to you from the day you were born. It may even have taken on a character of its own—like a pesky little being that has infiltrated every area of your life, sitting on your shoulder directing your every move. It's *Money Man! Money Man* is a metaphor for the chattering ego-mind that shouts in fear and plagues the person who is in poverty consciousness and worried about not having enough money, as well as the person who has plenty of money but worries about keeping it. *Money Man* is obsessive and is a figment in the imagination of any fear-programmed consciousness.

Unfortunately, *Money Man* manages to entrench himself so deeply in many people's lives that their soul-esteem becomes buried beneath crusty layers of fear and doubt. Just in case you find *Money Man* lurking in your consciousness, it's time to see him for what he is, meet him head on, and transform him into a supportive friend.

Before you begin trying to tame and subdue *Money Man*, let me ask you two questions. Is it your *intention* to be prosperous? Are you truly *ready* to have prosperity happen in your life? These may sound like silly questions, but your intention to be prosperous must be in alignment with your readiness and willingness to become prosperous. Many people think they want prosperity and as they apply the principles mentioned here, they even begin to experience prosperity miracles. All of a sudden they have nothing to worry about! But they are so used to worrying about not having enough money, or having too much money, that their imagination creates something else to worry about—and it usually involves money. The truth is, they weren't really *ready* to give up the worry addiction about money.

You'd be surprised at how the limiting beliefs of lack and loss may have anchored themselves into your subconscious mind. That pest, *Money Man*, wants to be noticed so badly that he keeps repeating these ideas without mercy. He pounds them into your head with tenacity and injects them into your heart relentlessly. It isn't that *Money Man* is bad, but he will do anything to get attention. When you learn to focus on yourself as a conduit for prosperity, and to fill the void created by not worrying with creative thoughts about good, *Money Man* will abandon the Poverty Ship, jump aboard your Financial Freedom Ocean Liner, and work his little head off.

You must bring yourself to a place of willingness, conscious decision and clear intention. Declare a firm decision to make the changes you must make in order to create healthy prosperity. As you feel the freedom of decision, start looking for new ideas. Be creative. Trust that new ideas are now forming. Take hold of them, bring them to a conscious level of mind, and feel the joy of new horizons. Problems are signals to the mind that something creative and new must happen in the mind. You are the director of your mind and you can change any situation for the better. Remember that prosperity manifests itself in direct proportion to the way you think, feel, believe and behave.

Albert Einstein said, "Imagination is more important than knowledge." Imagination has been given to you so that you can transcend your outer world. Whatever you focus on is what you tend to experience. Universal Energy flows through your thoughts, feelings and beliefs, so the more abundance and prosperity you can imagine and feel, the more the *Law of Attraction* will draw it to you.

Perhaps you happen to be one of those who already has a lot of money, but you're staying up nights worrying about what to invest in, how to avoid taxes, or how to keep from losing too much. If this is your mindset, then focus upon peace regarding money instead of fear. Remember that God is your Source.

With respect to the quantity of money you accumulate, it has everything to do with the state of your consciousness about money. In the chapter that discusses mental parallels, the consciousness (thoughts, feelings and beliefs) is compared to a container. If your consciousness container is the size of a five gallon bucket, it can only receive five gallons of good. Any excess would spill over and be lost. When you create a mental parallel that goes beyond the boundaries of your level of consciousness, you will not be able to integrate all of it into your limited awareness. If you manifest more prosperity in your life than your belief system can handle, something breaks down, someone gets sick, or some other emergency eats up the extra money. It's all a matter of consciousness.

For example, suppose that John has been studying these principles and seems to be getting the hang of manifesting more prosperity in his life. Perhaps John decides to attract at least

$25,000 more into his life during the next few months, and he manages to do just that. If John's consciousness container is only big enough to hold $10,000 more, he will subconsciously create new ways to lose $15,000 of that money.

You know what I'm talking about. Remember the times unexpected money came into your hands? You felt happy, so exhilarated by this good fortune. The next thing you knew, the car broke down, or the washing machine bit the dust, or someone got sick and ran up a big hospital bill, and the cost of the problem amounted to almost exactly the amount that you had received.

You must increase the size of your consciousness container if you want to receive enough money to meet your financial agreements, to invest, to share with others, and to spend for fun. To expand the container, identify your old beliefs and shift your focus to the positive opposite. Then work on embodying that new belief.

Can you identify your beliefs about money that you have had up to the present time? You might want to figure that out so that you can bring these blocks to a conscious level in order to disempower them. Give some time and thought to answering the following questions:

1. How much money can I envision having before it becomes too much money to manage, or too big a burden to handle?
2. How do I believe that money comes to me? Is it only by working hard?
3. What do I consider the source of my prosperity? (Be honest. Don't just say, "God is my Source" if you're worried about money. Dig deeper.)
4. Look at your present situation and ask yourself, "What have I believed in order to be in this situation?" (Take as much time as you need to answer this question, and come back later to add to it as old beliefs surface.)
5. Does resentment stir within you as you sit down to pay your bills?

You don't have to know where these ideas, feelings and beliefs come from, so don't waste your time analyzing what your parents had to do with it, or what events happened to plant these ideas in your head. The important thing is that you recognize your beliefs because then you can change them.

At this point it would be a good idea to use the Soul-Math Formula with respect to your prosperity consciousness. First use the diagnostic worksheet to analyze your thoughts, feelings and beliefs about money, and then create a correction worksheet by transforming all the negative factors into positive opposites. Notice the surprises and the information that you discover, and get busy making new choices and decisions about those factors that require change. Work on bringing all factors into alignment. Once you do, you will have started a spiritual momentum that cannot be denied. On the following pages (pages 240 and 241) are Soul-Math worksheets illustrating first a "scarcity consciousness," and then a "prosperity consciousness."

Exercise for Making the U-Turn

Think of something you would like to create with respect to abundance and prosperity.

Select one thought that *Money Man* keeps whispering into your head about *why* you think you can't have what it is you would like to experience. It might help to imagine this idea written on a blackboard. For example, "I think I can't be a prosperous person because that's what I've been taught to believe." Or "I think money is evil." Or "I'm not worth having a lot of money." Make sure this statement is accurate for you. If you want, you can imagine this negative idea written on a big balloon that you hold in your hand.

Now imagine that this self-defeating idea is fading out until it is dissolved from the blackboard. If you're holding a balloon, let go of it and let it float away out of sight. Take your time with this. Don't let Money Man annoy you, just ignore him.

When you are sure the old idea has disappeared, create a new thought in your imagination about why you CAN have what you desire. See someone handing to you the object of your desire. Or see yourself as part of the new circumstance or situation. Make it as real as you can. Write it or draw it on the clean blackboard in your imagination. Make the image of you already having what you want so real that you can almost touch, smell, see and feel it. In other words, *become* that which you desire. Embody it. Wear it. *Feel* what it's like to be in that experience.

It's important to create an image that evokes the feelings that you want to have. Why? *Because it is the feelings that you are really seeking.* For instance, if you think having more money will give you feelings of success, joy, freedom and ease, realize that it's actually the feelings you long for—not the money. In fact, if you were to manifest the money you think you desire and you don't manifest the feelings, you will continue to be unhappy. Keep constructing your desire in your imagination until you *feel* as though it's really happening.

Now create a positive declaration about this image. For example, "I *am* a prosperous person manifesting more and more money in my life." Then repeat that declaration several times daily for at least 21 days. You may want to create several positive statements of your own that you can also use. Be sure your declarations create the feelings inside you that match the feelings you would like to have as a result of manifesting this desire.

Once you have the vision in mind with declarations to help you keep it in place, get busy creating the feelings that you long for. You can do this in many ways (without money!) and you will speed up the manifestation process.

The Soul-Math Formula
Diagnostic Worksheet

I've created a scarcity consciousness _____ Date _____

Sample Worksheet

Example: Scarcity Consciousness

1. Existing circumstance needing correction

	Thought	x	Feeling	x	Belief	x	Action	=	Situation
	3. Record your typical thoughts as they relate to #1.		**4.** Record your typical emotions and feelings as they relate to #1.		**5.** What do you believe as related to #1? Dig deep!		**6.** Record current patterns of action and behavior.		**2.** How are things now?
	My job is my only source.		I feel locked in.		God isn't enough.		Same old thing, day in - day out.		My prosperity flow is blocked.
	My spouse is my source.		Some days I feel better.		I'm not enough.		I fall asleep in front of the TV every night.		Not having enough money has made me miserable in every area of my life.
	My skill is my source.		I feel limited.		I'm not good enough.		I eat to entertain myself.		
	My talent is my source.		I feel held back.		There's never enough.		I gossip a lot.		
	How could more money come to me than I make at my job?		I feel angy.		God and I are separate.		I love to tell my story.		
	I'm on a fixed income.		I feel poor and helpless.		I'm different from everyone else.		I can't do anything.		
	I never have enough.		I feel restless and bored.		I'm a victim.		I do things to distract myself from my money problems.		
	I don't have enough education.		It's hopeless.		I'm unworthy.		I'm waiting for some-thing to happen.		
	I'm too old/young.		I'm depressed.		I'm needy.		I've cut back spending.		
	If I just had more money!		I feel isolated.		Good doesn't last very long.		I avoid paying bills, depositing my checks.		
	I hate bills!		I'm worried.		Money is the root of all evil.				
	Somebody help me!		I'm afraid.		I can't have more than all the poor people.				
	I hate balancing my checkbook.		I feel uncomfortable about money.		Money means misery.				
			I'm impatient.						
			I have no motivation.						

Sample Worksheet

The Soul-Math Formula
Correction Worksheet

Example: Prosperity Consciousness

1. Existing circumstance needing correction — I've created a scarcity consciousness. **Date** ___

3. Record highest possible thoughts that would be in support of #2. — **Thought** x	4. Record highest possible feelings that would be in support of #2. — **Feeling** x	5. Record highest beliefs in support of # 2? — **Belief** x	6. What patterns of action would be in support of #2? — **Action** =	2. State desired result. — **Result**
God is my only Source. God's abundance is my abundance. Money is energy exchange. God is happening as me. Life is good. I am a spiritual being having a human experience. I am abundance. I am at ease about money. I rejoice in the prosperity of others. I am open and ready to receive. There are limitless ways for money to come to me.	I feel deep gratitude! I love the Lord my God with all my heart, all my soul, all my mind, and all my strength. God's Love fills me. I feel confident. I feel peace. I feel the joy of faith. I am worry free! I feel like giving. I feel light and joyful.	God is Abundance. God is Plenty. God is Enough. I am enough. I am abundance. I am plenty. With God all things are possible. God is my Source. I am worthy to receive. All is well.	Giving and participating in the Law of Circulation. I am loving. I am creating and producing. I am using my talents. I am responding to my Divine Director. I'm using positive declarations. I am acting prosperously. I am creating a plan for the responsible handling of my money.	Prosperity is flowing! I have enough money to meet my needs, to invest, share and enjoy. I am at peace. I am happy.

Another U-Turn Exercise

If your desire is to manifest more prosperity in your life, you must be creative about shifting your attention away from lack and toward abundance. On the next page is a form called *How Prosperity is Flowing in My Life*, that can be used to record the good that is already coming to you. There is more good than you might think in spite of what *Money Man* has been telling you. Make a copy of this page and carry it with you. Every time something comes your way, give it a dollar value and list it on your flow chart. If someone pays for your lunch, record it on your sheet. Suppose someone gives you free tickets to a concert or the theater—write it down. Whether you receive unexpected income, like the repayment of a loan you had forgotten about, or refunds, or even coupon savings, write it all down and add it up monthly. Don't overlook unexpected business that comes your way. Give it a dollar value and record it on your sheet. You'll be surprised how much abundance is already flowing into your life. It may not all be in the form of actual money, but it is, nevertheless, worth a dollar value.

I can't tell you how many people have been helped in shifting their position about money by using *The Ways in Which Prosperity is Flowing in My Life* exercise. It takes attention off the concept of lack and focuses it squarely on prosperity.

Now that you have identified the major blocks to creating a greater flow of prosperity in your life, let's think about what might happen when you successfully increase your flow of good and then it suddenly stops without warning. *Money Man* starts chattering and fighting for his life. I've heard people who are demonstrating wonderful examples of increase say things like, "Oh my goodness, so much good is coming to me, I keep thinking it's a dream and that I'll wake up any minute." Or "I asked for more business to increase my cash flow and now I have so much business that I can't handle it!" I call this kind of thinking *putting on the brakes*. Just the thought, "I can't handle this" is enough to block the flow. This negative declaration will have an effect similar to standing on a

The Ways in Which		
Prosperity Is Flowing in My Life		
Date	Prosperity Received	Value

garden hose and stopping the flow of water. It's important to keep your foot off the hose. When good is flowing, you must accept it with glad expectancy. Don't listen to *Money Man's* fearful chatter. Know that you are guided and assisted in the handling of the new amounts of money and the increased amount of work.

Have you noticed that many people who have become successful in bringing greater amounts of money into their lives are still complaining about never having enough money? If this describes you, you may be manifesting increased prosperity, but you have not yet learned to manage it. For example, you may have used up all of your increased wealth on a bigger and better house, a more expensive car, and grander vacations, and ended up without enough money to meet your financial obligations. You will find yourself in the same position and mindset that you were in before you attracted additional prosperity. You see, amounts do not matter. If your prosperity consciousness is tuned in to "not enough," you will always handle your money in such a way as to achieve "not enough."

So let's talk about handling money. Intelligent use of money is just as important as having more of it. People who have a defective mental pattern about money will continue in a pattern of need or "not enough," until they change the pattern to one of plenty. Most of the time, people who are in constant need are not very wise about handling money. Some debt is understandable but unrealistic debt points out an unsound attitude about money that gets dangerously close to falling out of integrity. Unrealistic debt means there is probably a delusion about money that supports a mistaken notion that some God will bail that person out and pay the bills. What a ridiculous notion. I *am* saying that Universal good is unlimited and that you can bring more money into your life from the One Source of all abundance. But I'm *not* saying that the flow will continue if it is abused. Honesty and integrity are major factors in a correct consciousness of healthy prosperity. Common sense is important. If you spend beyond your means, you are heading for big trouble. Your patterns about money in your consciousness must be honest, wholesome, and responsible.

Pointers for a Debt-Free Consciousness

1. Notice that the way you handle the outer details in your life is an indicator about what patterns exist in your consciousness. Make a commitment to putting your outer world in better order.
2. Keep your positive declarations going. Don't allow debts to keep you from feeling prosperous.
3. Establish a belief that it is easy to pay off your debts, no matter how out of control things seem to be.
4. Stop worrying about debt. Worry is non-productive.
5. Renew the trust you had in yourself about having enough income to handle your debt at the time you borrowed the money.
6. Figure the total amount you owe. Forgive any uncomfortable, unhappy or anxious feelings you have about the debt.
7. Picture your debt being paid off.
8. Don't be concerned about how long it may take because it will happen faster than you think when you commit to bringing the debt under control.
9. Get creative and budget your money. Plan a certain amount of your income each month toward debt reduction. Focus paying off one debt first. Then apply the amount you would have used on that debt to another. When you have paid the second debt off, take the money you would have used on that to double or triple the amount you have been paying on a third. Never use the money you have budgeted for debt reduction on other things.
10. Plan a plan and work the plan with honesty and integrity. As you apply money to a debt or pay a bill, think of it as honoring an agreement. Try writing "thank you" or some other statement of gratitude on the memo line of your checks.

What about people who already have healthy patterns with respect to money? I've watched others look upon them with envy, comparing their own financial state of affairs with the wealthy person. I've had people ask, "How come they have so much money and keep making more? Boy, are they lucky!" No, they're not lucky. They are simply at ease in their patterns of thinking about money. They never consider not having it and rarely worry about losing it. They focus on more instead of less.

You may ask, "What about people who are unscrupulous, have a lot of money, and do dishonest things with money?" To this I would say that unscrupulous people have a lack of reverence for other people and for Life Itself. Irreverence attracts misery. Remember the Law of Cause and Effect. I guarantee that people with an unhealthy approach to handling money will experience the law of retribution in some area of life.

As you expand your consciousness container with respect to prosperity, you will find more and more money showing up in your life. Discipline yourself to apply that money to your debt. When the time comes that you have extra money, even if you are still in debt, begin to create a surplus. This may start out as a savings account. Keep adding more to your savings each month. This gradually puts you in a position of financial flexibility, which leads to greater peace of mind about money.

Create a tithing program which includes tithing ten percent of your gross income to your source of spiritual nourishment, and ten percent to your savings to build a reserve. Tithing is a spiritual discipline and a method of lifting you out of a contracting, withholding, hoarding mentality.

Other Ideas for Increasing Prosperity Consciousness

1. Think of money as God in action, and accept it as a fact of life that no longer demands most of your attention. Because money is God in action, you can begin loving it.
2. Think of money as God's idea of circulation and a form of energy exchange. Begin to circulate money and give it with joy. Do not hoard it, box it in, or otherwise limit its freedom of movement.
3. Keep working to further convince yourself that you are worth more and more money.
4. Apply your thought creatively and don't waste your thinking on worry. Remember that the Universe responds in like kind, so worry will just produce more worry.
5. Accept your prosperity! Appreciate money and use it wisely. Rejoice in other people's prosperity.
6. Don't block your own prosperity by associating it only with bank accounts, investments, or career income.
7. Think of money as a flowing thing. Remember your *Ways in Which Prosperity Is Flowing* sheet.
8. Never allow yourself to become fearful about money again.

Earlier in this book I talked about the Law of Circulation. Just as circulation is a necessary process in the body, circulation is an important factor in the field of economics. Let yourself participate in the Law of Circulation and your consciousness container will expand and expand, because the Universe is flowing—always moving, always changing, always responding. Let your prosperity flow, let your life flow, let your thoughts flow in a positive direction. Work on getting the idea that there is plenty and more to spare—and never, never, never talk about lack or limitation.

Prosperity Declaration

As I relax and let go of fear and worry about money,
I accept the idea that there is always plenty.
I luxuriate in the idea of plenty.
I know that the Universe is
an Infinite Sea of Abundance,
and I soak it up and saturate myself with it
as it flows into my mind,
into my heart,
and into my world of affairs.
There is plenty of opportunity,
plenty of energy, plenty of money, plenty of faith,
plenty of trust, plenty of creative energy.
There is enough money in my life
to meet all of my agreements
and there is enough to share, invest, and enjoy.
I am so grateful. And so it is.

Listen to the Drummer

The lesson of My unfailing abundance is yet another that may seem challenging, My dear one. Quiet your mind for just these few moments and let yourself feel the opulence of My Presence all around you. Calm your body and mind and give yourself permission to throw off that which may seem less than the joy that is the hallmark of My abundant kingdom.

Is it so difficult to trust that My abundant universe supports you and meets your every need? You have heard it said that before you ask, I have answered. That is indeed the case, My beloved. The question is, what is it that you have planted in the soil of Universal Mind? If it is doubt, Divine Love will respond with doubt because it is doubt that is heard as your request. If it is lack and limitation, Love will respond with like kind because lack and limitation are the seeds to which I respond.

Learn this lesson well, My child. Understand that as you sow, so do you reap in your world of experience. If you would reap abundance, plant seeds of a consciousness that accepts My abundance without question. I know not of that which you term money, My dear one. I know only that I support you and fulfill your every intention.

If you desire that My energy be translated into the energy of money for your use in the human dimension, then let your intention be one of fearless reliance upon My ability to respond to your every desire. I do not simply speak of a consciousness that is desirous of greater prosperity, but also of the consciousness that has tasted wealthy abundance in terms of money.

Understand, My beloved, from My perspective it matters not at which end of the prosperity spectrum you find yourself, for in terms of Universal Energy it is all the same. If you find yourself in fear because you haven't enough, you are polarized at one end. If you find yourself with so much that you are in fear about handling it and keeping it, you are polarized at the other end. Find the balance point, My dear one. Find the point at which you can live your human experience in a way that is easy, joyful, lighthearted and happy. Find the path which gives you peace. When you do you will glorify My Presence as your experience of joy.

There is nothing to fear, My child. There is nothing to doubt, nothing to dread. Surrender to Me so that I may see through your eyes, think through your mind, and speak through your words. You are a blessed being of Light, My dear one. Live in abundance and joy.

I love you. All is well.

—The Drummer

*Every relationship that touches the soul leads us
into a dialogue with eternity, so that, even though
we may think our strong emotions focus on the
people around us, we are being set face to face
with divinity itself, however we understand or
speak that mystery.*
                                    —Thomas Moore

Chapter Twenty-Six
Falling in Love

Everyone has an instinctive desire to feel cared about,
loved, respected, valued and appreciated. At the same time, there
is a desire to love, respect, value and appreciate others. This
inner urge to give and receive love acts as a kind of magnetic
energy that attracts us to each other and compels us to want to *be*
something to someone. It's an internal tug that moves us toward
each other, because at the soul level we know that we share a
Oneness; we know that within another person we find our own
Self; within another person we see the Self that we all share— the
Self that is the Divine core of each person. In other words, it's
natural to desire connection. It's natural to be attracted to other
people and to enjoy being something to someone. It's natural to
recognize something deeply familiar about every other person.

Unfortunately, if the personality, or ego-self, regards itself as separate from the Oneness that connects all life, there is a feeling of disconnection and alienation from other people. The ego then tends to look upon the world as a threat and feels either very insecure or takes on a false sense of power. Either way, the ego approaches other people with suspicion, competition and insecurity, rather than trust and unconditional love. The same mistrust that the ego has of other people, it also feels toward God. E.G.O. is an acronym for "edging God out." In spite of this sense of separation, there is still a deep desire for connection that lives within the soul. That deep desire, however, may be distorted into a superficial attempt to love other people with a love that is built upon the shaky sands of human insecurity instead of upon the rock of solid soul-esteem.

It was Joshua Ben Joseph who prioritized the Ten Commandments and pointed out the two that superseded all the others. "The first is, the Lord our God, the Lord is one: and thou shalt love the Lord thy God from all thy heart, and from all thy soul, and from all thy mind, and from all thy strength. The second is this, thou shalt love thy neighbor as thyself. There is none other commandment greater than these." (Mark 12:28-33)

If you're like most human beings, you feel your love for God only sometimes, if at all. You might *think* that you love God, because to think otherwise might seem terrible to you and cause you to feel guilty. Or you might deny that loving God is important at all. You may even deny the existence of God. The truth is, you probably spend much less time thinking about your love for God than wondering about God's love for *you* as it relates to answering your prayers, healing your illnesses, supplying your prosperity, finding a new job, protecting, guiding, and otherwise blessing you. Your ego may be so busy trying to fix and control everything that you haven't enough of your heart, soul, mind or strength left with which to love God.

You may feel more love for God when you think your prayers have been answered, because you feel gratitude, and gratitude stirs feelings of love.

To decide to love God and to do so with all your heart, soul, mind and strength is the biggest U-turn you can make in consciousness. If you don't like the word "God," then call it Supreme Intelligence, Spirit, Love, or Harvey. The label doesn't matter. To love "That" with everything in you is to become one with "It." When you become one with It, you become a power-presence. You operate out of soul-esteem. You love with spiritual confidence.

More than likely you have personally experienced the human feeling of "falling in love." What happened to you when you fell in love with another human being? You probably laughed a lot, acted kind of giddy and daydreamed about what was going to happen next. You might have felt tingly all over as though you were sitting on top of the world. You may have found yourself thinking about that special someone almost to the point of obsession and staring off into space with a big smile. If you can remember how you felt when that feeling of having fallen in love was at its peak, you probably felt totally safe and invincible. You felt special, important and cared for and you were willing to do almost anything for that individual. Falling in love meant that you could feel that person's energy even when you were physically apart. It inspired within you a desire to express your love to that other person, and you noticed when he or she did something loving for you that deserved your praise and gratitude. This is what falling in love feels like.

After the initial stages of falling in love, the associated sensations and feelings begin to mellow and one of two things happens. If your ego is in control, you begin to vie for control in the relationship. The insecurities begin to surface, and the power struggle begins. However, if your love comes from a deeper place of unbroken wholeness, your love expresses itself as respect, support, teaching and learning. A loving relationship that allows God's Love to flow grows beyond the falling in love stage and takes on the look of a "team" or a spiritual partnership. What happens in such a relationship is actually the experience of your God-Self falling in love with the God-Self of another. It is the experience of God's Love moving through you and being released through you.

Little did the lyricist who wrote, "Love makes the world go 'round," realize that he was really describing spiritual energy. Jesus understood that energy. That is why he condensed the ten commandments into two which tell us to actively express our love for God and for each other in order to experience true freedom.

You may sometimes feel a deep love for God that doesn't seem to manifest in your world of affairs. If this happens, it indicates that you do not truly love the Lord your God with all your heart, soul, mind and strength. Some buried belief is stronger than your love for God. As a result, your love for yourself will also be conditional since you are an expression of God. When you put conditions on your love for God and for yourself, you block the flow of pure Unconditional Love from pouring into your consciousness and into your world.

The Master was right on target when He suggested that you love God first, because only then can you authentically love yourself. When you love your own soul, you can love other people. If you do not love God first, it is impossible to truly love your own soul. Your ego simply loves itself in a narcissistic way, and connection with others is like shifting sands in a strong wind. Your desire for love then takes on the feeling of "need."

It is natural to want to connect with others and natural to want a life partner. It is not natural to "need" someone else. When you operate out of soul-esteem, you come from a place of wholeness, not neediness, and every relationship is seen through the eyes of acceptance instead of suspicion; through the eyes of love and wholeness instead of need; and *not* through the filters of society, religion or other judgmental perspectives.

My first marriage was an example of connecting out of need. It looked like a mistake at the time and ended in a divorce proceeding that took about 30 minutes. There were no children to complicate things and not much money or property to divvy up. The only thing my husband wanted was the electric blender. As I walked from the courthouse to my car on the day of the divorce, I remember waiting on a street corner for a walk light. It dawned on me what had just happened. I was free. What a feeling! I wanted to jump up and click my heels. But I couldn't do that on the street corner. What would people think?

By the time I reached the parking garage, I noticed that my enthusiasm was fading. On the drive home (to Mom and Dad's house), reality set in. I was alone, and I felt lonely. The only thing I was sure of was my own insecurity. I had allowed the last three years to rob me of my identity. Who was I? What was next?

During the years that followed, I launched a successful interior design business, sold my oil paintings, and did a little teaching. Nevertheless, no matter how hard I tried, I didn't feel complete. There was always some part of me searching for the perfect partner that would make me feel whole. Part of me would *scope out* every man who crossed my path, wondering if he could be Mr. Right. During that time I did very little to rebuild my sense of self-worth. I just kept waiting for the right man to show up to do that for me. But no one showed up. My fears kept me isolated and caused me to believe I was untouchable and unapproachable.

After nine years of single life, I finally reached my wit's end. I concluded that I would never find my soul-mate and truly fall in love. I thought something was wrong with me, and that I didn't "appeal" to men. I hit an emotional wall and was ready to give up. But once I stopped trying so hard, an amazing thing happened. One dateless Saturday night, alone in my apartment, a transforming event occurred. I turned the lights out, lit some candles, put on a Chopin CD, and sat back to relax and do some serious thinking. I calmed my body and my mind and fell into a meditative state. Then it hit me. It wasn't necessarily a man I was longing for. What I *really* longed for were the *feelings* that I thought only a man could give me: feelings such as strength, self-respect, power, decisiveness, courage and confidence—feelings that I had always equated with masculinity.

The tears began to roll down my cheeks involuntarily. Not emotional tears but tears of breakthrough and healing. They were the type of tears that I would later learn to identify as my own unique "healing signal." It became clearer and clearer that I did not need a man in order to experience the qualities for which I was longing. It dawned on me that wholeness and completeness are inside jobs.

That night for the first time, I could look back on my marriage and see its value. I could see that it was a perfect mirror for where I was at the time. I had attracted another person who had the same insecurities and feelings of inadequacy that I had. He turned out to be one of my best teachers because he mirrored back to me what it was that I was ready to discover about myself.

I began talking to my Higher Self that night, out loud. The thought kept occurring to me, "If anyone were to walk in and see me doing this, they'd think I was losing it." Actually, I was finding *It*. My dialogue with God went something like this: "Dear God, I long to feel whole. Wholeness *must* be mine by divine birthright. Right here, right now, I claim my strength, my power, my ability to choose, and my self-worth!" Tears of healing came again, and I went on, "It's okay, God, if these attributes don't show up in the form of a person. I just want to feel wholeness within myself—with or without a man!" I cried and cried. I must have released years of pain and hurt in those tears. I surrendered, I let go, I released the past, and then I went limp. At that moment I felt it—that mystical marriage within myself; the coming together of my masculine and feminine natures; the unity with my God-Self; a completeness that had been missing. Suddenly nothing was missing. For the first time in my life, I experienced my own wholeness.

From that night on, it no longer occurred to me to search for a relationship. Instead, I began rediscovering myself. This was one of the first times that I recognized at a conscious level that I was taking care of my soul—and my soul was taking care of me. The men I encountered were no longer relationship prospects, just other people. I was able to look beyond the surface and meet God in everyone. I was on a spiritual high which lasted for several weeks.

After that, I settled down to a more practical awareness, but I still felt complete and whole all by myself. I understood from that night on that what I wanted to *have*, I must *be*. Every day I felt more strength, more confidence, more aliveness. My soul-esteem was on the rise. I found a church that felt right, enrolled in classes, attended workshops and seminars. I read constructive books. I meditated, exercised, and did things that made me laugh and have fun. I was rediscovering and learning to love my soul.

I did meet Mr. Right about one month after I stopped pursuing him. When Tom and I met, I knew that he wasn't my wholeness, but it was fun to watch my inner wholeness express itself with a wonderful partner. I didn't *need* him, but I did resonate with him. He encouraged me to follow my own dreams, and I was an enthusiastic player in his. We were married and enjoyed fourteen wonderful years together until one night Tom died as the result of a massive heart attack. I was alone again. But I didn't feel lonely. In fact, I felt my wholeness more than ever.

If you can identify with my experience, I encourage you to seek your own wholeness. Don't look for it outside yourself because you will never find it "out there." If you think you can find it outside, there will come a time when you will be faced with doing what I did—learning to love yourself enough to call forth your innate strength, courage, confidence, and self-respect—in order to develop soul-esteem. When you feel wholeness at the soul level, you begin to recognize those people who harmonize with you, respect you, accept you for who you are, and love you unconditionally. There is always someone there to assist you and mirror your sense of wholeness back to you. You will never be lonely again.

Two years after Tom's death, I opened my mind and my heart to the possibility of a new relationship—not out of need, but out of a desire to share my life with someone. A few months later, Roger came into my life. Yes, we fell in love and got married, but beyond that stage called "falling in love," we recognized a partnership with each other that continues to make our marriage sing with life. Roger is my cheerleader and has given me the support which helped me begin my ministry; together we founded The Soul-Esteem Center for Practical Spirituality. In addition, without his encouragement, I'm not sure when this book would have been completed.

What is it that happens when people connect at the soul-level? Love happens. Love is the healing consciousness in which wholeness takes place—in which miracles happen. Love is a transformative power. Love is the "glue" that holds things together. Love is the desire of God to express Itself through Its creation. It is a cosmic force that cannot be denied.

When you feel shut down or numb and seem incapable of feeling love, focus on something beautiful. An appreciation of beauty can bring you to the point of awe and enable you to touch the hem of bliss. This is love. Love is the most powerful way to create a flow between your soul and your body, or between your soul and another soul. Love seems to open all the channels and clear the pathways so that you can be aware of your oneness with all that is. When you are in a state of blissful love—not romantic love or sympathy—but a consciousness of unlimited good, unlimited grace, and unlimited life, you are in a healing consciousness, a transformative state of being. Where there is a consciousness of Love, there can be no fear, no doubt—only Love.

Remember that you can give away only that which you feel inside. If you harbor hate, hate is what you give away. If you harbor disrespect, disrespect is what you give away. If you harbor love and compassion, love and compassion are what you give to others. If you respond to hate with hate, or anger with anger, it is not because of what was directed your way, it is because that is what is inside you. The external circumstance serves only as a trigger. You can't get apple juice from a lemon no matter how hard you try. You can't give love away if what you have inside is hate—no matter how hard you try.

Until you begin to feel yourself generating love from within, the words "God," or "Love," will be empty words. But when you become so filled with Love that you begin to live in the world without reacting in any way that suggests that God is absent, you will experience falling in love with God. All of the love that you have for God will be a direct reflection of your love for your own soul.

What does falling in love with God feel like? It feels like true inner peace and total acceptance of self. It feels like awe, inspired by something beautiful; like belonging; like goose bumps on your flesh as you listen to extraordinary music; like a spacious joy and sense of ease; like true safety, security and protection. Being in love with God feels like being alive. It is God's poetry coming to you in seven languages; that of sight, sound, smell, touch, taste, intuition and synchronicity. Being in love with God feels like gratitude, unlimited surprise, the impulse to create and the irresistible desire to celebrate. It feels like laughter. It feels like the word, "Yes!"

One of the easiest ways to fall in love with God is to simply let God in. Most people try too hard, always grasping and trying to control things. Grasping will shut out that gentle feeling of being in love with God. When you open to God, grace occurs, and you experience a power in relaxing as you feel nature, drink in sunsets, smell the flowers, love the animals, the trees, wind, ocean, rivers and each other. All of this renews your love for God.

Einstein said, "You might as well not be alive if you are not in awe of God." *Let God in.* Let yourself discover the Divine in every other person, in all of nature, and within yourself. When that happens, you come to realize that you have fallen in love with God. You have a true sense of belonging to God's Universe—a feeling that you "fit" with all of Life. You honor every relationship as a temple of learning and rediscovery, and your level of spiritual confidence rises. Your outer confidence is also strengthened, your self-esteem takes hold and isolation melts away. You begin to merge and blend and dance with Life, and you realize that you *are* something to someone. You are the beloved of your Higher Self and you have fallen in Love with God.

Pierre Teilhard De Chardin wrote, "Someday, after we have mastered the winds, the waves, the tide and gravity, we shall harness for God the energies of love. Then, for the second time in the history of the world, man will have discovered fire." When love is understood by each of us, it will have a monumental impact on humanity.

Love is the energy that unites everything. It is the connective tissue of the Universe—of the body of God—like the connective tissue in our bodies which holds our bones in place.

If you were to injure the connective tissue in some part of your body, it would have a domino effect on other parts of your body. For example, if you were to damage the cartilage in your knee and continued to walk around on it, you would feel the effects in your lower back, and eventually the other leg and knee would be affected from trying to compensate for the injured knee. In this same way, when a single human being is injured by an unloving act, the soul of each of us feels the effect. When someone acts with ill-intention or mean-spiritedness, it interferes with the consciousness development that could lead humankind to "discover fire for the second time in the history of the world."

To love and be loved is your God-given heritage, a divine spark existing within everyone. The crucial challenge is to find that spark and fan it into a brightly burning flame. You may spend years falling in and out of love before you realize that there even *is* another dimension to love that you haven't as yet understood. As you focus more and more on Love, you will realize that every unfinished relationship that you have ever had must be healed. A healed relationship doesn't mean fixing it, or making it like it was in the beginning with all the bells and whistles, or that the person who left will return, or that you must return to a relationship with which you are finished. Healing a relationship can be accomplished without ever speaking to that person again or seeing that person in form again. Healing can be accomplished even if the other person has crossed over and no longer has a physical form. How? Because healing happens in your own consciousness.

Healing doesn't mean making or forcing something to look the way your ego wants it to look in physical terms. Healing is an energetic matter. A spiritual matter. When you heal a relationship spiritually, invisibly, energetically, you are free to set up a new mental parallel that will express in form and take the place of the hurt and the pain of the past.

As you expand the spiritual dimension in your life and in your loving, you begin to live your everyday life in a greater awareness of the NOW. You more easily let go of the mistakes, the fantasies of yesterday, *and* the fears about the future.

What are relationships for? Relationships offer you the opportunity to connect with others and to experience and love others as you love yourself. Relationships give God the opportunity to interact with Itself. Relationships are holy temples of learning and discovery.

A Course in Miracles says, "When you meet anyone, remember it is a holy encounter. As you see him or her, you will see yourself. As you treat him or her, you will treat yourself. As you think of him or her, you will think of yourself. Never forget this, for in the other person you will find yourself or lose yourself." Relationships exist to speed up the journey back to God. When a relationship is healed, the ego-self stops fighting to win, stops seeking justice, stops trying to manipulate everything to turn out the way it wants it to.

When separation is healed, when there is wholeness instead of fragmented parts of yourself, there can be no more hurt and no more pain. There is only Love. This is spiritual maturity. This is spiritual confidence. This is soul-esteem.

Love

I've been asked what love is.
I've asked myself what love is.
I've asked others what love is.
It seems that nobody knows.
But I know when I feel it,
I know when I have it,
I know when I give it
and I know when I live it.
That's the only answer I need.

Listen to the Drummer

I greet you, My beloved, with Love that is unfailing and limitless. I wrap you in the calmness of the moment.

You are never alone, dear one, never isolated, never separated from My oneness. Honor our connection and let your connection with others of My Creation be easy—for in every other person you shall find yourself—and you shall find Me. You need but look to see Me shining through the eyes of another.

Acknowledge the longing that surges through your soul to embrace the world in which you live. Recognize the deep desire for connection that lives within your soul—a desire to radiate love and loving kindness outward to all life everywhere. Let Love's healing energy burst forth from your heart center, touching everyone everywhere. Let it touch a loved one; a close friend; anyone with whom you have felt emotional separation. Let it dissolve all conflict and judgment.

When it seems as though you cannot resonate to the beat of the Drummer that is pulsating a graceful rhythm from the center of your being, focus your attention upon that within My creation which is beautiful. Notice the beauty of your world, My child. Let yourself be awed by it that you might thrill to the wonder of it all. Let yourself be moved by that beauty into love, that you may become open to the unlimited goodness that emanates from the One Source. Be aware that you can only give away that which you already have inside you, My dear one. So let there be Love. Let there be peace.

Remember, My beloved, that Love is the healing atmosphere in which wholeness takes place— in which miracles happen. My Love is the common denominator of all existence. It is that which binds it all together. My Love is My desire to express Myself through all of My creation.

Go forward in My strength knowing that the Love that flows through you is My Love. Wherever you are, know that it is My Holy Presence that walks with you, stands in the Light of Truth with you, guides you, and strengthens you.

I love you. All is well.

—The Drummer

Happiness is a Swedish sunset - it is there for all,
but most of us look the other way and lose it.
                                        —Mark Twain

Chapter Twenty-Seven
Soulercises
. . . to Keep You in Spiritual Shape

You've already been given many tried and true suggestions
in previous pages of this book about how to make the necessary
consciousness U-turns in order to move toward your ideal vision
for your life. This chapter includes some activities that may seem
simple but can be crucial in helping you complete and maintain the
consciousness U-turns. I have called these "soulercises," because
they are mental, emotional and even physical exercises that can
help shape your soul-esteem.

The first soulercise is to notice and put into practice the
"cosmic glimmers" that may come to you periodically. These are
spurts of enlightenment that dawn upon your awareness almost as
if you have plugged into some cosmic circuit and felt the shock of

contact. They can feel like flashes of knowing, or bursts of awareness, that I often describe as "ah-ha's." They have been symbolized in cartoons as light bulbs going off in the mind. They are divine sparks that enable you to penetrate the shroud of mystery and tap into the realm of pure spiritual Truth. Cosmic glimmers occur during discussions, during reflection or meditation, while spending time in nature, or they might be triggered by anything you see or hear. They can happen anytime, anywhere, and tend to increase in frequency as you do more and more soul-work.

Due to the rather elusive nature of cosmic glimmers, it's important to verbalize them and write them down immediately in order to anchor them into your consciousness. They act much like the dream that you know you had the night before, which slips away from your memory. More than likely, the glimmer will recur at some future time, but why wait when you can grab on to it and pull it into your awareness immediately? Talking or writing about these glimmers reinforces them so that you can put them to use and integrate them into your understanding more effectively.

The second soulercise is to put into practice that which you already understand. Avoid getting caught in the trap of concern about whether or not you thoroughly comprehend some spiritual idea or concept. Never allow yourself to feel inadequate or inferior because you don't "get" something—especially when the people around you seem to understand. Don't worry about what you do not grasp. Just get busy using the awareness you already have.

You've heard the expressions, "You snooze, you lose," or "What you don't use, you lose." These statements apply not only to the mind and body, but to the soul as well. Soul-work is about training, strengthening and developing your spiritual muscles into a state of spiritual fitness. It's crucial to use what you already grasp if you want to keep moving forward and not get stymied or paralyzed. Realize that what you need will dawn upon your awareness when you're ready. Don't worry about not being ready and don't move too fast. Above all, do not compare your progress to someone else's progress. No two paths are exactly alike. What is important for you is what you are actually using and implementing in your life. Concepts that you do not understand will show up as cosmic glimmers at the right time and in the right way.

One of the most important soulercises that you can do is one that promotes balance as it moves you out of stress and anxiety. It could be a "time out," or a vacation, perhaps meditation or contemplation—any activity that takes you into the soul-zone where you become awake and aware in the new now moment; a time when you can mentally, physically and spiritually loosen up and lighten up so that you are free to re-create.

One way to maintain balance is to look at life as a game. So many of the little things that happen from day to day can almost drive you berserk unless you take them lightly and make a game out of them in order to stay balanced and centered.

Here's an example: Have you ever asked yourself, "What happened to all the missing socks?" You know—the ones you need to make matching pairs as you fold the laundry. This dilemma could drive you insane as you swear up and down that matching pairs of socks went into the washing machine. I have nearly driven myself mad searching for missing socks. But I decided to make it a game, the object of the game being to end up with all matching pairs after each load of laundry. I even kept score for a time. I have a designated drawer for single socks just in case the mystery is solved and all the missing socks show up. Some of them do—between the cushions on the sofa, in a corner behind a chair, or as a victim of static cling in the leg of a pair of pants. But most of the time they just vanish into thin air. Every few months I count the unmatched socks, make a mental note of the score, and dump the contents of the sock drawer into the trash can.

Perhaps it's silly to spend valuable time trying to solve the missing sock mystery or keeping score or even making it a game. But sometimes it's this sort of creativity that helps me maintain my sense of humor and balance in the soul-zone.

Another soulercise that you may have sorely neglected is laughter. There is nothing like a good hee-haw to jolt you right into the soul-zone. There is no way you can laugh without being in the present moment. You cannot laugh and feel stress or anger at the same time. When you laugh, tension melts away. When you can laugh at something that happened to you, you are no longer controlled by it. When you find that you cannot laugh about something, you are bound to that thing so that it is in control instead of you.

One day I was speaking to my insurance representative on the telephone. He told me a great story about how his son taught him to keep his balance and perspective on life. One day while they were out running together, he noticed that his twelve-year-old son was smiling and chuckling to himself. When asked what he was laughing about, his son said, "Oh, I was just thinking about my *funny-thought*."

Dad replied, "What do you mean?"

"Well," said the son, "Every day I choose something that's happened as my *funny-thought* for the day. Then I think about my *funny-thought* as often as I can all day long and every time I do, I get to laugh—because it's so funny!"

Dad and son now share their *funny-thought* for the day every morning and enjoy both of them all day long. Dad said, "One day I laughed every time I thought about the guy I saw whose windshield wipers went out as it started to rain. He didn't let that stop him though. He just rolled the window down, stuck his head out, squinted against the raindrops, and kept going! Now that was a *funny-thought* that helped me keep my balance all day long."

Not long after learning about the daily *funny-thought*, I was having a much too serious day. So I decided to remember a funny situation that could become my *funny-thought for* the day. I recalled the time my two-year-old grandson opened the door while I was using the bathroom. He gave me an excited look, closed the door and disappeared. I could hear his little bare feet flapping on the kitchen floor as he ran off, turned around and came back. He opened the bathroom door and handed me a diaper! The memory of that precious moment made me laugh, and suddenly I wasn't so serious.

"Hey, this really works!" I thought. And that memory became my *funny-thought* for the day. What a great way to strike a balance, stay in tune with the lighter side of life, and guide yourself back into the soul-zone.

Recalling funny thoughts made me think about that one large genre of humor called *embarrassing moments*. Embarrassing moments are a fantastically rich source of funny thoughts which give us a world of opportunity to laugh at ourselves. Did you ever feel the rush of utter horror course through your body when you looked in a mirror and discovered part of your lunch stuck between your front teeth? How long had it been there?! Was it there when you were laughing in front of your boss—or your date?!

If you're a woman, have you ever come home after a day full of important meetings and found a glob of fuzzy lint smashed between your leg and your panty hose on the outside of your calf? And what about the toilet paper caught on the heel of your sexy satin dress shoe at the company banquet?

There's one consolation about embarrassing moments— we all have them! And, we have them for other people. Have you ever felt embarrassment for your friend who had lipstick smeared on her front teeth—and you didn't have the courage to tell her? Or maybe you couldn't bring yourself to tell your boss that his breath could kill flowers.

Once when I was working as a not-so-confident secretary, I was sitting at my desk and as I swiveled in my chair to get up, I looked down at my feet. Oh no! I was wearing one navy shoe and one black shoe! Same style—different colors. I swiveled back again with lightning speed and did everything I could to stay there all day with my legs under the desk. When my duties forced me to walk someplace, I tried to shrink into a little ball. What a miserable day.

Another time, just out of high school, I had a job with a big company. One day I rested my elbows on my desk with my chin in my hands and fell asleep. When I opened my eyes, I was looking at my supervisor's belt buckle about six-inches from my nose. My eyes rolled upward to find her glaring down at me. I was never so humiliated.

My mother told me about the time she was walking down

a busy city street wearing a wrap-around skirt. She grabbed the tie at the waistband to tighten it, and one side came off in her hand. The skirt fell around her ankles, she proceeded to trip over it, and she wasn't wearing a slip. Talk about wanting to disappear!

One evening I was standing in front of a class teaching with my fly open. A class member (a guy) said, "Uh, Phylis, you're front's open." I looked down and zipped up in front of forty people, and then I had to laugh. What at one time would have been an excruciatingly embarrassing moment was now an opportunity to laugh at myself and enjoy a good laugh with others.

One of the biggest turning points in my life came as the result of an embarrassing experience. I was taking a Dale Carnegie course and during one session we were expected to prepare a one-minute talk about an incident that got us excited—even angry. We were given "butterfly killers" (rolled-up newspapers) to beat on a sturdy table for emphasis as we gave our talk. The butterfly killer was meant to help us break out of our shells. I was a miserable failure. This was so difficult for me that I made myself sick. After my turn, I made it back to my seat, only to walk out before the class was over.

On the drive home, I cried and felt the feelings of mortification and embarrassment over and over again. What did they think of me?! What a quitter! I was never going back. That week the instructor called and said, "Phylis, I noticed you left class early." I replied, "Oh, Mike, I am so embarrassed. I feel awful!" He said to me, "Oh, I wouldn't feel that way if I were you, I don't think anyone noticed you were gone." WHAT? EVERYONE WASN'T WATCHING ME?! It was then that I realized that everyone in the class was primarily thinking about themselves, not about me. In fact, people in general are almost always thinking about themselves—hardly noticing what I'm doing. What a relief! My whole attitude changed from that moment on, and my self-confidence took a quantum leap. I did go back to the next class, completed the course, and ended up becoming an instructor myself—for seven years!

Many of us outgrow the discomfort of embarrassment. I

know that I have experienced less and less of it as my self-esteem has increased. Now I even enjoy those embarrassing moments. They relieve the tension and lighten everybody up—often at a time when we need laughter the most. And it's been proven how healing laughter can be.

Why in the world did God make embarrassing moments? God didn't make them. Embarrassing moments just happen sometimes. But they seem to happen more frequently to someone who is afraid of them. You'll know when you've passed the course on embarrassing moments when your self-esteem is high enough to help you laugh off an embarrassing incident and enjoy it instead of hate it. As your self-esteem increases, your soul-esteem is given more freedom to come forward. The more your soul-esteem deepens, the more your self-esteem becomes authentic and genuine. The two work together because you are both human and divine. The more they integrate, the more you express your innate wholeness.

Everyone has challenges, including moments during which one can choose to be embarrassed or choose to enjoy the situation. You will always have challenges and you will always have choices. Very little is beyond laughter and joy.

Paul Pearsall, author of *Super Joy*, describes super joy as "psychological hardiness that seems to guide some people through life; . . . regular and enduring celebration of the delight of daily living, the savoring of the moments of life; . . . a joy that feeds rather than takes from the human spirit; . . . persistent, unalterable strength; . . . natural human capacity for intense, volitional human elation; . . . the ultimate human experience, the transcendence of normalcy to a high-level well-being."

Remember that laughter is your proof that you have turned a problem over to your Higher Power. You know that a situation is being healed when you can laugh about it. If you can't laugh about it, you know you are still stuck in the problem. Being stuck in the problem keeps you from seeing the blessing hidden in the challenge.

Embarrassing moments as well as serious challenges have within them abundant blessings and opportunities for learning.

Laughter and rejuvenating time-outs are vital to your spiritual progress and to your human experience. When you get out of balance, the Universe has a way of forcing you to take time out. I know because when I tried to be my version of that silly "super woman" that so many of us try to be, instead of stopping to notice the beauty and love around me, I landed in Missouri Baptist Hospital for a six-day stay with pneumonia. A trip to Hawaii would have been cheaper and the scenery much better.

It's an old story. We become so busy, so intense, so involved in the outer world and daily activities that we become depleted. That's when it's time to "smell the roses." This means taking time out to appreciate the beauty of life by seeing it with new eyes. Take a moment to look deeply into the reflections in a pool of water rather than just passing it by. Go outside on a clear night and gaze at the stars in wonderment. Take a pleasure walk instead of a fitness walk—a walk where you notice the miracles, communicate with the children you see, talk to the animals, notice the colors, and dream your dreams.

Singer Bobby McFerrin sang the words, "In every life we have some trouble; when you worry, you make it double—don't worry, be happy!" The point is your emotional energies can be used for you or against you. Your emotions can uplift you or entrap you. Your emotions can be healing or they can make your life-energy go haywire by releasing huge amounts of poison in the physical body. When you become angry, you release an unbelievable number of toxins that not only do physical damage but distort perception and disturb the ability to enjoy greater loving and greater living.

One soulercise which is invaluable to your physical and spiritual health is the simple decision to not take everything that is said to you or done in your presence personally. When you are tempted to fall into this toxic trap, try using the title of Terry Cole Whittaker's book, "What You Think of Me is None of My Business," as an affirmation. When you are caught in this paranoia trap, the real problem is one of low soul-esteem. That is, you have forgotten that you are a being of Light. As a result, there is a tendency to take what everyone says to heart as though all of it has something to do with you. In reality, it has more to do with the other person's issues.

Your soul-esteem comes from deep within your soul. It doesn't have anything to do with anyone else in the outside world. It is not founded on the approval of others—it is the innate acceptance of yourself as a child of the Divine. When you think that everything someone says or every expression on someone's face is some insult or barb directed at you, you must tune up your soul-esteem by turning to your faith that God is your partner, your source, your support, your creator and your closest friend. Understand that other people's perception of you is that which they see as they look through the lenses of their own consciousness. You must learn to be detached from others' perceptions, stand tall in your own soul-esteem, and love the God-Self of you as well as the God-Self of others. Then you will be free to smile at them and handle the situation in a way that is poised, lighthearted and loving.

The most important spiritual goal of every soulercise is to rediscover the soul and learn to let the personality of the soul shine through the human personality as a power-presence. The object is to become more and more spiritually fit so that your soul will take over and take charge of the personality instead of it being the other way around. It's important to exercise the spiritual muscles to the point that your soul begins to guide and direct the ego in a way that is authentically powerful and masterful. Get into the soul-zone, loosen up and lighten up, laugh yourself into a joy, and savor the journey. Take the time out to plug into your natural source of energy—your God-Energy, and one day you will look in the mirror and see a power-presence smiling back at you with love and spiritual confidence.

The Cosmic Glimmer

That spark of awareness comes as if out of the blue,
a flash of knowing, a burst of spiritual energy,
a divine spark that pierces the illusion of mystery
between me and the Divine.
Those rare moments of Truth
can feel like a shock to the system
from the power of its impact.
I have seen beyond the veil.
I have gazed for one brief instant
into the sea of spiritual possibility—into the Void—
into the glory of the Light Itself.
The cosmic circuits open, the gap opens wide,
and I shudder from the thrill of *knowing*.
The cosmic glimmer changes me.
Now that I have glimpsed the higher dimensions—
I will never be the same again.
There is no going back.
The path to enlightenment will transform every distraction
into a remembrance that enriches me
and reveals to me once again
that which I had forgotten.

Listen to the Drummer

Stop trying so hard, My beloved. Rest awhile as you let the illusions of conflict and competition fall from your awareness. Let the distractions of the human drama fade from your mind and melt from your heart as we once again enjoy our sacred connection.

Listen for the rhythm of My unbroken continuity. Notice Me, My beloved. Notice Me as the I Am of your soul, as the very beat of your heart. Notice Me in the tree outside your window, in every flower, cloud and wisp of air that touches your cheek. Notice Me in those mysterious events that happen to show you the way. Notice Me everywhere—always ready to fill your need — always ready to answer your question—always ready to guide you along your way safely. Can you trust Me that much?

Let My laughter fill your soul, My dear one, as you remember the life-giving quality of such expression. Come, see the world from My high place where the human condition has no power to weigh heavy upon the soul.

I say to you now, My beloved, put on the armor of light. Let My light surround you, infill you, bless you and harmonize all that concerns you. As you do so, you shall be guided by the angels of My Presence so that you will know how to meet every circumstance. And as you do, you will add your light to the world. This is your contribution to the world, My child—to remember that you are a light in the midst of what seems to be darkness. Let My light shine through your physical form—through your mind, through your heart, and through every action you take.

Take time to rest, My child. Take time to use the Earth as the playground I meant it to be. Glorify Me and share in the joy that I feel as I express through you. Be not misguided by others who are sleepwalking through their human experience. Wake up, My child, to the glories of My creation and the possibilities that it offers you.

It is possible, My dear one, to live in the world, but be not of the world. It is possible to attain freedom from bondage to personal ego. It is possible to rise above the illusion of separation. It is possible to create your world by seeing your world through new eyes. See a new vision, My child. Use your divine faculty of imagination and build your vision as we would see it together.

In this short time that we have been in conscious communion, many of your questions have already been answered in this Oneness. All you have now to do, My beloved, is carry out the answer to the question.

I love you. All is well.

—The Drummer

Part Six
Contact

*I do not know if it is the "mystic" sense I possess;
but certainly it is perceptive. It is the faculty that
brings distant objects within the cognizance of the
blind so that even the stars seem to be at our very
door. This sense relates me to the spiritual world.
It surveys the limited experience I gain from an
imperfect touch world, and presents it to my mind
for spiritualization. This sense reveals the Divine
to the human in me, it forms a bond between earth
and the Great Beyond, between now and eternity,
between God and man.*

—Helen Keller

Chapter Twenty-Eight
Your Built-In GOD System

No one can deny that there are impressions and insights that defy all reasoning processes, transcend the five senses, and occur without effort. They are unpremeditated, sometimes abrupt impulses, nudges, promptings, feelings, or knowings that seem to come from an unseen Source. These impelling forces are higher faculties of the soul being brought into use and are usually referred to as "intuition." Your intuition is your built-in guidance system, a set of sensing faculties beyond the rational processes of the physical mechanism. These faculties include direct knowing, soul-sight, soul-sound, soul-touch and even soul-taste and aroma!

You might call this array of soul-senses your built-in GOD system, or your *Guidance Of Divinity* system. When you are tuned into your GOD system, you are guided and protected. The spiritual waking up process is faster when these faculties are operating because you learn and remember with much less interference from the physical plane. Following your intuitive guidance system enables you to bypass a lot of pain and repetition that can happen when you struggle to learn something only from the five sensory perspective.

Direct knowing is a form of intuition based on perceiving and understanding without interference or interruption and with a certainty that is beyond doubt. It is mostly a *feeling* that is so overwhelming that it cannot be denied. You may have heard yourself say, "I know, and I know that I know!"

Direct knowing can be improved and developed like any other spiritual faculty. How? By practicing. Consciously acknowledge your internal promptings, trust them, and act on them. You might start the developmental process by having another person ask you direct questions that you answer based upon the feelings that immediately come to you. Go with your first impression so that you don't get confused by logic, reasoning, and opinions. Don't worry, stew, wonder, analyze, or ask questions about your first impulse. As long as it won't hurt you or anyone else, follow the impulse. Then afterwards simply notice how "on target" you were. Start small and work up to the big stuff after you have built some self-confidence. Don't force it and don't let any tension about it come to your consciousness. At some point you will learn to recognize what an intuitive prompting feels like, and what *knowing* feels like to you, and you will get better and better at distinguishing direct knowing from wishful thinking or logic.

If you think back, you may remember times when you had an intuitive "hunch" about something. Perhaps you followed it and never found out whether or not you were on target. Or perhaps you *didn't* follow it and later found out that your hunch had been right. You may have found yourself saying, "Something told me to do it the other way," or "I should have followed my intuition."

I remember a powerful incident many years ago when I was a teenager. It was one of my first conscious experiences of my own GOD system. One weekend there was a big picnic planned. I had looked forward to it and even bought a new outfit to wear. A friend was to pick me up in her new red convertible, so I was dressed early and eagerly awaiting her arrival the day of the picnic. As I waited, I felt an intense sensation sweep over me that carried with it the message, "Don't go." I told my mother about the feeling and she encouraged me to pay attention if I felt strongly about it. My ego put up a fight for a few minutes because it didn't want to miss out on this picnic. But I couldn't squelch the clear warning that told me to stay home.

When my friend drove up with several other friends, honking the horn and yelling the way teenaged girls in a red convertible do, I went to the car and told them I was staying home. I waved good-bye and walked back into the house with my chin dragging, feeling a mixture of disappointment, self-pity and relief.

In those days there were gangs in our cities just as there are today. There weren't as many and they didn't use guns, but they were just as rough and mean and carried broken bottles, brass knuckles and various other weapons. An infamous motorcycle gang showed up at the picnic that day, terrorizing everyone and injuring several people. I was grateful that I had listened to my GOD system.

Perhaps the reason I listened to my built-in GOD system on the day of the picnic was that I was open to the powers beyond the physical senses. I had been consciously working on my soul-esteem from the time I was eleven years old. I didn't call it that then, but that's what it was. I also give my angels credit for looking after me and really teaming up that day to get my attention. From that day on I have become more and more aware of the messages that come through my various intuitive faculties.

Direct knowing is developed as you learn to trust in Universal Goodness and Infinite Intelligence. That which knows can know through you. As you increase your spiritual confidence in your direct knowing, your soul-esteem will reach new heights. Your soul-esteem is your soul's sense of self worth, just as your self-esteem is your personality's sense of self worth.

Besides direct knowing, part of your GOD system involves *seeing* without the physical eyes. I call it *soul-sight*, or *in-sight*. This faculty of inner vision is mentioned in the Bible many times. It is called the *single-eye*. The single eye is a metaphor for seeing only that which is of the Light. *"The light of the body is the eye; if therefore thine eye be single, thy whole body shall be full of light. But if thine eye be evil, thy whole body shall be full of darkness."* (Matt. 6:22) We are being counseled to see things from God's perspective, from a vantage point of goodness and wholeness, rather than from a fragmented human perspective.

You are—I am—every person is—essentially a spiritual being. This world is essentially a spiritual world, and the world is governed by spiritual laws. When you let yourself *fall in love* with your inherent spiritual nature, or essence, you begin to build soul-esteem by trusting your GOD system. As you begin to *see* things the way they *really* are, you realize that what you see through your human eyes may not always be what it seems. The master teacher, Jesus, said *"Judge not according to appearances but judge righteous judgment."* Judgment here means discernment, not criticism. You judge righteous judgement by *seeing* with the single eye—the eye that beholds goodness—the eye that beholds divinity in all that is.

When using the faculty of physical sight you behold and interpret whatever you look upon through the filters of your own consciousness: that which you think, feel and believe. This means that what you see may seem different from that which someone else sees. If a hundred different people were asked to look at the same panoramic view and describe what they saw, there would be one hundred different descriptions. Your view of the world is seen through lenses ground to fit your own personal prescription. If you live entirely according to the information coming through those lenses, you live in a world according to *that* information and only that information.

Your spiritual vision, your in-sight or soul-sight, can take you beyond these limited perceptions. It enables you to look again, to see through the eyes of your soul, to see from God's perspective. Habakkuk of the Old Testament referred to God this way: "Thou that are of purer eyes than to behold evil." God does not see evil or sin or the condition of want or lack of any kind. So practice expanding your vision to see God as Spirit, as perfect Principle, as a Presence that knows nothing of sin. Then practice seeing your world and every person in that same way.

For example, God is Love and wholeness even when you are filled with anger. God is the divine potential in you even when you think you are inadequate or useless. The moment you decide to *see* things differently—the moment you release your bitterness or rise above guilt, or stop feeling sorry for yourself, it will dawn upon you that God's Love was always there even in the midst of your misperceptions. God doesn't forgive—God gives. There is nothing to forgive in His sight, for "His eyes are too pure to behold iniquity." The fact is, you have already been receiving your retribution through the *Law of Cause and Effect.*

Through your human eyes you may see yourself as guilty or wrong or as falling short in some way, but your spiritual vision can cleanse the lenses of your physical eyes so that you begin to see things differently. The moment you see the Light, you stop seeing the darkness. Let these words become your mantra: "God of Light, help me see things differently." Look at everything through the eyes of Spirit. When the human world presents you with ugliness or disappointment, use your soul-sight to move to another level of perception that realizes things are not as they seem to your human eyes and filters. Such a vantage point will liberate you from the human condition of limitation and judgment and move you into the expansiveness and peace of soul-esteem.

Just as soul-sight is the spiritual correlative to human eyesight, the human sense of touch also has a correlating spiritual faculty. To *touch* means to allow some part of the body, especially the hands, to come into contact with someone or something so as to *feel* the nature of that which has been touched. Soul-touch is the sensation, or a feeling, of having been touched by Spirit.

There is unlimited evidence of Spirit's amazing touch

everywhere you look. All you have to do is notice. All you have to do is increase your awareness and allow yourself to feel the presence of Spirit in order to be touched at the soul level. As you attempt to increase the touch of Spirit in your experience, begin with the thought that everything contains the possibility of holiness—even the most unholy of circumstances. It is easy to detect the touch of Spirit as you stand under an umbrella of stars, or sit in reverence as you watch a magnificent sunset, or drink in the beauty of a flower. The trick is to find divinity, or the touch of Spirit, in everyday life—even in the problems of life.

Learning to perceive the touch of Spirit in the most mundane of circumstances or finding it in a challenging situation requires *noticing* the presence of Spirit at the *level of your soul*. This is a *feeling* of elation, of being filled to overflowing with love, reverence or awe. It is something that rises up from inside of you. One friend of mine confided to me recently that she can tell when she is touched at the soul-level because her skin starts tingling from head to toe. She has been building her soul-esteem on a conscious level for only the past several years and this is a new development for her.

On Sunday mornings I conduct a service at The Soul-Esteem Center called *The Gathering*. I've had so many people tell me that they feel the touch of Spirit during this time more than at any other time. Perhaps that's because those who walk through the doors into *The Gathering* step out of the everyday world and walk into the soul-zone. They walk into present time awareness, into an atmosphere of safety and peace—a place where their divinity is acknowledged and recognized. They then become ready to let the transforming energy of Love touch their souls.

The touch of Spirit is all around you, all of the time. If you learn to enjoy the touch of spirit and to be happy with the refreshing, healing elements that are always available to you, you learn how to be really alive in every present moment. And then no matter what you are doing, you encounter the touch of spirit—as you wash the dishes, look at a flower, or gaze into the eyes of another human being.

Another spiritual faculty that might be considered part of your built-in GOD system is the *taste* of Spirit. Life is a banquet spread before you and you get to choose what it is that you taste, shaping your spiritual taste buds in the process. You've heard of doing a *taste test*. Life offers you the ultimate taste test. You have the opportunity to distinguish the flavors of life that you like from the flavors you don't like. Just as your human taste buds learn to distinguish the sweet from the sour and the salty from the bitter, you learn to discern what your spiritual tastes are. You may have a "taste" for adventure; your experience of life may be tasteless or bland; you may dish out hurt to other people and you will sooner or later get a taste of your own medicine. If you have become bitter, or sour on life, it's as if everything you taste makes your mouth pucker and your body contract with the unpleasant sensation.

You may have noticed that when you eat too much salt or too much spicy food, your taste buds become dull so that you're not receptive to the subtle, natural flavors. In the same way, if you taste the "good life" to the point of excess, you dull your senses so that you no longer notice the subtle flavors of life. In order to taste anything at all, you crave something stronger, or grander, or juicier, or more powerful. This craving usually takes the form of greed, gluttony, covetousness, lust or envy.

When you spend time in the temple of nature, or when you come together with people of like mind, you are able to easily taste the many delicious flavors of Spirit and you savor, appreciate, relish, and partake. Your spiritual taste buds are satisfied because your soul is filled with spiritual nourishment of divine origin called *manna*. Being in nature, doing meditation, praying and spending time with happy and spiritually minded people will cleanse the senses so that you can actually taste the delicate flavors and the richness of Spirit at the same time.

I remember when I spent some time at a Florida spa and embarked upon a seven-day water fast. After six days my body said, "Enough." Such a fast shuts down the digestive system so that when the fast is broken it must be done very carefully. You have to prime the pump so to speak and get things moving gently and slowly. The method suggested at the spa was to break the fast with orange juice. Someone handed me half of an orange with the instructions to "Lick it, suck on it, but no fair eating it." I sat my weak body down on a chair, took the orange in both hands, and closed my eyes. I hunched over the treasure in my hands and approached that orange as though I were offering the most sincere prayer I'd ever prayed. I squeezed the orange a little bit so that there was juice lying on top, and then touched my tongue to the juice. The power of the first taste almost hurt. My whole body tingled with the sensation of the incredible flavor as it awakened everything all the way down to my toes. My taste buds had been cleansed and the taste of that orange made my whole body sing. I realized that until that moment I had had no idea about how an orange could actually taste. For days I was amazed at all the new tastes that I had never before noticed in the foods I ate.

The same thing is true about experiencing Spirit. You may have to fast from those things that contaminate and coat your consciousness in order to appreciate the subtleties, the zing, the sweetness, the smoothness of Spirit. Fasting happens every time you stop indulging in old patterns of limiting belief. Fasting from negative thoughts, feelings and beliefs allows you to tune into your GOD system and use your intuitive faculties to pick up the higher frequencies of Spirit. When you fast, you perform a kind of *sensory cleansing* which enables you to make new and higher choices. Your spiritual faculties then become more receptive, more sensitive, more inviting to the things of Spirit. As you practice spiritual fasting and exercise your power of choice and decision in a new way, you continue to open up to new spiritual tastes and possibilities. You nurture your soul and increase your soul-esteem.

Soul-sound is another part of your built-in GOD system. You are more than likely familiar with phrases such as "the voice of God," or "the still small voice," which imply that you hear beyond the range of sound heard by the human ear.

Within the scope of human perception, you might associate the idea of sound with the human voice or music. I'm sure you're familiar with the discord and irritation caused by loud lawn mowers early on a Saturday morning, or a group of motorcycles disturbing a quiet dinner, or a crowd of loud voices when you're trying to have a private conversation. There are grating noises, screeching sounds, thudding sounds, and rattling and creaking noises. We hear sad sounds, happy sounds, moaning sounds and sounds of discovery and surprise. But rarely the sound of silence. There is so much sound bombarding us in the third dimensional world, it's no wonder that we rarely hear the soul-sound of the inner voice—the sound of Spirit.

Most humans are so acclimated to outer sensory stimulation that they generally forget how to listen from within. The key to tapping the inner voice lies in becoming quiet and in stilling the mind so that you can hear the subtle, gentle whispers of the God within. Meditation, long walks in nature, visualization, exercise, driving on a country road, all offer ways to calm the mind so that you can perceive the sound of Spirit.

What does Spirit sound like? It sounds like the voice of conscience that whispers inside you. When you reject this voice, you are not following your GOD system. In her book called *Ye Are Gods*, Annalee Skarin tells of a young woman who described repentance as a wormy feeling you get when you do something you shouldn't. This is a good way to describe how the voice of conscience sounds when it knows something must change for the better.

Sometimes the sound of Spirit sounds like the voice of approval. It may come in the form of a pat on the back that carries with it warm affection and fills your whole body with that "good feeling." This is not the voice of the ego with its loud declaration of self-righteousness—it is the sound of Spirit that you might classify as sacred feedback.

How do you know you're hearing the voice of Spirit? You know by the resulting feeling of profound inner peace. This is the peace that passes all understanding—an inner tranquility that emerges from a place deep within the soul. From this place, you can transcend any human chaos that may be happening in your outer world. The sound of Spirit may be accompanied by a surge of new energy and vitality, because when you tune into your GOD system, you allow the life force to move through you and your world of affairs more easily.

Another sign that confirms that you are listening to Spirit is the support you receive. It will be as if invisible hands are helping you, guiding you, and providing for you in everything you do.

Sometimes you may choose *not* to listen to the sound of Spirit, but to the false voice of your ego. Remember that ego is an acronym for *edging God out*. Some very definite signs that you are edging God out are the uncomfortable feelings of anxiety instead of peace, difficult barriers instead of an easy flow, critical judgment instead of unconditional love, and confusion instead of mental and emotional clarity. The voice of ego often sounds like the voice of fear that encourages anxiety and even dishonesty. The voice of Spirit is committed to the Truth.

Practice listening to the sounds of Spirit through the voice of a friend, the stirrings of nature, or the cadence of beautiful music. Notice the warm sensation in your chest or stomach when Spirit speaks to you. Practice noticing the lightness in your heart, the feelings of enthusiasm, and the movement toward peace and tranquility. This is Spirit's way of guiding you into your best choices and decisions.

Experiment with the clues, the synchronicities. Follow the guidance and stay spiritually confident. Listen with soul-esteem and over time you will become more and more skilled at discerning between the voice of Spirit and the voice of ego. You will learn through practice to choose the inner voice as the one to guide you as the truest friend you've ever had.

This brings us to the last of the physical senses, the sense of smell. It may seem unusual to correlate the physical sense of smell with a spiritual faculty—that's why I call it the *aroma of Spirit* instead of the *Smell of Spirit*. Your olfactory sense is a highly discriminatory faculty, much like taste. U.S. philosopher,

Eric Hoffer, said that "Self-esteem and self-contempt have specific odors; they can be smelled."

You use your sense of smell as a warning system. When you get a *whiff* of something rotten with respect to food, you don't eat it. When you *smell a rat*, you don't get involved with that situation. When a criminal flees from the scene of a crime, the police try to *sniff him out*.

If I were to ask you what Spirit smells like, you would more than likely think of roses or some other pleasant smelling flower or a type of perfume or incense. You might describe it as a clean smell, a sweet smell, or a pleasing fragrance. It would not be an aroma to which you would wrinkle your nose in response. The aroma of Spirit would always be described as pleasant, inviting and inoffensive.

The sense of smell from a spiritual perspective is like all the other spiritual faculties. It is part of your GOD system that helps you identify the forgotten yet familiar realm of Spirit.

A Word of Caution

I recently ran into someone who had attended *The Gathering* one time a couple of years ago. She said to me, "I haven't returned because the energy of the room didn't seem right to me." It may have been more accurate if this person had said, "My energy of consciousness didn't resonate with the consciousness of the group."

The energy of any room is a product of the consciousness that fills the room. Every Sunday morning at about 9:30 a.m. before the 10:00 a.m. service, those of us on the team conducting the service form a circle and pray together. We turn our attention to the Presence of God, to unconditional Love, and we open ourselves to feel the touch of Spirit. We rededicate ourselves to serving God and to acknowledging the Presence of God in every person. We fill the room with cleansing, loving Light energy and with uplifting, inspiring live music. The room then fills with loving people. If a person doesn't like the energy, it's because his or her energy doesn't resonate with the group consciousness. The room itself doesn't have anything to do with it. Nor does it have anything to do with the consciousness of the group or individual being either good or bad.

Be careful about trusting everything you see or hear. Just because it comes from somewhere beyond the five senses does not necessarily mean that it is ordained by God. There may be all sorts of gibberish going on in the brain and depending on your state of consciousness, you may think you are hearing or seeing *signals* or *signs* from God. Not always so. It takes practice to learn how to discern whether or not your feelings are from your Higher Self, or just a creation of your ego mind.

Remember the law that says, unless you observe something it isn't real for you. The point is that you have the power to *choose* that which you *observe* and make *that* your reality.

Keep this in mind: There is no struggle in Spirit. That which is of Spirit is filled with peace. The effect is always restorative, healing and never carries with it any critical judgment or mental analysis. If you receive a *message*, or hear a *voice*, or feel a *touch*, or *see* something out of the ordinary, always ask yourself how you feel. False impressions or sensations will carry with them a sense of struggle and a lack of peace. There will be mental questioning, analyzing and positioning. This is not Spirit speaking. This is your personality speaking. True impulses from God produce harmonious adjustments and healing. Heaviness is lifted and burdens melt away. Good happens.

Listen to the Drummer

Hello once again, My dear one. As your human senses become stilled, let your gifts of Spirit engage themselves. Allow yourself to see with My eyes; hear beyond your human ability to listen; touch with a spiritual sensitivity that can be experienced only by your soul; taste the flavors of My Presence and notice the aroma of My Spirit.

Transcending the five sensory world makes no sense to your human senses, My child. But as you tune into the Drummer that sits at the center of your being, you will notice the impulses, the inner promptings, the feelings and the knowings that comprise your built-in guidance system. These are your soul-senses, My dear one. They cannot be accessed through the rational processes of your human mechanism.

Listen to the Drummer, My beloved. Trust the rhythm of your higher faculties without interference or interruption from human doubt and fear. Keep your eye single and judge not according to appearances. Come with Me to My vantage point and look at your world from the grander perspective.

See Me in the tree outside your window—in every flower, every cloud, every wisp of air that touches your cheek. See Me in those mysterious events that happen to show you the way. Hear Me as the voice that speaks from inside you. Feel My touch as the beauty of your world embraces you. Notice Me everywhere, always ready to fill your need, always ready to answer your question, always ready to guide you along your way safely. Can you trust Me that much?

Oh yes, My beloved, I hear your impatience. I hear your doubt as you wonder when you will receive My touch, or hear My voice. Do not cloud your spiritual faculties with impatience and doubt, My dear one. Every waking moment during which you live your human experience you are being led, guided, directed and protected. Such guidance is so easy and smooth that you may not notice My hand in it. Do not chastise yourself. Simply pay closer attention. I will lead you out of any difficulty and all things will be made new. I love you. All is well.

—The Drummer

The natural expression of the angels is Truth.
If we deny the truth about ourselves and accept
the illusion of limited, powerless, victimized humans,
we repress the energy of the angels. But when we
fully accept the eternal verities of life, our hold on
the energy is released and the angels can begin to
bring everything up to the divine standard.
                                    —John Randolph Price

Chapter Twenty-Nine
Angel Synchronicities

The word *angel* means *messenger of God.* Based upon
the premise that God is the One Presence and the One Infinite
Intelligence, angels could be conceived of as thoughts moving from
God Mind to human awareness. Angels, or any other archetypal
concept, can be regarded as thought-forms within the Mind of
God. Since God is the One Infinite Spirit, the all-encompassing
and loving Divine Presence that is eternal, everywhere present,
all-powerful, and all-knowing, it follows that everything lives and
moves and has its being *in* God and is some part of the One
Infinite Spirit.

From this perspective, God's angel-thoughts could take
any form depending upon the individual consciousness or belief
system of the person who has the angel encounter. For some,
angels might show up in the form of the traditional winged beings
of light with very physical characteristics, or they might show up
as a voice from nowhere, or as a gentle tap on the shoulder. They
sometimes appear directly or in visions or dreams. Their

presence might be sensed in the midst of music or singing, or they may be seen as shafts of light or as light glimpsed out of the corner of one's eye. Their presence can also be felt by an almost overwhelming feeling of Love that washes over you.

Angels are always proving to us the sacred truth that All Is One. They are always there to nudge you, coach you and guide you, wake you up to avoid an accident, or protect you from harm. These loving, protecting messengers are often responsible for the many meaningful coincidences, or synchronicities, that are happening in our lives in increasing numbers today. I don't know about you, but I truly believe that angels have disguised themselves as pets or other human beings like you or me. Each of us gets to play the role of *angel* on occasion when we're moved to "be there" for someone else.

You might be experiencing angel whisperings when you have an idea or when you create something. Since God is everywhere present, God's thought *is* the very creative process that pours Itself through all forms of Its expression. That expression might manifest as art, dance, music, writing, or any other process whereby you are instrumental in the transformation of something from its beginning as an idea, to its manifestation in form. All creativity is spiritual in nature and is a demonstration of your co-creative connection with Spirit.

The angels of God's Presence touch your consciousness to help you participate in the creative process. It is written that God created man but little lower than the angels and crowned him with glory and honor.

Stories of angel encounters are no longer limited to the world of religious mysticism. Book after book is being published with more and more stories of rescues, guidance, inspiration, loving protection, and divine intervention. Angels have gone mainstream and are bringing the mystical into everyday life.

A friend of mine, who is a nurse in the Surgical Intensive Care Unit at St. Anthony's Hospital in St. Louis, Missouri, tells me that the nursing staff has been recording cases of angel sightings since 1987. These particular angels seem to always show up as children between five and seven years of age and are often seen just prior to a patient's death. Over and over these children have been seen by the patients outside the windows or playing at the foot of a bed or by the nurse's station, and even in the unit's public bathroom.

Another friend feels the presence of her angel by a sensation on her face that feels like wings lightly brushing her skin. I personally identify my angels as they announce themselves to me in the form of energy fields of various colors.

An increasing number of us are evolving to the point of being able to see, hear, and touch more of the invisible world. It's been said that the veil is getting thinner between Spirit and form. The process of spiritual development is being assisted by unseen forces more than ever before. Maybe that's because more of us are consciously yearning to remember and understand our connection to the Divine and have *asked* to be guided and assisted in our human experience. It's amazing how quickly we are responded to when we remember to ask.

My sense of it is that the angels and guides are gathering closer to us. They are assisting us in making a great paradigm shift from old energies to new, from religion to spirituality, from limited thinking to vast panoramas of possibility. The thoughts of God, as angelic beings, are here to help us through a time of madness. Their assignments are to help us prove that the Divine Light of God shines in the souls of everyone, everywhere. As a result, more and more people are having angel encounters.

An angel encounter is an experience or a *happening* that defies human reason. Angel encounters might be described as incidents of divine intervention, rescue, blessings, *in the nick of time* help, meaningful coincidence, comfort, guidance, invisible support, selfless behavior, or some other incredible experience that transcends time and space and touches our lives as if with a magic wand.

My husband Roger and I put many of our angel encounters in the category of "synchronicities." We talk with each other a lot about synchronicities. In fact, Roger talks to everybody about synchronicities. He has become absolutely enchanted with noticing the ways in which synchronicities accelerate when you have the presence of mind to notice them and when you simply ask your angels for assistance.

Psychologist Carl Jung first used the term *synchronicity* in 1930 in reference to unpredictable, impressive and startling happenings that seem to be connected and cannot be explained by any apparent physical cause. A synchronistic experience is the same as a meaningful coincidence.

From a spiritual perspective, synchronicity refers to the many ways in which God shows up for us in just the right way, at just the right time. It's one of the primary ways in which we *experience* and *know* God. We cannot conceive of what God is with our ordinary minds. The only way we can *know* God—is to *experience* God. And the more we let ourselves flow in Universal Energy, or the *stream of consciousness*, the more we experience God *as* synchronistic occurrences.

A synchronistic occurrence is really an *allowing*. It isn't as unpredictable and startling as Jung thought it to be. In fact, the more we begin to trust that everything is in its right place, that everything happens at the right time, the less we are surprised by meaningful coincidences, or angel encounters, or messages and guidance from the invisible realm.

Some time ago, Roger and I decided to take a much needed vacation, but we couldn't decide what we wanted to do or where we wanted to go. We went into the silence and asked the appropriate questions. What came to me was a clear answer in my head that said, "Phylis, what you *do* doesn't matter. Where you *go* doesn't matter. What *does* matter is that you take a break from routine—from deadlines—from schedules—from *shoulds* and *have to's*. Stop thinking for awhile and take time out to touch, feel, enjoy and rest. You can do that anywhere, and you can do it while doing whatever you're doing."

And so we decided to stop trying to come up with the perfect plan and agreed instead to take a *synchronicity vacation*. We decided to trust God to see that we were in the right places, experiencing the right things, at exactly the right times. We decided to forget about time frames, schedules, planning, concern or worry. We trusted God to work everything out as we just moved with the flow of divine synchronicity.

We realized that if we were to take a synchronicity vacation, there were several requirements. First of all, we would have to stay very aware and awake in the present moment in order to *notice* the synchronistic happenings—or angel encounters as they showed up.

Secondly, we would have to stop all judgments so as to not get caught up in comparisons, opinions and emotional reactions that might steer us away from a really important clue.

Next, we decided to stop all impulses to control anything. Wow! No wonder we hadn't heard of anyone taking a synchronicity vacation before!

We then agreed to follow our internal GOD (Guidance Of Divinity) systems and act on our intuitions with soul-esteem. In other words, we chose to trust Spirit with utter faith and sheer abandonment. We knew that if we could move ourselves into such a place, we could expect everything we thought, said and did to be supported by the Universe.

Roger and I had a long talk about this vacation and how much fun it would be to trust God that much and just sit back and collect the blessings. We reviewed the requirements and agreed to do the best we could to comply.

We had planned to take off on Monday, June 1, on my birthday, but Roger was experiencing a severe cold and I was just getting over one, so we put off our departure until Tuesday. Tuesday came and he still needed rest, more than he needed a lot of traveling, as did I, so we didn't leave on Tuesday morning.

We began to wonder when the positive synchronicities would begin. Little did we know they already had. On Monday we had noticed a wet spot on the carpet in our first floor bathroom. Roger had mentioned it to me, but we got busy and forgot about it since we rarely use that bathroom unless we have guests in the house.

It wasn't until 5:00 p.m. on Tuesday that for some unknown reason I was literally guided into that bathroom and once again noticed the wet spot. I reached down and touched the carpet and realized that the whole bathroom floor was saturated. I looked a little closer and finally noticed that the shut-off valve was dripping and couldn't be stopped. I put a bowl under it to catch the water, called the plumber, and the problem was solved in a couple of hours.

That night I packed, and the next morning both of us felt rested and healthy. We left on Wednesday morning. I drove away saying, "Thank you, God!" Can you imagine what we would have come home to if we had taken off for eight days with that leak in our bathroom? This was a divine synchronicity, an angel encounter. Perhaps if we had been more awake to the nudges and promptings, we would not have needed colds to keep us home!

We set out on our adventure in the direction of Branson, Missouri. When we arrived in the Branson area, Roger was guided to call Treehouse Condos on Indian Point, and they just *happened* to have one condo available, with a deck overlooking the lake. That Friday I decided that I wanted to see the Shoji Tobuchi show, so I asked Roger to call and get tickets for Friday night. He almost laughed in my face, and said, "We might get some tickets during the week, but not for a Friday night in June—especially when we're calling the same day!"

I said to him, "So where's your trust, Synchy?"

He smiled, recovered his soul-esteem, and called for the tickets. They just *happened* to have two seats—second row center.

And so it went, one thing after another—finding ourselves in the right place at the right time. Whatever we decided to do, a way opened up for us to do it. Even the temperature cooperated. I don't do well in really hot weather, and by the time we started our trip on Wednesday, the temperature had dropped into the seventies and low eighties, with light breezes and lots of sunshine. It stayed that way until we arrived back home. We truly enjoyed a synchronicity vacation—with lots of angel encounters.

When you're in the flow, you put up no resistance. God's Mind becomes your mind, and God's thoughts become your thoughts. You become a clear channel, unobstructed, unadulterated and unpolluted by distorted thinking and beliefs. How do God's thoughts, pure God Consciousness, become *conscious* to you? They become conscious through many avenues—through other people, through your intuition, through revelation, through meaningful coincidences, or synchronicities, or through angel encounters.

We have come a long way since Carl Jung talked about meaningful coincidence and synchronicity as chance happenings, unpredictable occurrences, or startling and amazing surprises. As you get a handle on how the Universe operates, these encounters become commonplace. In fact, you can expect them and need not be surprised when they happen because you literally are the creator of these occurrences rather than the random target of some ethereal marksman. During the flow of positive synchronicity, you are never in a victim consciousness and you never sit back and feel sorry for yourself. Instead, you embrace life with a sense of joy, wonder, amazement and belief in wholeness and harmony.

I'd like to share with you another of the many angel encounters that I have experienced. Rather than *seeing* an angel, I felt a touch and heard a directive. This happened when I was traveling back and forth between St. Louis and Orlando, attending ministerial school. One Saturday, I finished a school day and headed for the Orlando airport to catch my flight back to St. Louis. It was really important that I get back because I was scheduled to deliver two Sunday sermons the next morning. It wasn't a full flight, so I asked for an upgrade and was given a seat in first-class.

I boarded the plane, settled down into my big first-class seat with a glass of orange juice, and began going over my talks for the next day. I had plenty of time to review my notes, and then noticed that the plane hadn't moved in almost an hour. Just then the Captain's voice came over the speaker system and said, "Well, I guess you noticed we're still sitting at the gate. This plane has a defective part, and we're trying to find a replacement. As soon as we do, we'll get this thing fixed and we'll be on our way. Anyone who must make flight connections, please deplane and we will help re-route you. Thank you for your patience."

I felt a little anxious, but I put my concerns aside and closed my eyes and relaxed. I then experienced a feeling that might be described as a tap on my right shoulder. It was so strong and physical that I opened my eyes and looked around. No one was there. But I felt it again—stronger this time. It was a feeling that I have since described as a cosmic kick in the pants. It was as if something was pushing me out of my seat.

I cooperated with this angel encounter, got up, pulled my carry-on out of the overhead compartment, and walked off the plane. I had no idea what I was going to do, or why. I walked out into the terminal and stood looking back at the gate. There was a long line of people waiting to reschedule flights in order to make connections. I listened to a voice that said, "Get in the line and wait."

About 30 minutes later, I found myself at the head of the line. Behind the counter was a stone-faced airline employee named Lewis. Lewis was a nice-looking, young African-American with a Jamaican accent. He had been well trained and knew how to hide his emotional reactions to the disgruntled passengers as they complained about the situation. From what I could tell, the airline knew that this flight would never leave Orlando that night. I also knew I had to be in St. Louis in time to get a good night's rest for my early morning assignment. It was clear that I was meant to make a soul-connection with Lewis, or why would I have been guided to stand in this line for 30 minutes? So I looked beyond the expressionless face that Lewis displayed, and I greeted the One that was both he and I.

When my turn came, I leaned on the counter with both arms, put my chin on my hands, and looked directly into Lewis' eyes. I felt the connection. I patiently explained my dilemma to Lewis and from that point on, Lewis took over angel duty. He hesitated, as if making some connection inside himself, and then he turned away and picked up a telephone. He spoke into it behind a cupped hand so that no one could see or hear what he was saying. He hung up the receiver and with the same stone-like expression, he motioned me to stand aside and wait.

I waited for another 20 minutes while Lewis served the remaining passengers waiting in line. Then he motioned me over, wrote something on a card, and handed it to me as he held a forefinger up to his lips in a "mum's the word" gesture.

He had handed me a boarding pass. He walked me over to Gate 10, pointed to a seat, and said, "Wait here." I did. I waited for at least another thirty minutes. But suddenly, quietly, the door to Gate 10 opened. A flight attendant appeared. She motioned me toward her, scooped me through the door and closed it behind us.

On the way to the plane she explained that this flight had made an emergency landing—something about running low on fuel due to resistance from heavy head winds in route from Puerto Rico to St. Louis. The crew decided to land in Orlando just long enough to refuel. There was one empty seat on the plane.

I was home and in bed by 10:00 p.m.—just in time to get the rest I needed. All of this happened because I responded to my built-in GOD system that supplied me with directions that I felt and heard. It happened because I listened and responded to the messengers.

I encourage you to open up to angel consciousness. If it feels better to you to call it divine intuition, meaningful coincidence, divine guidance, or the voice of God, call it whatever you choose. The point is you don't have to wait for times of physical danger, critical situations, or disaster in order to call upon God for help. When you bring yourself into alignment with God's Energy, when you are *in the flow*, you can literally call the shots.

It is written, "Ask, and it shall be given you; seek and ye shall find; knock and it shall be opened unto you; For everyone that asketh receiveth; and he that seeketh findeth; and to him that knocketh it shall be opened. ... In all ways acknowledge Him and He will make plain thy paths."

Listen to the Drummer

Greetings, My beloved. Come into the safety of My atmosphere. Stop for a few moments and listen for the beat, the rhythm, the song, the glory of My Presence at the very heart of your being. How are you, My child? Are you aware of the Love that surrounds you? Let yourself drink it in and satisfy your soul, just as you would quench your thirst with living water. Feel the pulse of My Life within you.

Yes, My dear one, My Life is within you and all around you. My Life takes many forms, all designed to meet your needs, lift your spirit and inspire your soul. It is out of My Life that you have been created and it is within My Life that you live and move and have your being. Let the fire of Spirit rise within you to explode in the creative power of your imagination. Let your soul soar with confidence into the dimension of thought that has no boundaries or limitations. That realm of thought is the energy of My Mind. You have heard it said that within My house are many mansions. This is the same as saying within My Mind are many dimensions.

I speak now about the angels of My Presence, dear one. Just as you are a blessed manifestation of an idea that began in My Mind, so are the angels and divine beings of all dimensions thought-forms within My Consciousness. Oftentimes the angels bring to you My wisdom, My touch, My ideas, and My guidance. So much of the communication that takes place between us is brought to you on the wings of these angelic beings. Do not question this, My dear one. Simply accept and enjoy it.

You are indeed surrounded by guides and angels that come to you in an infinite variety of ways. The Drummer that sits at your Holy Center is an angel of Light that lives as you. Always be ready to receive the whisperings of My angelic kingdom and always be ready to be the angel that you are for someone else. Angels are always proving the sacred truth that All Is One.

It is up to you to allow the angels to be a part of your experience. Remember to ask, My dear one, for the code of the angels is one of honor with respect to your freedom of will and the sacredness of our communion. Angels will never interfere except in cases of your safety, and sometimes not even then. It is the asking that invites them to be active in your life. You have been told to ask and it shall be given. This is a directive that must be adhered to if you would engage the activity of the angelic kingdom.

My Kingdom is one glorious wholeness, My dear one: one continuous, eternal, abundant flow of Love and Light. Bask in it. Let My angels hold you up and surround you and bless you with My gift of peace. Let yourself be aware of My Presence at the center of your soul. The beat is sounding louder and louder. Keep marching, My dear one, keep marching.

I love you. All is well.

—The Drummer

If you want to go east, don't go west.
—Ramakrishna

Chapter Thirty
There's No Business Like Soul Business

The most noble purpose on this Earth is to cultivate soul-esteem and to participate in assisting others to do the same. You foster soul-esteem through the evolutionary process of waking up to your own soul and exercising your spiritual faculties and sensitivities.

Soul-esteem is spiritual confidence that blossoms as you integrate your human self with your soul-self. This integration expresses through your personality as a power-presence—a demonstration of your whole self in the human dimension. Soul-esteem is the self-esteem of the soul, and when it is developed to a point of spiritual maturity your personality's self-esteem reaches peak performance.

Developing soul-esteem requires effort. It requires mental, physical, emotional and spiritual dedication. Unfortunately, many of us have been so caught up in the illusions of the outer world that we have forgotten why we're here. We think we're here to be successful, make money, have great relationships, and experience perfect health. We forget that our primary purpose for being here is to conduct soul business. It is to discover our true Self, to know God as the Love that is within each one of us, and to bridge the gap between the human self and the soul-self. Everything else is a by-product.

The idea is to put first things first and to commit yourself to soul-work as your top priority. "Seek ye first the kingdom of God, and all these things shall be added unto you." As you elevate your consciousness, you experience changes in your outer world. As within, so without. When you live with this motivation, you literally consecrate your life to God.

A consecrated life is a life that is ready at all times to do the Will of God. It is a willingness to allow God to be fully expressed through you. A consecrated life is not concerned with the importance of results because results are God's business. This does not mean you are to give up your hopes and dreams or stop setting goals and planning. It means that as you participate in life as a co-creator with God, there is a point at which you must relinquish any effort to force results to appear as your ego-self wants them to appear. You must be willing to let the Energy of God fill your vision and your desire naturally—without being glued to an outcome.

It may seem difficult to have a vision or plan and be intent upon bringing that idea to fruition, while at the same time staying open at the top and flexible about what's going to happen. If you hold fast to your dedication to discover your true Self, however, to know God as the Love that is within you and to heal the separation, you will be living the spiritual life. You will be cultivating soul-esteem and your plan will unfold naturally.

At this point you may still be asking yourself, "Is it really that crucial to make the business of soul my first priority?" The answer is yes, because if you don't, you limit yourself to the human, material approach to living. You limit yourself to ego-control, human power, and all the fears that accompany such dependency.

You might say, "But my life is working fine the way it is. Things are going well for me and my family—I'm healthy and prosperity is flowing. Why should I concern myself with soul-esteem?" This is a subtle, seductive trap that's easy to fall into. When you are comfortable physically and financially, there may be a tendency to become spiritually lazy. Why? Because you may be one who rates your degree of spirituality by how successful and comfortable you are physically. You may find yourself turning to spirituality only when things are *not* going so well in your physical world.

It is true that your outer world is the effect of your inner world, and when your outer world is not the way you want it to be, you can change it by using spiritual principles. This is all true, but if you use spiritual methods in an attempt to manipulate and control the human world, you are operating as though there is an outside power on one hand, and your mind on the other. You have not integrated one with the other so that you are thinking with the Mind of God. You are simply using spiritual principles, or laws, to make things happen the way your human ego-mind wants them to happen. The problem is, this only works for awhile. Something will finally happen in the human world to point out the fallibility of such an approach to life.

So what is your job if you choose to live the spiritual life and cultivate soul-esteem? Your job is to maintain a consciousness of oneness with your Higher-Self, your God-Self, and to resonate with the higher energies of Spirit which are the energies of abundance, harmony, wellness and high intention. When you come into such sacred agreement with God through this kind of spiritual thinking, feeling, belief and action, you become God's channel for the expression of all divine ideas. This truly is living the consecrated life.

All of creation exists in the "God-Stuff" that already exists as potentiality. You co-create with God by arranging and re-arranging that God-Stuff, kind of like molding and remolding clay into various forms. The forms that you create can be beautiful or ugly, big or little, perfect or distorted, depending upon how you mold them. You mold this invisible essence with your thought, fueled by your feeling and belief. How you transform your beliefs, train and focus your thoughts and feelings, and put all of it into action, is really what soul-business is all about.

You are Divine. You are a being of Light, an expression of Love, and the essence of you, the soul of you, is experiencing the human world. Consider that all of us—you and I—have agreed to come into physical form to help transform the human condition so that we can all express as divine humans. Consider that our main mission is to restore the physical world to that original Garden of Eden where we all know our Oneness and each individual soul is perceived to be part of the Whole. Consider that we are not just here to expand our soul's consciousness, but to penetrate the human illusion of separation. This idea is nothing new to most spiritual thinkers, but it's time we embody this idea and stop merely talking about it. *It's time we identify more with the soul-self and less with the human personality.* It's time we give the business of the soul our primary attention.

I see wonderful ways in which more and more of us are awakening to our soul-selves. If you look around, you will see that there are more and more people responding to their own soul. Those who are not—those who are oblivious to their soul—display that isolation in their human experience. I truly believe that violence and crime are committed by human beings who are mentally and emotionally cut off from their soul. When people ignore their own soul, they automatically separate themselves from Spirit. Notice that I said they separate *themselves* from Spirit; from the perspective of Higher Truth, there is no separation. The separation or isolation of the human spirit is an illusion. But as long as the illusion is believed, one acts out of the illusion of separation and the results are a life of isolation, struggle, stress and manipulation. Life is lived according to the toss of the dice, according to the survival of the fittest.

The true nature of your soul is revealed when you understand the true nature of God. The true nature of God is the benevolent, all-loving, all-accepting, all-knowing, all-powerful spiritual *Presence* that you turn to when you close your eyes to meditate or pray. It is that which you become when you give your love away. It is that which you are as you respond to the world with soul-esteem. The true nature of God *is* the true nature of your soul when you free yourself from all the illusory limitations of the personality.

As you practice taming the personality and listening to your own inner voice, you will be less and less controlled by the outer world, more and more sensitive to the needs of your soul, and willing to follow the lead of your true Self.

The Soul-Math Formula, Consciousness U-Turns, and many more tools in this book are designed to help you tame the personality and develop soul-esteem. They can help you deprogram the mental, physical and emotional levels of your being so that you can once again make full use of your power of will. As your soul-esteem becomes stronger and stronger, you will experience what it means to live in the world but not of the world. You will be able to look upon the ugliness of the human condition without falling apart at the seams. You will have a multidimensional awareness that lives above the world of dark energy. Remember that where there is Light there can be no darkness at all. Where there is Love there can be no fear. The whole process of reclaiming your power of spiritual confidence has to do with living in the Light and shaping that Light with the highest possible thoughts, feelings, beliefs and actions.

Your unlimited power includes your ability to think in a way that uses God's Mind as your mind. It includes your God-given powers of choice and decision and your incredible spiritual faculties. It is time now to turn away from outside human forces and influences and to listen for the beat of your Inner Drummer.

Be patient with yourself as you journey into soul-esteem. Stay in the soul-zone and walk with unbendable faith. You will know the Drummer when you tune into the rhythm of Spirit, and you will fall into step with an indescribable sense of joy and lightness.

Writing this book has been an opportunity for me to empty my cup by sharing my experiences, understandings, inspirations and thoughts. I know that you have been guided by your Inner Drummer to receive something within these pages that you are *ready* to receive. Let go of what doesn't fit for you at this time and put to use that which does. Blessings to you, my dear friend. I now free my own mind to go on from here as a willing and open vessel ready to receive the next cosmic glimmers as they illuminate my ongoing spiritual adventure.

Enjoy the final chapter filled with soul-esteem declarations to fortify your spiritual treasure chest. Thank you for sharing my journey, and God bless you on yours.

The Angels Tell Me

As I sit in the quiet
with the rain beating out a rhythm on the roof
and the birds singing in the wet, happy trees,
I open to the voices of the Angels.
As I begin to cross into dimensions unknown yet familiar,
I hear my own voice become that of those
who know me better than I know myself.
I'm told that all that I do is part of the Mission—
part of the Plan—part of the Great Work.
I was asked to recall that the human personality
once longed for forum—
but at the same time was afraid of too much attention.
Now is the time for no such longing
and no such fear.
Now is the time to dance in the sun.
Now is the time to rejoice.
Now is the time to shine.

Listen to the Drummer

It is with Infinite Love that I once again embrace you, My dearest child. I celebrate with you as you take down the defensive walls of your human imaginings and walk with Me in the Light. I rejoice with you as you look beneath the packaging of the human world to discover the priceless gift that you are to Me and to your Holy Self. I acknowledge you as you discover your many powerful gifts, some of which still lay dormant in the depths of your soul. I rejoice with you as you discover that you are Divine. You are a being of Light, an expression of My Love. The very essence of you—the soul of you—is that which will never die, that which is eternally part of Me.

You have been told how important it is to express your gratitude to Me. But I tell you this, My dear one. I do not need your gratitude. You need your gratitude. Gratitude is that which tears down the walls of separation that your mind has constructed. Gratitude turns your attention from what you think is missing to that with which you are blessed. There is so much more that can bless your life, My child, as you take down the walls of resistance and false belief. You are doing a good job, My beloved. Even as I speak you are lifted into a higher level of faith—a place where you will discover more and more of the gifts that await you.

Actually, it is I who am grateful, My beloved. It is I who glories in the expression of Myself through you and as you. You give Me creative expression. You give Me the joy of interaction. You give Me the glory of Love and compassion. You are My precious child, My Divine Spark, My Life in action.

Is it not marvelous, My dear one, to realize the power and wholeness that exist as we love each other beyond measure? Is it not marvelous to experience our Oneness as we breathe together in conscious unity? You need never worry about things or circumstances, My dear one. You need only love Me as I love you. That is the all of it.

Go forth this day believing and trusting in My Life as your life, My Infinite Intelligence as your intelligence and My joy as your joy. Let this day be a day of personal victory, heartfelt glory and boundless love. You are My beloved in whom I am well pleased. I love you. All is well.

—The Drummer

*If you really want peace of mind and inner
calm, you will get it. Regardless of how unjustly
you have been treated, or how unfair the boss has
been, or what a mean scoundrel someone has proved
to be, all this makes no difference to you when you
awaken to your mental and spiritual powers.*
                                        —Joseph Murphy

Chapter Thirty-One
Soul-Esteem Declarations

One of the most helpful tools to assist you in making your consciousness U-turns are declarations, or affirmations, designed to reprogram the mind. In Chapter 24 you learned about how to create a positive declaration. Here is an alphabetical list that addresses specific areas of concern. You may also use it as a guide in creating your own declarations.

Abundance
I rest secure in God's abundance as I open myself to the unlimited and inexhaustible supply of this great universe.

Acceptance
I suspend all resistance, resentment, or rebellion as I move into poise and acceptance, knowing that the workings of Spirit are safe and easy.

Action
I let fear and procrastination melt away as I translate Spirit's loving energy into perfect right action.

Anger
I lift myself above the insanity of anger and let Love restore my peace, calm my fears and bless my relationships with joy.

Anxiety
As I focus my attention upon peace, my trust in God is renewed, my body relaxes and anxiety dissolves into freedom and harmony.

Beauty
I now turn my attention to that which is beautiful—a flower, a baby, a sunset, or the sound of music—and I am lifted into gratitude and the ecstasy of God's Kingdom.

Body
I honor, respect and bless my physical body as excellent in all respects and as a magnificent vehicle for the expression of God's perfect Life Force.

Career
My perfect life's work is that which is before me to do in every present moment; it is divinely inspired and serves to give my soul expression.

Change and Transition
I confidently surrender to the flowing changes of life with a forgiving mind and a flexible spirit.

Choice
I acknowledge my power of choice as a divine attribute and from this moment on I make bold, confident choices inspired by Spirit.

Conscience
My conscience reflects my Holy Self. It is my inner guide and the divine compass of every action I take.

Courage
I claim the quality of courage that lifts me out of fear and into the power of Love before which all obstacles vanish.

Death
I relinquish all fear about death and recognize it as nothing more than the turning of a page, the movement from one room to another and the ongoingness of Life eternal.

Decision
I make my choices confidently and precisely as I invoke the quick and perfect response of Spirit.

Depression
I pull myself out of the depths of hopelessness by choosing life, and with my choice I rise out of doom into the glory of hope.

Desire
As I let go of ego-longings, I make it my highest desire to live my life in peaceful accordance with the harmonies of Spirit.

Divine Inheritance
Nothing can keep me from the Love of God, a peaceful heart, and abundant living. This is my Divine Inheritance.

Doubt
As I practice the presence of God, I release all doubt. My thoughts are clear, my feelings are focused on love, and I execute my every action with confidence and ease.

Ease
I let go of the idea of struggle and I gracefully move into a sense of ease in everything I think, say and do.

Ego
Every day my ego-self surrenders more and more to the

Higher Self of my being so that I function as a power-presence: confident, loving, joy-filled and happy.

Empowerment
I release any ego-desire to manipulate or control as I call forth the authentic power that lives at the center of my being. I function from a place of integrity, sincerity and loving intention.

Energy
Unlimited Universal Energy moves through me and as me to accomplish every undertaking with strength and vitality.

Enthusiasm
Enthusiasm is God within inspiring me to live with passion in a state of joyful participation and positive expectation.

Envy
I know that nothing can be personally owned but everything is mine to enjoy, honor and embrace with lightness and peace.

Evil
I put on the armor of Light and I step into the Truth that God's goodness prevails and fills all the dark places.

Faith
Love is perfecting all that concerns me. I embody the faith of God and go forward with spiritual confidence and inner peace.

Fear
I call forth my power of will to calm my fears and move me into God's Love with confidence, courage and unbending faith.

Forgiveness
I now transform my perception of those who seem to be acting as adversaries, and I see them as powerful teachers in my life.

Giving
I turn my attention from any form of getting and get busy giving to life through my ideas, talents, self-expression and loving compassion.

God's Will
God's Will is the highest vision for my life and expresses through me now as my highest thought, feeling, belief and action.

Grace
I upgrade all personal effort and striving to a state of mind that allows the power of God to move through me as spiritual poise, rhythmic self-expression and gentle power.

Gratitude
I move into gratitude and thanksgiving for the many blessings in my life, knowing that I am *already* blessed with whatever it is that I desire or need.

Guidance
My sense of intuition is attuned to God's direction as I move ahead with spiritual confidence—free from fear and trusting Infinite Wisdom to make clear my way before me.

Habits
I now use my power of will to choose new habits of life that are healthy patterns of respect for my body, mind and spirit.

Happiness
I stop seeking happiness outside myself, realizing that I am already surrounded by and infilled with the Holy Presence of God. This is true happiness.

Harmony
I see beyond the difficulties of the human world and see God's wholeness and harmony taking place in all my concerns.

Health

I call forth a consciousness of health that corresponds with the Divine Standard in the Mind of God.

Heart

My heart is cleansed of all heaviness and hurt and is filled with the joy and lightness of Holy Spirit.

Heaven on Earth

I am lifted beyond self-concerns into a loving openness and peaceful acceptance that creates for me a heaven on Earth.

Inspire

I now arouse the Divine Influence within me to shine forth as unlimited energy, ideals, passion and creativity.

Joy

I let the Light of Joy fill my soul and bubble up to saturate my heart and mind with fearless rejoicing.

Judgment

I move off any willful positions and release all critical judgment. In doing so I find profound peace and oneness with all that is.

Life

I am plugged into the Infinite, charged with Life, energized by Spirit and powered by God!

Life Eternal

I know that beyond my human experience of life, my soul lives as a part of God's Life—a part of Life Eternal.

Light

All darkness and fear are dissolved as the Light of God surrounds me and fills me with Its radiance.

Loneliness

I am never lonely, for God's Love comforts me, soothes my pain and lifts my soul into loving self-expression.

Love

Divine Love now dissolves all difficulties, heals all sense of separation, and reminds me that I am one with God.

Mind

As I use my mind to think only the highest possible thoughts, the Mind of God expresses through my every idea and vision.

Money

The energy of money is flowing freely in my life. I accept and handle it with love and spiritual confidence.

Nonjudgment

I let go of the need to be right as I place my attention upon balance, open-mindedness and infinite possibility.

Old Age

I am youthing as the cells of my body vibrate to the Divine Standard. I am vibrant, whole and alive with Spirit.

Order

I cooperate with the high idea of divine order. Everything is in its right place at the right time for the highest good of all.

Past

I accept that the past has brought me to this place in time on my perfect path to self-realization, and I release all that has gone before with love and gratitude.

Patience

I place all that concerns me in a pattern of unfoldment that is in God's time, not mine. I relax and know that all is well.

Peace

I surrender all tension and negative emotion as I stop trying so hard and I let peace prevail in every cell of my body and in every thought and feeling.

Plenty

I know there is plenty of love, plenty of energy, plenty of joy, and plenty of trust in God's abundance in my life right now.

Power

The power of God's Love and Wisdom now replaces any temptation to force, control or manipulate as I let go and let God.

Power-Presence

As I let God's attributes express as my attributes, I become a power-presence in my world.

Prosperity

I allow God's unlimited energy to flow through me and all of my affairs, dissolving all blocks and prospering my life in unlimited ways.

Purpose

My purpose is to give, love and serve, and I bring that purpose to every activity, large and small.

Relationships

I surrender all neediness as I open myself to right relationships. All of my interactions are temples of learning within which to experience love, cooperation and harmonious expression.

Release

I surrender the need to control or cling to any person, place or thing, and I am free and willing to make new choices. I am supported, guided and protected by God and know that nothing can be truly lost or abandoned.

Respect
As a child of God, I attract respect in every circumstance. I likewise treat others with love and respect.

Risk
Risk is not a danger, but a doorway to greater living. I choose my next step wisely and confidently.

Search
I need not search in desperate need, for the Presence of God lights my path and clears the way before me.

Self-Esteem
I call forth the spiritual confidence that lives within my soul to shine forth as self-esteem in my human experience.

Spiritual Confidence
I raise the level of my human self-confidence as I allow a deeper confidence to emerge from the depths of my God-Essence.

Success
I see myself as successful as I learn from my mistakes and take the next steps with courage and spiritual confidence.

Synchronicity
I expect God's clues to show up in the right way and at the right time as synchronistic events that meet my needs in every present moment.

Thoughts
My thoughts are the highest possible intentions and I see in my mind's eye only truth, beauty and wholeness for everyone.

Time
I spend my time in a way that is filled with joy and peace and create a continuum of powerful new now moments.

Truth

I now stand tall in the sincerity and integrity of God's Truth and surrender the opinions of my human ego to the grander Truth which harmonizes all situations in my life.

Will

My will is my director, and I let it be used by the Will of God to make wise choices and decisions through me in support of my life purpose.

Wisdom

Divine Wisdom directs me and guides me in making the best choices for everyone's highest good.

Work

I am attracted to the work that supports my life purpose. I bring dedication, enthusiasm and creativity to my work no matter what it is that I find myself doing in the moment.

Worry

All worry is now replaced by unwavering faith that Spirit is moving through all that concerns me and directing my attention to that which is constructive, productive and rooted in peace.

For information on talks and seminars
presented by Phylis Clay Sparks, contact:

Soul-Esteem™ Publishing

105A Progress Parkway
Maryland Heights, Missouri 63043
Telephone: (314) 576-5508
Fax: (636) 536-4730
e-mail: soulesteem@aol.com
Web site: www.soul-esteem.com

NOTES

NOTES